TOPICS IN CONDITIONAL LOGIC

D1447236

7-22-80

Dear John,

I take it you still haven't received your review copy. I'm sorry about that. I am enclosing a copy for you to evaluate. I'm afraid I have to ask you to return it since I only have a couple of copies myself. I sincerely appreciate your willingness to act as an outside evaluator for my promotion.

I'm also inclosing another reprint that just arrived.

Warm regards,

Don

DONALD NUTE

University of Georgia

TOPICS IN CONDITIONAL LOGIC

D. REIDEL PUBLISHING COMPANY

DORDRECHT:HOLLAND / BOSTON:U.S.A.

LONDON:ENGLAND

Library of Congress Cataloging in Publication Data

Nute, Donald, 1947–
    Topics in conditional logic.

    (Philosophical studies series in philosophy; 20)
    Bibliography: p.
    Includes index.
    1.   Conditionals (Logic)   2.   Modality (Logic)
3.   Semantics (Philosophy)   I.   Title.
BC199.C56N87   160   79–27088
ISBN 90–277–1049–X

Published by D. Reidel Publishing Company,
P.O. Box 17, 3300 AA Dordrecht, Holland

Sold and distributed in the U.S.A. and Canada
by Kluwer Boston Inc., Lincoln Building,
160 Old Derby Street, Hingham, MA 02043, U.S.A.

In all other countries, sold and distributed
by Kluwer Academic Publishers Group,
P.O. Box 322, 3300 AH Dordrecht, Holland

D. Reidel Publishing Company is a member of the Kluwer Group

Printed in The Netherlands

For Jane and Virginia Nute

TABLE OF CONTENTS

TABLE OF CONTENTS

PREFACE AND ACKNOWLEDGEMENTS

As the title indicates, I use formal methods in this book to attack a variety of problems involving conditionals in one way or another. Some of these problems concern the analysis of conditional constructions as they are used in ordinary discourse. Others involve analysis of the relationship between conditionals and causation, or of the relationship between conditionals and temporal asymmetry. Included also are discussions of different kinds of conditional probabilities. Besides using formal methods in exploring these topics, I also treat the formalizations as subjects of inquiry in their own right and determine some of the interesting properties of the formal systems developed along the way.

The first thing I try to do is to make some progress toward getting clear about how we use and understand both indicative and subjunctive conditionals, counterfacual and otherwise, as they occur in ordinary speech and thought. Although few fences are erected between the English and the symbolese, I try to take into account the possibility that persons who are not well versed in the techniques of formal semantics might nevertheless recognize the important role conditionals play in our speech and thought. In the first two chapters, I try to make the move from the discussion of examples drawn from everyday thought and discourse to the construction of formal systems and semantics as gently as possible. I attempt to show how the formalization develops naturally as a way of characterizing one aspect of more ordinary ways of thinking and talking. The resulting formal semantics is based upon the sort of deliberation in which we engage when we decide whether to assert or deny a conditional, and the resulting conditional logic is based upon the patterns of argument which we intuitively accept as valid. The goal is descriptive and the criterion for success is the degree to which the resulting formalization adequately captures the logical structure of ordinary usage.

Elsewhere, my goal is not so obviously descriptive. In fact, it is probably impossible, in general, to distinguish clearly between the descriptive and the prescriptive aspects of formalization and the use of formal methods in the analysis of philosophical problems. I think, though, that formal methods do not differ in this respect from any other methods used by philosophers.

This book was made possible by a generous grant given to me while I was

ix

on leave from the University of Georgia during the academic year 1976–77 by the National Science Foundation and by a grant from the University of Georgia which supported my research during the summer of 1978. I am indebted to Mr. William Mitcheltree and the editor of *Noûs* for giving me permission to include materials from Nute (1980) and Nute and Mitcheltree (1980) in Chapter 4, and to the editors of *Reports on Mathematical Logic* for permission to include material from Nute (1979) in Chapter 7. I thank Professors Bernard Dauenhauer, Michael Dunn, David Lewis, Barry Loewer, John Pollock, George Schumm, Robert Stalnaker, Marshall Swain, and Bas van Fraassen, Mr Ed Lester, Mr William Mitcheltree, and Mr Dan Turner for helpful discussions and criticisms, and in some cases for allowing me to see their work before publication. I also thank Mrs Beverly Chandler, Mrs Lucile Epperson, and Miss Ellen Johnson for secretarial help which was frequently given above and beyond the call of duty. I wish finally to express my special appreciation to my collaborator and friend Professor James Fetzer and to my wife Jane.

CHAPTER 1

THE BASIC ANALYSIS OF CONDITIONALS

1.1. CONDITIONALS AND FORMALIZATION

All of us use conditional constructions all the time. We use them to ask questions, to give commands, to make assertions, to make promises, and to do many other things. It seems perfectly obvious that we must each of us know a great deal about how conditional constructions function, about what constitutes an adequate answer to a question phrased using a conditional construction, about what must be done to obey a command made with a conditional construction, about what must be the case for a conditional assertion to be true, about what must be done to fulfill a conditional promise, and so on. Language is conventional and the function of conditional constructions must be determined by the way that we normally use them. So we can't fail to use them correctly most of the time. Of course someone might try to use a conditional construction in a way in which it is not normally used. When this happens, something goes wrong, some kind of mistake has been made. But in a certain sense every speaker of English knows how to use conditional constructions. What I want to do in this chapter is to begin to make precise and explicit and to explain this knowledge which we all share.

The paradigm conditional construction is the 'if-then' construction. Examples of sentences involving this construction include 'If he is late, then he will miss the train', and 'If his alarm clock had not been unplugged, then he would not have missed the train'. A common variant of this construction omits the word 'then'; we would probably omit 'then' in both of the examples already given. We nearly always omit 'then' when asking a question, giving a command, etc., as in 'Will you go if I do?' and 'Don't pay them if they won't give you an itemized bill'. Sometimes we form conditionals by omitting both 'if' and 'then' and using the subjunctive mood of the verbs, as in 'Had he overslept, he would have missed the train' and 'Were I wealthy I would not toil'. So we see that there are a number of forms that conditional locutions can take. I am here interested in conditional assertions whatever the exact form of the conditional construction used, although I will for the most part consider examples in which the verbs used are in the subjunctive mood. The mood of the verb does have some effect upon the meaning and use of the construction, and I will consider some of these differences later.

1

In this chapter, I will develop a formal language, a formal logic or calculus, and a formal semantics. I will show that these three items bear certain relations to each other. The formal logic and the formal semantics will 'fit' each other in a way that we express by saying that the logic is sound and complete with respect to the semantics. Many like myself find the investigation of formal systems intrinsically interesting, but there are reasons for being interested in the particular formalizations developed here other than their intrinsic fascination. The logic to be developed is intended to capture something about the way we use the conditional construction in English to make assertions and to compose arguments. The semantics is intended to capture something of the conventions which govern our ordinary use of conditional constructions, and of the conditions which make our conditional assertions true or false. In other words, I will be using the techniques of formalization as a tool in my effort to explicate the implicit knowledge of and about conditional constructions which we share.

When we use formalization as an analytic tool, we typically focus upon some part of ordinary language which we wish to clarify, or upon some concept, or set of concepts, which we wish to understand better. Everything besides those items which we are investigating gets pushed under a rug. The rug that they get pushed under is the convenient sentence letter, predicate letter, impersonal individual constant, etc. We use some special symbol to represent that linguistic structure or that concept which has momentarily caught our interest and lump all else into our p's and q's and our F's and G's. The analysis then takes the form of sets of formation rules in the formal language, sets of axioms and rules in the logic, and abstract structures in the formal semantics. To connect the non-formal linguistic structure or concept with the formalization, we devise some uniform method for pairing off the informal claims which might be made using the structure or concept being analysed with expressions in the formal language. This also has the effect of pairing off informal arguments with sequences of formal expressions and of pairing off the meanings of our informal claims with structures or parts of structures in our formal semantics.

The starting point for a formalization of conditional assertions in English must be an examination of our intuitions concerning the ways conditional constructions can be used and of the sorts of things we do in trying to evaluate conditional statements and to decide whether to accept or reject them. These intuitions, I think, are nothing more than partial verbalizations of our implicit understanding of the common conventions which we have together adopted to govern our use of conditional constructions. The truth conditions for conditional assertions or statements simply are a part of the conventions we have adopted. What we take to be a good reason for accepting or rejecting a conditional must, in the final analysis, be the same thing as what makes the conditional true or false. It is important that this assumption about language be made clear at the outset, since otherwise, many of the things I say in this chapter may sound confused. Language is conventional and is therefore not sacrosanct. Intuition reports linguistic convention (at least in this case and in the sense I mean it) and is therefore also not sacrosanct. Conventions can and sometimes do change. When conventions change, so do the intuitions which report them. Sometimes there can be very good reasons for changing both conventions and intuitions, but more about that shortly.

Beginning with some preformal intuitions about conditionals, I shall formulate an artificial language within which we can symbolize various English sentences, a logic or formal calculus which is intended to reflect our intuitions about what is and what is not a good argument involving the sentences which can be symbolized in our artificial language, and a formal semantics which reflects our intuitions about what makes the sentences which we symbolize in our artificial language either true or false. To the extent that these constructions are guided by ordinary usage and intuitions, our formalization is descriptive. But, as I have already hinted, our formalization may also turn out to be normative. We may find that certain sequences of sentences in our formal language turn out to be (or not to be) derivations in our logic at the same time that informal arguments corresponding to these sequences of artificial sentences are not (or are) intuitively valid. We may find that some artificial sentence is (or is not) satisfied by some structure in our formal semantics even though the corresponding English sentence is not (or is) intuitively true. If and when this happens, we will discover that our initial preformal or unreflective intuitions and our formalization do not exactly 'fit' each other. We might try to improve the fit by putting them together a bit differently. We do this by changing our method for symbolizing English sentences in the artificial language. We may also try to get a better fit by altering the logic and/or the formal semantics. But there is also a third alternative. If we are strongly committed to the symbolization and also strongly committed to the axioms and rules of the logic, and to the basic structures of the semantics, we may alter our intuitions to better fit the formalization. (Less drastically, we may form intuitions to fit some feature of the formalization where we had no preformal intuitions at all.) Where we actually change our intuitions, we could see what we are doing as bringing our personal understanding of the conventions governing the use of conditionals more closely into line with the implicit, communal conventions, or we could see what we are doing as actually *reforming* our conventions in order to bring *them* into line with some general principles about linguistic conventions to which we have become committed and with which our original conventions do not agree. An excellent example of such a principle might be consistency, should it turn out that our initial conventions seem to commit us to both the truth and the falsity of a single statement in English. To the extent that our exercise in formalization results in an alteration of our original intuitions about conditionals, our formalization will be normative.

It should always be kept in mind that our original goal in formalization is descriptive. We are trying to explicate some linguistic or conceptual knowledge which we all share. Our formalization should reform our intuitions only rarely. A strong commitment to the notion that formalization should be used primarily as a descriptive tool motivates the whole of the next chapter in which I defend a rather controversial thesis about the logic of conditionals.

A more modest reform which formalization may result in, a kind of reform which doesn't really require us to change any original intuitions, is the abandonment of monism. This consequence of the formalization of conditionals is, I think, inescapable. We may be inclined, at first, to think that conditional constructions are used in only one way to make assertions. We should, if this is true, have only one conditional logic and only one conditional semantics. We should, that is, subscribe to a sort of monism concerning conditionals. Such a monism is, I think, mistaken. We use conditionals in a variety of ways, each with its own logic and truth conditions. It is easy to confuse our intuitions about one usage with those about another. It is easy to confuse two very similar but distinct linguistic conventions. Part of the service which formalization performs is to allow us to sort out these various intuitions and group them together into compatible sets. In this chapter, I will try to sort out and formalize one of the most common linguistic conventions involving conditionals, although I do not think that this is the only convention which governs our use of conditionals, nor even that it is the only such convention which is very common. There are other, equally important usages about which I shall try to say more in later chapters.

The formal language, logic, and semantics to be developed in this chapter are not novel. Although I arrived at them, at least in part, independently of other authors, they are nevertheless very similar to suggestions made by other authors. In some cases, the results at which I have arrived are identical to those of other authors. A number of the similarities and differences are pointed out in the third and fourth chapters. What I have tried to do in this chapter which is different from what some other authors have tried to do, including what I myself have tried to do in earlier papers dealing with conditionals, is to spell out explicitly and in some detail the way in which the formalization is grounded in preformal intuitions and the way in which these preformal intuitions evolve into a formalization and subsequently become altered in the process. I hope that the manner in which I present this material will render it coherent to readers who do not themselves normally use formalization as a tool of analysis.

1.2. HYPOTHETICAL DELIBERATION

It is a basic assumption of this work that a conditional sentence can be used to say something which is either true or false. I will call such a bearer of truth-value a *conditional proposition*. The truth conditions for conditional propositions are closely related to the tests we use in deciding whether to accept or reject them. There is one kind of thought process in particular, in which we very often engage when we are evaluating a conditional and deciding whether to accept or reject it, a process which I will call *hypothetical deliberation*. A careful account of hypothetical deliberation will provide us with an analysis of one way in which conditional constructions may contribute to the truth conditions for propositions which these constructions are used to express. Where its employment is appropriate, hypothetical deliberation is itself in a certain sense the *meaning* of the conditional construction.

We begin our analysis in this section by providing an initial, partial account of hypothetical deliberation.

I will represent a conditional symbolically as $A > B$ where A is the antecedent and B is the consequent of the conditional.

The evaluation of conditionals proceeds through a search for counterexamples. When we have occasion to decide whether $A > B$ is true or false, we try to imagine a reasonable situation in which A would be true and B would be false. We treat A as a hypothesis and B as a conjecture and we investigate the connection between the two. Of course, a major portion of this analysis consists in the unpacking of the term 'reasonable'. Even when we have developed some rather extensive and interesting principles concerning the features a suitable notion of reasonableness must satisfy, the reasonableness condition will remain rather vague and indeterminate.

This indeterminacy is not a fault of the analysis, however, for vagueness is an important feature of the ordinary conditionals which we are trying to explain and we should expect our analysis to preserve this vagueness and to pinpoint its causes. How this can be done will become clearer as we proceed.

Where A does not logically entail B, it should always be possible to imagine a situation or *way things might have been* in which A is true and B is false. If every such situation counted as a counterexample, then only logical entailments would be approved through the process of hypothetical deliberation. But we see a difference between entailments and the broader class of intuitively true conditionals when we examine hypothetical deliberation more closely. For example, one can surely form a thought-picture of this volume floating to the ceiling. Such a thought-picture offers a putative counterexample to the conditional 'If this book were released in mid-air, it would fall to the floor'. Yet one would not admit that the possibility of forming such a thought-picture shows that the conditional is false.

The first conclusion to be drawn from this example is that we may accept a certain imaginary situation as being a counterexample to an entailment without accepting that same imaginary situation as being a counterexample to the corresponding simple conditional. The second conclusion to be drawn is that although it may be difficult to explain *why* a particular imaginary situation would or would not be a reasonable candidate to consider as a counterexample to a particular conditional, it is clear that such principles of reasonableness are involved in hypothetical deliberation.

If subjunctive conditionals are related to, or in any way say anything about what actually happens in the world, then what actually happens must somehow enter into our hypothetical deliberations. Suppose I suggest to my class that if I were to let go of a piece of chalk, it would float to the ceiling. Then I do let go and the chalk falls to the floor. The situation which actually occurs in the classroom is a counterexample to my conditional assertion. Whenever the antecedent of a conditional turns out to be true, one of the situations which *must* be considered in our hypothetical deliberation is the actual situation.

The actual situation may play an even more important role in our hypothetical deliberations. Some authors, including Stalnaker, Lewis, and Pollock, suggest that for the most common sort of conditional, if A is true then the *only* situation we need to consider in evaluating A > B *is* the actual situation. We do frequently employ such a principle in our hypothetical deliberations, but I do not think that we always employ such a principle. If we did, we would always infer A > B from A & B. But sometimes we reject this inference. Sometimes we reject A > B out of hand if we see no *connection* between A and B. What we have, then, are two *different* intuitions about conditionals. We need to investigate these competing intuitions further.

Stalnaker seems to recognize only one of these intuitions. It is claimed in Stalnaker (1968), that a connection between antecedent and consequent is a sufficient but not a necessary condition for the truth of the conditional. I know of no reference in Stalnaker's work where he tempers this claim or considers the possibility of more than one use of conditionals, one of which requires a connection between antecedent and consequent, and one of which does not. Lewis (1973) admits at least the formal possibility of a conditional for which A & B could be true while A > B was false, but he does not seem to have given the possibility any serious consideration. The logic which Lewis develops in which we can have $(A \& B) \& \sim (A > B)$ is also a logic in which we can infer from A > B and B entails C, that A > C. This is a feature which Lewis's conditional logic **VW** shares with earlier systems which I have developed. But Pollock has convinced me in correspondence that we cannot have a conditional which requires a connection between antecedent and consequent, and for which the inference from A > B and B entails C to A > C is also intuitively valid. Suppose, for example, that A > B is 'If I push the button, the doorbell will ring' and C is 'The doorbell exists'. There is certainly a connection between my pushing the button and the doorbell ringing, and the ringing of the doorbell surely entails the existence of the doorbell, but there is no connection between my pushing the button and the existence of the doorbell. If we are using conditionals in a way which requires a connection between the antecedent and the consequent, then we are not using conditionals in a way which allows the inference from A > B and B entails C to A > C.[1]

The answer to the problem of the conflicting intuitions is clear: we use conditionals in compliance with more than one set of conventions. Put another way, there are at least two different *kinds* of conditionals in common use, each governed by its distinct set of conventions: one which requires a connection between antecedent and consequent, and one which does not. Pollock (1976) is the only author I know who has spelled this out clearly before now, and has made an attempt to analyze the kind of conditional which requires a connection in a way which does not assume the validity of the inference from A > B and B entails C to A > C. Pollock calls these *necessitation* conditionals. Although I had worked on the analysis of such conditionals previously, I had fallen into the error of supporting a logic like Lewis's **VW**.[2] In the remainder of this chapter I will consider only those conditionals which do not require a connection between antecedent and consequent.

When B is true and we are considering a condition $A > B$ which does not require a connection between antecedent and consequent, how do we go about evaluating $A > B$? What we do is to consider whether there is what Pollock calls an *antagonistic* connection between A and B, that is, we consider whether A's being true would *interfere* with B's being true. We feel obliged to admit that the truth of A *does not* interfere with the truth of B when A & B is true, even if before learning that A & B is true we believed that the state of affairs asserted to obtain by A is of a sort which *might* interfere with the obtaining of the state of affairs asserted to obtain by B. In such a case we would say perhaps that we had good reason to think that $A > B$ was false, but that as things turned out $A > B$ is true.

In the case where $\sim A \& B$ is true, we are likely to accept $A > B$ unless we note the sort of antagonistic connection between A and B mentioned before. This suggests that if $\sim A \& B$ is true, then either the truth of A wouldn't interfere with the truth of B (in which case $A > B$ would be true), or the truth of A would interfere with the truth of B (in which case $A > \sim B$ is true). So from B we should be able to infer $(A > B) \vee (A > \sim B)$.[3] But this isn't acceptable. Suppose, for example, that B is 'My roof does not leak' and A is 'A heavy branch fell on my roof during last night's storm'. In fact, my roof does not leak and no branch fell on it. But neither $A > B$ nor $A > \sim B$ is true since heavy branches falling on roofs *can* cause them to leak but such accidents don't *always* produce leaks. The most we can say is that if B is true and the truth of A clearly *would not* interfere with the truth of B, then in our hypothetical deliberations we will only consider situations in which B remains true.

The conclusion of the last paragraph suggests that when A is true, since A's truth does not interfere with the truth of anything which is actually true, we are obliged to consider only the actual situation in our deliberations, since this is the only situation in which we do not reject some of our actual truths. But I think this is not quite correct, even if we are not considering a conditional which requires a connection between antecedent and consequent. The difficulty for such a view arises when we consider conditionals with disjunctive antecedents. Consider, for example, 'If either Carter or Ford had won the last Presidential election, then Amy Carter would be living in the White House'. Both the antecedent and the consequent of this conditional are true, but the conditional itself is false (at least according to my intuitions and to the intuitions of all 'non-philosophers' upon whom I have tried this example). The reason we reject this conditional is because we do not think of the antecedent as stating a single condition which a situation either does or does not satisfy. Instead, we treat the two disjuncts as stating two separate conditions which must be treated separately in our hypothetical deliberations. Since one of these conditions stands in an antagonistic connection with the consequent of the conditional, we reject the conditional. I think examples of this sort cast sufficient suspicion upon the principle, that we only consider the actual situation when evaluating conditionals with true antecedents, to justify omitting this principle at this point. I am trying first to develop only those features of hypothetical deliberation which are relatively uncontroversial. Once a basic analysis is put together which most writers accept as the core of their own more complete analysis, we will consider which additional, controversial principles we need to add. In fact, the whole issue of disjunctive antecedents is controversial and their discussion will take up the whole of the next chapter.

What kind of connection would make a conditional *prima facie* plausible? Certainly a logical or semantical connection that would ensure analyticity would suffice. Such a connection is involved in the counterfactual, 'If I were a bachelor, I would have no legitimate offspring'. Inductive connections or connections based on observed regular concomitance may also suffice. This is the sort of connection involved in our earlier example, 'If this volume were released in mid-air, it would fall to the floor'. Deontic connections may be invoked in support of a conditional as in, 'If he deserts his family, he is immoral'. These are but a few of the kinds of connections that might link the antecedent and consequent of a conditional. Each of these kinds of connections dictates certain restrictions on what will count as a counterexample to the conditional under scrutiny.

Before continuing with our investigation of the word 'reasonable' and what it means within the context of a discussion of hypothetical deliberation, let us review the basic position of the analysis being developed. Hypothetical deliberation involves what Stalnaker (1968) calls a 'thought experiment'. In performing this experiment, we mentally construct situations in which the antecedent of the subjunctive conditional is true, looking for such a situation which is reasonable (given the antecedent) and in which the consequent of the conditional is false. Let's call these situations which we construct during hypothetical deliberation *hypothetical situations*.[4] If we are able to construct a reasonable hypothetical situation which disconfirms the conditional being evaluated, we judge the conditional to be false. If we decide that such a counterexample cannot be constructed, we judge the conditional to be true. If we are not sure of the proper restrictions that should be placed upon the construction of counterexamples, we withhold judgment and perhaps ask for clarification.

Some of the situations which occur to us in our hypothetical deliberations may turn out to be 'confirming examples' rather than 'disconfirming examples'. Suppose I am deciding how to vote in a Presidential election and I believe that we should decrease our military spending. I would then be concerned to know whether it is true that military spending would be cut if Foghorn were elected. If I thought there was no connection between Foghorn's election and military spending, I might reject the conditional out of hand and simply say to myself that there is no reason to think it is true. However, I know that a plank in Foghorn's campaign platform is the reduction of military expenditures. The connection is there, but how strong is it? To reject the conditional, I need to find a reasonable situation, perhaps even a probable situation, that would prompt Foghorn to act differently than he has promised. I know that our NATO allies oppose any decrease in our military spending, so one situation I am likely to consider is that in which Foghorn is elected, tries to decrease the military budget, and is faced with an outcry from our NATO allies. Considering this possibility, however, I might decide that Foghorn would not submit to such pressures and that he would seek a reduction in spending anyway. In my deliberations, I have considered certain possibilities which do not disconfirm the conditional, yet it is certainly reasonable that I should consider the likely reactions of our NATO allies in evaluating this particular conditional. Of course, should I reject the conditional and should Foghorn subsequently be elected and reduce military spending, then I will be proven wrong. Unfortunately, we sometimes have to evaluate conditionals before all the evidence is in.

It may not be improper for us to consider confirming situations in our hypothetical deliberations, since this will not lead to error in our conclusions, but some situations will be so obviously confirming that they will never occur to us in our actual deliberations. In the case of the example we just considered, 'If Foghorn were elected President, military spending would be cut', we would not give a moment's attention in our deliberations to a situation in which Foghorn is elected, he makes a sincere effort to keep his campaign promises, the Congress gives him unquestioning support, and no political or military crises of even the slightest significance occurs anywhere in the world during his term of office. It would not in fact occur to us to consider such a situation since it so obviously confirms the conditional being evaluated. We do not waste time on such situations when our program calls for us to seek out counterexamples. A confirming situation may be considered, but this will normally occur only when the situation holds some initial promise of disconfirming the conditional being evaluated.

Another reason why a situation might not even occur to us in our hypothetical deliberations is that it is so obviously unreasonable. Consider once again, 'If Foghorn were elected, military spending would be cut'. We might object that military spending would probably be increased if Foghorn were to win and the earth were to be invaded by the Martian Anti-littering League. But this possibility is too ridiculous even to occur to us in our deliberations. We might consider some situations which upon reflection we deem unreasonable, but such outlandish cases as this one will not occur to us at all. We might, for example, initially consider the possibility of war breaking out in some part of the world, but decide that the political situation is actually improving and therefore reject that possibility. Or in the case of releasing this book in mid-air, if I used this example in the classroom some student might consider the possibility that there is a piece of metal concealed in the cover of the book and a powerful magnet in the ceiling which will attract the book and prevent it from falling to the floor. (Some students have very suspicious natures.) Upon further reflection, however, the student is likely to decide that this possibility would require more effort on my part than my past record of pedagogical devotion indicates and therefore reject this possibility as too unlikely to consider seriously. Yet this situation may not be too unreasonable to at least occur to the student.

The variability of the notion of reasonableness is even more radical than has been indicated so far. We may actually apply different criteria of reasonableness to the same antecedent on different occasions. Let's look at an example of two different occasions on which we might evaluate the same conditional differently due to different standards of reasonableness. On one occasion, we are arguing with someone about the relative effectiveness of the military technologies of various cultures throughout history. On the other occasion, we are arguing about the effectiveness of various military strategists. On the first occasion, but not on the second, we might apply standards of reasonableness to our attempted counterexample construction which would justify us in saying that if Julius Caesar had commanded the United Nations forces in Korea, he would have employed catapults and the North Koreans would have annihilated his forces without any assistance from the Chinese. On the second occasion, but not on the first, we might justifiably say that if Julius Caesar had commanded the UN forces in Korea, he would have employed nuclear weapons and annihilated both the North Koreans and Chinese.[5] The context of the occasion of deliberation in each case dictates the restrictions placed upon the deliberations. In one case Caesar is limited in his choice of weaponry by the technology of the Roman Empire, while in the other case he is limited by the much more advanced technology of the early 1950s. Conditionals are notoriously vague, and at least one reason for their vagueness is the sort of variability in the standards of reasonableness applied to counterexample construction that we are considering here.

Another complication involved in the notion of reasonableness being explored here, is the fact that there may be situations which are reasonable to consider when we consider one antecedent, but which are not reasonable to consider when another antecedent is being entertained. What I have in mind here does not involve applying different reasonableness conditions, as did the Caesar-in-Korea example. I am talking about cases in which we do not change our reasonableness conditions at all. For example, we decided that we would not consider invasion by the Martian Anti-littering League in deciding whether Foghorn would decrease military spending if elected. But this would certainly be a reasonable situation to consider if we were trying to decide whether, for example, military spending would have decreased if our past space explorations had resulted in our learning that there were other sentient beings in the solar system. What is not a reasonable counterexample for one conditional may well be a reasonable counterexample for another, and this may be so even when there is no reason to think that our criteria for what shall count as reasonable have undergone any change.

In hypothetical deliberation, many situations will not be considered because they are so obviously unreasonable or because they so obviously confirm the conditional being evaluated. What we consider are situations which hold some initial promise both of being reasonable, in the sense of 'reasonable' being applied at the time, and of disconfirming the conditional considered. But there is an even more important practical reason why we do not consider all the situations, reasonable or otherwise, in which the antecedent in question is true. That reason is that there are simply too many of these situations. In their totality, two situations could differ according to the exact weight of the Liberty Bell. We would consider these differences to be unimportant for the purposes of evaluating most conditionals unless, of course, the conditional being evaluated explicitly concerned itself with the exact weight of the Liberty Bell. In our deliberations, we do not provide complete details of the situations we are considering. Complete details are beyond our competence. Instead, we lump situations together which are alike in the features we take to be relevant to our deliberations and cover the rest with a sort of unconscious *ceteris paribus*. Because of this, we may lump two situations together when we are considering one conditional that we would differentiate if we were considering another. Examples would be, 'If Foghorn were elected President, he would wear a tie to his inauguration', and, 'If Foghorn were elected President, military spending would be cut'. Here we have the same antecedent occurring in both conditionals and yet the situations that would actually occur to us in our deliberations might be rather different. Considerations of this sort led Gabbay (1972) to suggest that the restrictions placed upon our counterexample construction depend both on the antecedent and on the consequent of the conditional. I think this is mistaken, at least if the two conditionals are evaluated on the same occasion. Although the two conditionals do not have the same counterexamples, if any, and although different situations will actually be attended to in evaluating the two conditionals, I would still claim that any situation which it is *reasonable* to consider in evaluating one will also be reasonable to consider in evaluating the other. A presentation of some reasons for rejecting Gabbay's view can be found in Chapter 4.

At this point, we need to consolidate our observations about hypothetical deliberation. This can be done by providing a set of idealized instructions for such deliberation. These instructions are *ideal* because of considerations like those of the preceding paragraph.

Step 1. Consider all situations in which the antecedent A of the conditional under consideration is true. In particular, what actually happens is one of the situations which must be considered if A is actually true. Call this class of situations $S(A)$.

Step 2. Eliminate from $S(A)$ all situations which do not satisfy the relevant conditions of reasonableness. Do not reject the actual situation if it is in $S(A)$. Call the resulting class of situations $R(A)$.

Step 3. Eliminate from $R(A)$ all situations in which the consequent B of the conditional under consideration is true. The resulting class of situations is $R(A) - S(B)$. Class $R(A) - S(B)$ is a class of counterexamples to the conditional being considered.

Step 4. Reject $A > B$ *on this occasion* if $R(A) - S(B)$ is not empty. (Remember that the standards of reasonableness may change from occasion to occasion.)

Step 5. Accept $A > B$ on this occasion if $R(A) - S(B)$ is empty.

Essentially, these instructions are complete. We can expand upon them only through a further examination of the notion of reasonableness involved in Step 2. We have observed that different standards of reasonableness may be employed under different circumstances, but there are certain common features which every legitimate notion of reasonableness must share. It is to a determination of these common features that we must now turn.

There is an important connection between the kind of reasonableness we are considering and the notion of impossibility. Surely if it is impossible that a sentence B should be true, then there are no reasonable situations in which B is true. Because of this, we have the following condition.

Reasonableness Condition 1. If it is impossible for sentence B to be true, then $R(A)$ does not contain any situations in which B is true, i.e., $R(A) \cap S(B)$ is empty.

There is a sort of converse to Reasonableness Condition 1 which also seems to me to be true. No matter how bizarre or improbable an antecedent may be, so long as the antecedent is not impossible, there will be some situations which it is reasonable to consider in evaluating conditionals with that antecedent. We are quite sure now that Mars harbors no intelligent life, but there might have been Martians if things had worked out differently. Since there might have been Martians, we can certainly consider what would have happened if our Mariner landing craft had discovered them. Perhaps they would have tried to communicate with the craft, or perhaps they would have attacked it. In trying to decide what they would have done, we consider situations in which there are Martians. After all, our topic *is* conditionals and the mere falsity of an antecedent should not interfere with our search for a counterexample to the conditional. It is only when the antecedent is impossible that the attempt at constructing a counterexample is quashed at the outset. Thus, we have our second condition.

Reasonableness Condition 2. $R(A)$ is empty only if A is impossible.

An interesting consequence of Reasonableness Conditions 1 and 2 can be drawn immediately:

Uniformity Principle. If $R(A)$ is empty, then there is no situation in $R(B)$ in which A is true, i.e., $R(B) \cap S(A)$ is empty.

Some other interesting consequences follow from our first two reasonableness conditions. As it turns out, we can define necessity and possibility in terms of conditionals. Suppose A is possibly true. Then by Reasonableness Condition 2, $R(A)$ is not empty. Now $R(A)$ is a subclass of $S(A)$, the class of situations in which A is true. Furthermore, both A and $\sim$ A can not be true in the same situation, so $R(A) = R(A) - S(\sim A)$, and $R(A) - S(\sim A)$ is not empty. It follows that $A > \sim A$ is false, i.e., $\sim (A > \sim A)$ is true. Now suppose $\sim (A > \sim A)$ is true. Then $A > \sim A$ is false and $R(A) - S(\sim A)$ is not empty. Since $R(A) = R(A) - S(\sim A)$, $R(A)$ is not empty. So by Reasonableness Condition 1, A is possibly true. If we let $\Diamond A$ be the proposition that is true just in case A is possibly true, we must conclude that $\Diamond A$ is logically equivalent to $\sim (A > \sim A)$. Similarly, if we agree that A is necessarily true just in case $\sim$ A is impossible, and we let $\Box A$ be the proposition that is true just in case A is necessarily true, we can show that $\Box A$ is logically equivalent to $\sim A > A$. These results may seem strange at first, but they are less strange upon reflection. Consider the case of $\Box A$. If $\sim A > A$ were true, then every reasonable situation in which $\sim$ A is true would be a situation in which A is true. So every reasonable situation in which $\sim$ A is true would be a situation in which both A and $\sim$ A is true. But there are no situations in which both A and $\sim$ A are true, so there aren't any situations which are *at all reasonable* in which $\sim$ A is true. But this is just another way of saying that $\sim$ A is impossible or A is *necessarily* true.

These results for the modalities can be used to establish an additional reasonableness condition for our analysis. It is commonly held that $\sim \Diamond A$ is equivalent to $\Box \sim A$. Using the results just obtained, this means that $\sim\sim (A > \sim A)$ (or rather the equivalent $A > \sim A$) is logically equivalent to $\sim\sim A > \sim A$. This in turn implies the following:

Reasonableness Condition 3. $R(A)$ is empty if and only if $R(\sim\sim A)$ is empty.

So far we have provided an initial, informal semantics for a certain class of conditionals. This semantics is the direct result of our examination of what I have called hypothetical deliberation. This account provides a basic understanding of certain conditionals of ordinary discourse, upon which we may build a more sophisticated understanding later. In developing this informal semantics, we have looked only at hypothetical deliberation *in vacuo*. By this, I mean that we have not explicitly looked at the ways in which we might use conditionals in *arguments*. We have only looked at a kind of thought experiment we employ in coming directly to decisions about conditionals. But conditionals often occur as premises and conclusions of arguments, and such occurrences *in situo* will certainly affect our decisions about the truth and falsity of the conditionals according to the way in which they are involved in arguments with other conditionals and other propositions. To improve our analysis, we need to extend the scope of our examination to include hypothetical inference as well as hypothetical deliberation.

1.3. SOME INTUITIVELY VALID INFERENCE PATTERNS

To produce an adequate account of conditionals, we need to supplement our discussion of hypothetical deliberation with an examination of those inference patterns involving conditionals which we intuitively take to be valid. In this section, we will be proposing two interesting forms, which valid arguments, with conditionals as premises and conclusions, may take. First, however, we will develop a formal language for conditionals which will facilitate our discussion.

The primitive symbols of our conditional language will consist of the following:

1. denumerably many propositional letters $P_1, P_2, \ldots$;
2. brackets, parentheses, and braces;
3. the negation operator $\sim$;
4. the conjunction operator &;
5. the disjunction operator $\vee$; and
6. the conditional operator $>$.

The set CL of well-formed formulas or wffs of our language is the smallest superset of the set of propositional letters which is closed under compounding by means of the logical operators in the usual ways, taking care of punctuation as needed. Additional symbols for material implication ($\rightarrow$), material equivalence ($\leftrightarrow$), possibility ($\Diamond$), and necessity ($\Box$) are defined as follows:

DEFINITION 1.2.1. $A \rightarrow B =_{df} \sim A \vee B$

DEFINITION 1.2.2. $A \leftrightarrow B =_{df} (A \rightarrow B) \& (B \rightarrow A)$

DEFINITION 1.2.3. $\Diamond A =_{df} \sim (A > \sim A)$

DEFINITION 1.2.4. $\Box A =_{df} \sim A > A$.

Negation has the usual truth-functional interpretation, as do conjunction and disjunction, except, perhaps, when they occur in the antecedent of a conditional. Until we begin to provide axiomatizations of conditional logics and to develop formal semantics for conditionals, we will read these symbols in the usual ways. I will also use capital letters 'A', 'B', etc., as variables ranging over wffs, and hence in a sense as propositional variables.

We first note that '>' should not be transitive, i.e., that the following thesis is not in general true:

Transitivity. $(A > B) \rightarrow ((B > C) \rightarrow (A > C))$

Yet a restricted version of transitivity may be acceptable. Transitivity is *prima facie* attractive, but examples from ordinary conversation convince us that it is to be avoided. The following is such an example:

(1)   If Thurston were to work less, he would be less tense.

(2)   If Thurston were to lose his job, he would work less.

(3)   If Thurston were to lose his job, he would be less tense.

If we had this argument presented to us in the course of an actual conversation, we might first accept (1) without reservation, then reluctantly accept (2), and finally object that something has gone wrong since (3) is clearly false. Actually, we have misgivings as soon as we hear (2), and we are inclined at that point to rescind our approval of (1). We might try to explain this change of heart concerning (1) by suggesting that the reasonableness conditions we employ in evaluating (1) *before* we hear (2), are not the same conditions we employ in evaluating (1) *after* we hear (2). Such an explanation is going to complicate our semantics considerably. Fortunately, a simpler explanation is available. Once we hear (2), we begin to think in terms of Thurston's working less *because* he loses his job whereas before hearing (2) we were thinking in terms of Thurston's working less *other things being equal*. Our misgivings about our response to (1) do not indicate that we have changed our minds about what would be the result of Thurston's working less *other things being equal*; instead, we have misgivings because we see that the argument is going in a direction which explicitly requires that other things are *not* equal. Given the direction that the argument is taking, it appears that we evaluated the wrong conditional when we evaluated (1). What we should have been evaluating is:

(4)   If Thurston were to lose his job and work less, he would be less tense.

It is really this new premise which, along with (2), gives (3), but this new premise is false. However, if (2) and (4) *were* both true, then (3) would be true as well. Thus, we reject unrestricted transitivity in favor of a restricted transitivity thesis:

(RT) $((A \& B) > C) \to ((A > B) \to (A > C))$

RT is a theorem of conditional logics developed by Stalnaker (1968), Åqvist (1971), Lewis (1973), Chellas (1975) and Nute (1975). A similar principle is proposed for the logic of indicative conditionals by Adams (1975). We will certainly want our account of conditionals to support RT.

How does accepting RT affect our informal semantics for conditionals? RT requires that whenever $R(A \& B) - S(C)$ is empty and $R(A) - S(B)$ is empty, then $R(A) - S(C)$ is also empty. Put differently, this means that whenever $S(C)$ contains $R(A \& B)$ and $S(B)$ contains $R(A)$, then $S(C)$ contains $R(A)$. This will be assured if $R(A \& B)$ contains $R(A)$ whenever $S(B)$ contains $R(A)$. Is this a reasonable principle? $R(A)$ is the set of reasonable situations in which A is true. If all such situations are also situations in which B is true, it certainly makes good intuitive sense to say that all reasonable situations in which A is true are also reasonable situations in which both A and B are true. This gives us an additional reasonableness condition:

Reasonableness Condition 4. If $R(A) \subseteq S(B)$, then $R(A) \subseteq R(A \& B)$.

The second thesis I wish to recommend in this section is the following *Conditional Additivity* thesis.

(CA) $((A > B) \& ((C > B)) \to ((A \vee C) > B)$

We get a corresponding reasonableness condition:

Reasonableness Condition 5. $R(A \vee B) \subseteq R(A) \cup R(B)$.

Thinking about it, Reasonableness Condition 5 is obvious. The reasonableness situations in which $A \vee B$ is true are going to come from among the reasonable situations in which either A or B is true. Even when a different informal account of conditionals is given, philosophers have with very few exceptions adopted CA as an intuitively valid principle for conditionals.

Additional principles are suggested for conditionals by an examination of conditional inference, but these other principles are more controversial than is RT. Although the informal semantics developed here differs from that developed by other philosophers, the corresponding claims about which wffs in CL are valid are almost universally accepted. In other words, we have reached that stage at which we can say no more about our semantics without committing ourselves to the validity of controversial theses. This is a good place to stop at least long enough to formalize the semantical insights achieved thus far.

1.4. FORMAL SEMANTICS FOR
HYPOTHETICAL DELIBERATION

Our fundamental observation about hypothetical deliberation was such that deliberation proceeds through a search for counterexamples. In carrying out this search, we examine various hypothetical situations, considering whether certain propositions are true or false in them. For the purposes of developing a formal semantics the *only* feature of hypothetical situations that we are concerned with *is* that propositions are true or false in them. We might in fact think of a hypothetical situation as a function from CL (the set of wffs of our conditional language) into the set of distinct truth values $\{T, F\}$. But as I noted earlier, I will not identify hypothetical situations with such functions. Another term that has been used for the kind of entities we have been calling hypothetical situations is 'possible world'. This term is used by Stalnaker (1968), by Lewis (1973), and by many other authors and it is explicitly used as a synonym for 'counterfactual situation' by Kripke (1972). Instead of using these terms as synonyms, we will use 'hypothetical situation' for the entities entertained during actual hypothetical deliberation and we will use 'possible world' as a technical term for the corresponding functions from sentences to truth values. If S is a hypothetical situation, the possible world w_S corresponding to S will be a function from CL into $\{T, F\}$, such that for each A in CL, $w_S(A) = T$ if, and only if, A is true in S, and $w_S(A) = F$ if, and only if, A is false in S. A basic notion in our formal semantics will be the notion of a possible world set.

DEFINITION 1.3.1. A possible world set is a non-empty set W of functions from CL into $\{T, F\}$ such that for every $w \in W$ and $A, B \in CL$:

1. $\qquad w(\sim A) = \begin{cases} T \text{ if } w(A) = F \\ F \text{ otherwise} \end{cases}$

2. $\qquad w(A \ \& \ B) = \begin{cases} T \text{ if } w(A) = T \text{ and } w(B) = T \\ F \text{ otherwise} \end{cases}$

3. $\qquad w(A \lor B) = \begin{cases} T \text{ if } w(A) = T \text{ or } w(B) = T \\ F \text{ otherwise} \end{cases}$

Surely all truth-functional tautologies are true in every hypothetical situation and surely all contradictions are false in every hypothetical situation. Our technical notion of a possible world, being the formal counterpart of the informal notion of a hypothetical situation, reflects this. The two conditions in our definition of a possible worlds set insure that every possible world maps every tautology to T and every contradiction to F. We now have, in possible worlds sets, a technical device which corresponds to a combination of our informal notion of a hypothetical situation, and our informal notion of a sentence being true or false in a hypothetical situation. We also have the sense in which conjunction and disjunction are truth-functional.

The other fundamental concept involved in our informal semantics is that of reasonableness. Some putative counterexamples to a given conditional are reasonable while others are not. Of course, any counterexample to any conditional is just a hypothetical situation satisfying certain conditions. The function of the notion of reasonableness in our analysis, is to eliminate certain hypothetical situations from consideration as we seek counterexamples. In other words, a reasonableness condition tells us which worlds we may look at in our search for a counterexample. Reasonableness conditions generally depend in certain ways upon the way things *actually are*. For example, when my students considered the hypothetical 'If this volume were released in mid-air, it would fall to the floor', they assumed in their deliberations that the 'laws of nature' do not change. They did not consider any situations in which physical objects *repelled* each other according to their masses and distance. But why is this a consequence of our assumption that physical laws remain constant? Because bodies do not *actually* repel each other in the manner indicated. If bodies actually *did* behave in this way, we would in our hypothetical deliberations consider *only* hypothetical situations in which this 'Backwards Law of Gravitation' held. This is an example of how our reasonableness condition depends upon the actual situation. This feature of reasonableness conditions must be taken into account in defining the formal counterpart of a reasonableness condition, i.e., a class-selection function on a possible worlds set.

DEFINITION 1.3.2. A *class-selection function on a possible worlds set W* (*CS-function on W*) is a function f from CL × W into $\mathscr{P}$ (W).

Intuitively, what a class-selection function does is tell you, once you know what the actual situation is and given a wff A, which hypothetical situations (possible worlds) are reasonable (selected) candidates for the role of counterexample to conditionals with A as antecedent. This is a function not only of

A but also of *one of the hypothetical situations* because our reasonableness conditions usually *depend indexically* upon certain aspects of the actual situation. By this I mean that we assume that certain things about the actual situation do not vary, things to which we may only be able to refer indexically. Putting together the notions of a possible worlds set and a CS-function, we have the notion of a class-selection model.

DEFINITION 1.3.3. A class-selection model (CS-model) is an ordered pair $\langle W, f \rangle$ such that W is a possible worlds set and f is a CS-function on W.

Not just any class-selection function will do as a representation of a reasonableness condition. Step 1 of our idealized instructions for hypothetical deliberation tells us that a class-selection function should pick out for A only worlds in which A is true and should include the 'actual' world in those it picks out if A is true. And our Uniformity Principle tells us that a class-selection function which picks out nothing for A should not pick out for B any worlds at which A is true. Reasonableness Conditions 3, 4 and 5 further restrict our choice of selection functions. These conditions will be made precise below.

We now have available all the technical machinery we need to provide a complete formal counterpart to our idealized instructions for hypothetical deliberation. Suppose we are evaluating the hypothetical $A > B$, possible worlds set W is the formal counterpart of the set of all hypothetical situations that could possibly enter into any hypothetical deliberation, class-selection function f on W is the formal counterpart of the reasonableness condition we are using on this occasion, and $\alpha \in W$ is the possible world which tells us which wffs are actually true. Then the formal counterpart of $S(A)$ is $W/A = \{w \in W : w(A) = T\}$, the formal counterpart of $R(A)$ is $f(A, \alpha)$, and the formal counterpart of $R(A) - S(A)$ is $f(A, \alpha) - W/B$.

Since α is the possible world corresponding to what actually happens, $A > B$ is true if and only if $\alpha(A > B) = T$. But $A > B$ is true if and only if $R(A) - S(B)$ is empty, i.e., if and only if $f(A, \alpha) - W/B = \emptyset$. Notice that the condition $f(A, \alpha) - W/B = \emptyset$ is equivalent to the condition that $f(A, \alpha) \subseteq W/B$.

We can collect these formalizations of notions developed in our discussion of hypothetical deliberation and valid inference patterns into the concept of a basic class-selection model.

DEFINITION 1.3.4. A *basic class-selection model* (*BCS-model*) is an ordered pair $\langle W, f \rangle$ such that:

(1) $\langle W, f \rangle$ is a CS-model;

(2)   for all $w \in W$ and $A, B \in CL$,

   (a) $f(A, w) \subseteq W/A$;
   (b) if $w(A) = T$, then $w \in f(A, w)$;
   (c) if $f(A, w) = \emptyset$, then $f(B, w) \cap W/A = \emptyset$;
   (d) if $f(A, w) \subseteq W/B$, then $f(A, w) \subseteq f(A \& B, w)$;
   (e) $f(A \vee B, w) \subseteq f(A, w) \cup f(B, w)$.

(3)   for all $w \in W$ and $A, B \in CL$,

$$w(A > B) = \begin{pmatrix} T \text{ if } f(A, w) \subseteq W/B \\ F \text{ otherwise} \end{pmatrix}.$$

A wff A *is true* (*in a BCS-model* $\langle W, f \rangle$) if and only if $W/A = W$. A wff A *is BCS-valid* if and only if A is true in every BCS-model. As our reasonableness condition changes from one occasion to another, so will the corresponding selection function and hence the intended model. We intuitively call a proposition involving a conditional construction *valid* (or perhaps *necessary*) only if it must be true regardless of the specific reasonableness condition being employed. The corresponding *formal* notion of validity is that of truth in all BCS-models.

We now have a formal semantics which captures the conclusions of our discussion of hypothetical deliberation. Of course, this semantics is ideal in the same way that our instructions for hypothetical deliberation were ideal. We would still need to know exactly what the actual situation was like, we would still need to have a complete grasp of our reasonableness condition, and we would still need to be able to review every hypothetical situation in order to determine what conditionals are true. But we do have a much firmer grasp now on the notion of *validity*. Regardless of the fact that our formalization idealizes the notions involved in our analysis of hypothetical deliberation, any wff which is BCS-valid will be justified by our *actual* hypothetical deliberations.

1.5. THE WEAK CONDITIONAL LOGIC W

A *tautology* is any wff $A \in CL$ such that for every possible world w, $w(A) = T$. A *conditional logic* is any set $L \subseteq CL$ such that every tautology is in L and if $A, A \rightarrow B \in L$, then $B \in L$. Members of a conditional logic L are also called *theorems* of **L**. In this section, we will identify the conditional logic determined by the class of all BCS-models.

Consider the following inference rule:

NEC.   From A, to infer □A.

We say a conditional logic is **L** closed under NEC just in case □A ∈ **L** whenever A ∈ **L**. We say a conditional logic **L** contains a formula like

(A1) $□(A → B) → (□A → □B)$

just in case **L** contains every substitution instance of that formula. Let W be the smallest conditional logic which is closed under NEC and contains (A1)–(A7), where (A2)–(A7) are as follows:

(A2) $□(A → B) → (A > B)$

(A3) $(A > (B → C)) → ((A > B) → (A > C))$

(A4) $(A > B) → (A → B)$

(A5) $□ \sim A ↔ \sim ◊A$

(A6) $((A \& B) > C) → ((A > B) → (A > C))$

(A7) $((A > B) \& (C > B)) → ((A ∨ C) > B)$

It can be shown that for each member A of **L** there is a finite sequence of wffs the last member of which is A and every member of which is either a tautology, a wff of one of the forms (A1)–(A7), or follows from earlier members by *modus ponens* or NEC. Such a sequence is called a *derivation in* **L** *of* A. We say that A *implies* B in a conditional logic **L** just in case A → B ∈ **L**. We say a *set* Γ of wffs *implies* A in **L** just in case there is some finite subset Δ of Γ such that the conjunction of the members of Δ implies A in **L** in the sense already defined. A set Γ of wffs is **L**-*consistent* is and only if there is some wff A such that Γ does not imply A in **L**. A set Γ of wffs is *maximally* **L**-*consistent* if and only if Γ is **L**-consistent and for every wff A, A ∈ Γ or $\sim$ A ∈ Γ.

Since every conditional logic contains all tautologies and is closed under *modus ponens*, we say that all conditional logics are *extensions* of the classical propositional calculus. Certain familiar results are true for all extensions of the propositional calculus, and hence for all conditional logics. Let **L** be a conditional logic. If Γ is an **L**-consistent set of wffs, then there is a maximally **L**-consistent set of wffs Δ such that Γ ⊆ Δ (Lindenbaum's lemma). A set of wffs Γ is **L**-consistent if and only if every subset of Γ is **L**-consistent (Compactness Theorem). A set Γ of wffs implies A → B in **L** if and only if Γ ∪ {A} implies B in **L** (deduction theorem). A set Γ of wffs implies A in **L** if and only if $\Gamma \cup \{\sim A\}$ is not **L**-consistent. These and similar results will be assumed in the remainder of this work.

It can be shown that **W** contains a number of interesting formulae. A few of these are listed in the next theorem.

THEOREM 1.4.1. **W** contains the following formulae:

(a) $\quad \Box A \rightarrow (B > A)$

(b) $\quad ((A > B) \& (A > C)) \rightarrow (A > (B \& C))$

(c) $\quad A > A$

(d) $\quad \Diamond A \rightarrow ((A > B) \rightarrow \sim (A > \sim B))$

(The proofs for Theorem 1.4.1 are left to the reader.) Parts (a) and (b) of Theorem 1.4.1 will be particularly useful later in this section.

We want to prove three things about the system **W**. First, we will show that **W** is consistent. Second, we will show that every member of **W** is BCS-valid and hence would be justified and accepted through application of our idealized instructions for hypothetical deliberation. Third, we will show that every wff which is BCS-valid is also a member of **W**, and hence that our weak system of conditional logic completely captures the notion of validity defined by our idealized instructions for hypothetical deliberation. In other words, we will show that **W** is a consistent logic which is determined by the class of all BCS-models.

A conditional logic **L** is said to be *consistent* if and only if it is **L**-consistent. We will prove a general result about the consistency of conditional logics first and then apply this result to **W**. For any $A \in CL$, let A^+ be the result of replacing every occurrence of '>' in A by '→'. We note that $(A > B)^+ = (A \rightarrow B)^+ = A^+ \rightarrow B^+$, that $(\sim A)^+ = \sim (A^+)$, and that $(\Box A)^+$, $(\Diamond A)^+$, and A^+ all imply each other in any conditional logic. For any conditional logic **L**, we will call an ordered pair $\langle A, R \rangle$ an axiomatization of **L** if and only if A is a set of wffs including all tautologies (axioms), R is a set of inference rules including *modus ponens*, and for every $A \in CL$, $A \in \mathbf{L}$ if and only if there is a finite sequence of wffs with last member A such that every member of the sequence is either a member of A or follows from previous members of the sequence by one of the rules in R. As we noted earlier, the set of wffs of one of the forms (A1)–(A7) together with the rule NEC constitute an axiomatization for **W** when added to the set of tautologies and *modus ponens*. We then have the following result:

LEMMA 1.4.2. Let **L** be a conditional logic such that $\langle A, R \rangle$ is an axiomatization of **L** satisfying the following two conditions:

(1)   if $A \in A$, then A^+ is a tautology;

(2)   if $A_1^+ \ldots A_n^+$ are tautologies and some inference rule in R allows us to infer B from $A_1 \ldots A_n$, then B^+ is a tautology.

Then **L** is consistent.

Proof. Assume the hypothesis. By the definition of an axiomatization, if $A \in L$, then A^+ is a tautology. Let $A \in CL$. If **L** is not consistent, then $\sim (A \rightarrow A) \in L$ and $(\sim (A \rightarrow A))^+ (= \sim (A^+ \rightarrow A^+))$ is a tautology. But this is false, so **L** is consistent.

THEOREM 1.4.3. **W** is consistent.

Proof. Inspection shows that if A is an axiom of **W**, then A^+ is a tautology; and if A^+ and $(A \rightarrow B)^+ (= A^+ \rightarrow B^+)$ are tautologies, so is B^+. Furthermore, since $A^+ \rightarrow (\Box A)^+ \in W$, if A^+ is a tautology, so is $(\Box A)^+$. So by Lemma 1.4.2, **W** is consistent.

THEOREM 1.4.4. (Soundness for **W**). Every member of **W** is BCS-valid.

Proof. By the definition of a tautology, every tautology is BCS-valid. It is also clear that *modus ponens* preserves BCS-validity. So we need only show that every axiom of **W** is BCS-valid and that NEC preserves BCS-validity. Let $\langle W, f \rangle$ be a BCS-model and let $w \in W$. For (A1) and (A2), we need to show that $w(\Box A) = T$ if, and only if, $f(\sim A, w) = \emptyset$. Assume $w(\Box A) = T$. Then $w(\sim A > A) = T$ by Definition 1.2.4. Let $w' \in f(\sim A, w)$. Then $w'(A) = T$ and $w'(\sim A) = T$, both by Definition 1.3.4. But by Definition 1.3.1, this is impossible; so $f(\sim A, w) = \emptyset$. Assume conversely that $f(\sim A, w) = \emptyset$. Then it is vacuously true that $w'(A) = T$ for all $w' \in f(\sim A, w)$, and $w(\Box A) = T$. Assume $w(\Box (A \rightarrow B)) = T$ and $w(\Box A) = T$. If $w' \in f(\sim B, w)$, then $w'(\sim B) = T$, $w'(\sim A) = F$ since $f(\sim A, w) = \emptyset$, and hence $w'(\sim (A \rightarrow B)) = T$. But if $w' \in f(\sim B, w)$, then $w'(\sim (A \rightarrow B)) = F$ since $f(\sim (A \rightarrow B), w) = \emptyset$. So $f(\sim B, w) = \emptyset$ and $w(\Box B) = T$. To establish (A2), assume $w(\Box (A \rightarrow B)) = T$ and suppose $w' \in f(A, w)$. Then $w'(A) = T$, and since $f(\sim (A \rightarrow B), w) = \emptyset$, $w'(\sim (A \rightarrow B)) = F$ and $w'(A \rightarrow B) = T$. So $w'(B) = T$ and $w(A > B) = T$. To establish (A3), assume $w(A > (B \rightarrow C)) = T$ and $w(A > B) = T$. Let

$w' \in f(A, w)$. Then $w'(B \to C) = T$ and $w'(B) = T$, so $w'(C) = T$ and $w(A > C) = T$. Next assume $w(A > B) = T$ and $w(A) = T$. Since $w(A) = T$, $w \in f(A, w)$. But then since $w(A > B) = T$, $w(B) = T$, establishing (A4). For (A5), we first need to show that $f(A, w) = \emptyset$ if and only if $f(\sim\sim A, w) = \emptyset$. If $f(A, w) = \emptyset$, then for all $w' \in f(\sim\sim A, w)$, $w'(A) = F$. But for all $w' \in f(\sim\sim A, w)$, $w'(A) = w'(\sim\sim A) = T$. So $f(\sim\sim A, w) = \emptyset$. The converse is proved by a parallel argument. Now we observe that $w(\square \sim A) = T$ if and only if $f(\sim\sim A, w) = \emptyset$, if and only if $f(A, w) = \emptyset$, if and only if $f(A, w) \subseteq W/\sim A$, if and only if $w(\sim \lozenge A) = w(\sim\sim (A > \sim A)) = w(A > \sim A) = T$. For the case of (A6), assume $w((A \& B) > C) = T$ and $w(A > B) = T$. Let $w' \in f(A, w)$. Since $w(A > B) = T$, $w' \in f(A \& B, w)$. But then since $w((A \& B) > C) = T$, $w'(C) = T$. Hence, $w(A > C) = T$. Finally, for the case of (A7), assume $w(A > B) = T$ and $w(C > B) = T$. Let $w' \in f(A \vee C, w)$. Since $f(A, w) \subseteq W/B$ and $f(C, w) \subseteq W/B$, $f(A \vee C, w) \subseteq f(A, w) \cup f(C, w) \subseteq W/B$ and $w'(B) = T$. So $w((A \vee C) > B) = T$. This establishes that all instances of (A1)–(A7) are BCS valid. Now assume A is BCS-valid and let $w \in W$. If $w' \in f(\sim A, w)$, then $w'(\sim A) = T$ and (since A is BCS-valid) $w'(A) = T$. But this is impossible. So $f(\sim A, w) = \emptyset$ and $w(\square A) = T$. Therefore $\square A$ is BCS-valid and NEC preserves BCS-validity. Then by the definition of W, every member of W is BCS-valid.

We call a conditional logic L a $\square$-*normal extension* of W if and only if $W \subseteq L$ and L is closed under NEC. Where L is a $\square$-normal extension of W, let $W_L = \{\Delta \subseteq CL : \Delta$ is maximally L-consistent$\}$, and for each $A \in CL$ and $\Delta \in W_L$, let $f_L(A, \Delta) = \{\Delta' \in W_L : \{B \in CL : A > B \in \Delta\} \subseteq \Delta'\}$. We can think of a maximally L-consistent set Δ of wffs as a function which maps all and only members of Δ to T and maps all other wffs to F. Construed in this way, the members of W_L are possible worlds. For any consistent normal extension L of W, $W_L \neq \emptyset$ by the Lindenbaum lemma and hence $\mathscr{M}_L = \langle W_L, f_L \rangle$ is a CS-model. We call $\mathscr{M}_L$ the *canonical CS-model for* L.

THEOREM 1.4.5. If L is a consistent $\square$-normal extension of W, then $\mathscr{M}_L$ is a BCS-model.

Proof. Assume the hypothesis. It remains to be shown that $\mathscr{M}_L$ satisfies conditions (2) and (3) of Definition 1.3.4. Let $\Delta \in W_L$ and $A \in CL$. Suppose $\Delta' \in f_L(A, \Delta)$. Since $A \to A$ is a tautology, $A \to A \in L$, and $\square(A \to A) \in L$ by NEC. By (A2) and *modus ponens*, $A > A \in L$, $A > A \in \Delta$, $A \in \Delta'$ by the definition of f_L, and $\mathscr{M}_L$ satisfies condition (2a) of Definition 1.3.4. Suppose $A \in \Delta$. If $A > B \in \Delta$, then since $(A > B) \to (A \to B) \in \Delta$ by (A4), $A \to B \in \Delta$

and $B \in \Delta$. So $\{B \in CL : A > B \in \Delta\} \subseteq \Delta$. Hence, $\Delta \in f_L(A, \Delta)$ by the definition of f_L, and $\mathscr{M}_L$ satisfies (2b). Suppose $f_L(A, \Delta) = \emptyset$, $B \in CL$, and $\Delta' \in f_L(B, \Delta)$. Since $f_L(A, \Delta) = \emptyset$, $\Gamma = \{B \in CL : A > B \in \Delta\}$ is not contained in any maximally L-consistent set of wffs and by the Lindenbaum lemma, Γ is not L-consistent and Γ implies $\sim A$ in L. By the compactness theorem, let $B_1 \ldots B_n \in \Gamma$ such that $(B_1 \& \ldots \& B_n) \to \sim A \in L$. Then $\square((B_1 \& \ldots \& B_n) \to \sim A) \in L$ by NEC and $A > ((B_1 \& \ldots \& B_n) \to \sim A) \in L$ by Theorem 1.4.1(a) and *modus ponens*. By (A3) and *modus ponens*, $(A > (B_1 \& \ldots \& B_n)) \to (A > \sim A) \in L \subseteq \Delta$. But since each $B_i \in \Gamma$, $A > (B_1 \& \ldots \& B_n) \in \Delta$ by repeated use of Theorem 1.4.1(b) and *modus ponens*. So $A > \sim A \in \Delta$ and $\sim \lozenge A (= \sim \sim (A > \sim A)) \in \Delta$. By (A5) and *modus ponens*, $\square \sim A \in \Delta$, and by Theorem 1.4.1(a) and *modus ponens*, $B > \sim A \in \Delta$. Hence, $\sim A \in \Delta'$ and $\mathscr{M}_L$ satisfies (2c). Suppose $f_L(A, \Delta) \subseteq W_L/B$ and let $\Delta' \in f_L(A, \Delta)$. Then $\Gamma = \{B \in CL : A > B \in \Delta\}$ implies B in L. Let $B_1 \ldots B_n \in \Gamma$ such that $(B_1 \& \ldots \& B_n) \to B \in L \subseteq \Delta$. $\square((B_1 \& \ldots \& B_n) \to B) \in \Delta$ by NEC, $A > ((B_1 \& \ldots \& B_n) \to B) \in \Delta$ by Theorem 1.4.1(a) and *modus ponens*, $A > (B_1 \& \ldots \& B_n) \in \Delta$ by Theorem 1.4.1(b) and *modus ponens*, and $A > B \in \Delta$ by (A3) and *modus ponens*. If $(A \& B) > C \in \Delta$, then since $((A \& B) > C) \to ((A > B) \to (A > C)) \in \Delta$ by (A6), $A > C \in \Delta$ by *modus ponens*. So $\{C \in CL : (A \& B) > C \in \Delta\} \subseteq \Delta', f_L(A, \Delta) \subseteq f_L(A \& B, \Delta)$, and $\mathscr{M}_L$ satisfies (2d). Next suppose $\Delta' \in f_L(A \lor B, \Delta)$. If $\Delta' \notin f_L(A, \Delta) \cup f_L(B, \Delta)$, then there are $C, D \in CL$ such that $A > C, B > D \in \Delta$ and $(A \lor B) > C$, $(A \lor B) > D \notin \Delta$. But $C \to (C \lor D) \in \Delta$, $\square(C \to (C \lor D)) \in \Delta$, $A > (C \to (C \lor D)) \in \Delta$, $(A > C) \to (A > (C \lor D)) \in \Delta$, and $A > (C \lor D) \in \Delta$. Similarly, $B > (C \lor D) \in \Delta$. $((A > (C \lor D)) \& (B > (C \lor D))) \to ((A \lor B) > (C \lor D)) \in \Delta$ by (A7), so $(A \lor B) > (C \lor D) \in \Delta$ and $C \lor D \in \Delta'$. But since Δ' is maximally L-consistent, $C \in \Delta'$ or $D \in \Delta'$, which is impossible. So $\Delta' \in f_L(A, \Delta) \cup f_L(B, \Delta)$ and $\mathscr{M}_L$ satisfies (2e). Finally, it follows immediately from the definition of f_L that $\mathscr{M}_L$ satisfies condition (3) of Definition 1.3.4, so $\mathscr{M}_L$ is a BCS-model.

THEOREM 1.4.6 (Completeness of **W**). Every BCS-valid wff is a member of **W**.

Theorem 1.4.6 follows from Theorem 1.4.5, the consistency of **W**, and the fact that any wff which is contained in every maximally **W**-consistent set of wffs is a member of **W**. Since **W** is both sound and complete with respect to the class of all BCS-models, we say **W** is *determined* by the class of all BCS-models.

NOTES

[1] This applies only to conditionals in ordinary usage. In *scientific* contexts, we may wish to allow this inference.

[2] Lewis nowhere says that **VW** is *intended* to capture the logic of a conditional whose truth requires a connection between antecedent and consequent, nor should anyone infer from my remarks that Lewis had this in mind. He considers **VW** apparently only as a formal possibility which is determined by a certain class of models of the sort developed in his semantics. I mention this logic here only because it is one of the few conditional logics developed in the literature in which $(A \& B) \rightarrow (A > B)$ is not a theorem.

[3] Many will recognize the thesis $B \rightarrow ((A > B) \vee (A > \sim B))$ as a weakened version of Stalnaker's Conditional Excluded Middle: $(A > B) \vee (A > \sim B)$. Both of these, I think, are too strong.

[4] The notion of a hypothetical situation requires some comment. This notion is akin to that of a counterfactual situation discussed by Kripke (1972) and that of a possible world discussed by almost everyone. First, a hypothetical situation is a way things might have been or might be. I include among hypothetical situations the way things actually are. Second, I am a realist with regard to hypothetical situations, since I think that they in some sense do exist. They are actual. But unlike Lewis (1973), I do not think that the actual world is a hypothetical situation. We occupy the actual world, but we do not occupy a way things might have been or might be. We don't even occupy the way things are. I also don't think hypothetical situations exist outside the actual world. Hypothetical situations are actual and occupy the actual world. In a sense, the world itself contains all its possibilities, all the ways it is, might have been, and might yet be. Finally, I wish to emphasize the use of the word 'construct' in my account of hypothetical deliberation. This is important if we are to avoid certain supposed problems concerning the identification of individuals across worlds, and it has to do with the way in which we apprehend different situations. A metaphor of 'construction' rather than one of 'discovery' seems best to capture this apprehension. (A further discussion of this view can be found in Kripke (1972) and Nute (1978a).) We might think of hypothetical situations as enormous states-of-affairs, only one of which obtains, or as enormous properties which the world could have, but only one of which it does have. Then *merely* hypothetical situations exist in exactly the same sense that other unrealized states of affairs or uninstantiated properties exist. This will be anathema for anyone with a considerable nominalist bent, but it is my view on the matter nevertheless. Perhaps the nominalist can make some sense out of my discussion by taking hypothetical situations to be nothing more than maximally consistent sets of sentences; I cannot. When we engage in hypothetical deliberation, we do not consider sets of sentences nor do we consider things which exist outside the actual world and hence beyond our ken. Instead, we consider actual ways things might have been or might be.

[5] William Mitcheltree suggested to me that Caesar would use catapults to deliver nuclear weapons, thereby annihilating the UN forces without the aid of either the North Koreans or the Chinese.

CHAPTER 2

CLASSICAL VS NON-CLASSICAL LOGICS

2.1. DEFINING THE ISSUES

Most philosophers writing recently on the logic of conditionals have accepted all the theses of our weak conditional logic **W**. No one, though, has seriously suggested that **W** exhausts the logic of conditionals. Indeed, almost everyone writing in the area has suggested some proper extension of **W** as the correct logic for conditions. The significance of **W** is that it appears to be one of the strongest conditional logics we can put together without generating some disagreement among the majority of these philosophers who have expressed an opinion on the subject. Of course, even **W** is too strong for necessitation conditionals. For the conditionals we are now considering, though, we will take **W** to be a *lower bound* on the proper logic for such conditionals. An *upper bound* is provided by the following thesis:

Triviality. $(A > B) \rightarrow \Box(A \rightarrow B)$

Triviality is much too strong. Any normal extension of **W** which contains Triviality will also contain the following objectionable theses:

Transitivity. $((A > B) \& (B > C)) \rightarrow (A > C)$
Transposition. $(A > B) \rightarrow (\sim B > \sim A)$
Weakening Antecedents. $(A > B) \rightarrow ((A \& C) > B)$

In fact, any $\Box$-normal extension of **W** which is closed under any of Triviality, Transitivity, Transposition, and Weakening Antecedents is closed under all four.

W is itself too weak to be the logic of any ordinary language conditional. The most striking absence that occurs to us when we look at **W** is the lack of certain kinds of substitution principles. While **W** is closed under a rule of substitution of provable equivalents within consequents, it is not closed under the corresponding rule for substitution of provable equivalents within antecedents. Chellas (1976) formulates such rules:

RCEC: From $A \leftrightarrow B$, to infer $(C > A) \leftrightarrow (C > B)$

RCEA: From $A \leftrightarrow B$, to infer $(A > C) \leftrightarrow (B > C)$

W is closed under RCEC, but not RCEA. Any □-normal extension of W which is closed under RCEA would also be closed under a general rule for substitution of provable equivalents:

SE: From A ↔ B, to infer C ↔ D, provided that D is the result of replacing one or more occurrences of A by B in C.

Chellas calls conditional logics which are closed under SE *classical* while conditional logics like W which are closed only under RCEC he calls *half-classical*. Must a reasonable conditional logic be classical?

Stalnaker has suggested in conversation that the intent of philosophers working in so-called intensional logics has always been to analyze intensional constructions as standing for functions of the contents of other expressions. The only real difference between intensional and extensional logic is that extensional logic treats logical operators as standing for functions of the references, designations, etc., of other expressions, while intensional logic treats at least some logical operators as being functions of the senses or other non-referential content of expressions upon which they operate. In the case of propositional or sentential logics of the sort we have been considering, the difference is that extensional logics are truth-functional, while intensional logics are not. Accepting the position that provably equivalent wffs must share exactly the same content, Stalnaker maintains that intensional logic must be classical by original design. He therefore proposes that non-classical logics are so different from those which historically have been called intensional that they should be called by a new name such as *hyperintensional*. So W is non-classical (Chellas) or hyperintensional (Stalnaker). Stalnaker is of the opinion that the conditional constructions used in ordinary discourse are all intensional, i.e., classical. I am not so sure he is right about this. I think there is considerable evidence that many of the conditionals used in ordinary discourse are non-classical or hyperintensional. But even so, W's complete lack of substitution principles for antecedents remains suspect. Perhaps we do not want to adopt RCEA for certain conditionals, but it seems likely that we will want to allow *some* wffs to be substituted for others within the antecedents of conditionals.

Whatever else we say about A > B, its content would appear to be a function of the contents of A and B. We should therefore be able to substitute for A any other wff which has the same content as A in A > B. But how do we decide when two wffs have the same content? Calling the content of a wff a *proposition*, what we seek is an identity criterion for propositions. Provable equivalence is one such criterion. Another would be provided by identifying the content of a wff with the class of hypothetical situations in which the wff is true. The now-famous counterpart to this suggestion is the dictum that a proposition *is* a class of 'possible worlds'. Actually, by accepting either of these criteria, we commit ourselves to RCEA. Is there any reasonable alternative to this pair of identity criteria? Recent developments in relevance, entailment, and epistemic logics suggest that there must be ways of thinking about the contents of wffs which do not commit us to the view that provably or even truth-functionally equivalent wffs must have exactly the same content.

As the reader has probably anticipated, this discussion is motivated by the fact that I will be developing a non-classical conditional logic in this chapter. A good deal of the chapter is devoted to considering arguments for and against the adequacy of such a logic as an analysis of ordinary language conditionals. These arguments will frequently depend upon examining examples taken from ordinary discourse. I do not think that a conclusive argument is given in what follows for the view that many ordinary language conditionals are non-classical, but neither do I think overwhelming arguments have been presented, here or elsewhere, against this position. I do think good and considerable evidence supports the position that we should take seriously the possibility that a non-classical logic can be developed which most adequately represents the logical structure of a large portion of those conditionals used in ordinary discourse.

Once a case has been made for a non-classical conditional logic, such a logic will be developed. This new logic will be much stronger than **W**, containing many substitution principles for antecedents that **W** lacks. We will also continue our development of semantics for conditionals, defining a special kind of BCS-model with respect to which our new non-classical or hyperintensional logic **H** is both sound and complete.

Finally, before beginning the development of a non-classical conditional logic in earnest, I would like to point out that later chapters will be concerned with an examination of alternative attempts to develop a classical conditional logic. I am not sure that all ordinary language conditionals are non-classical. I am not even certain that conditionals are ever used hyperintensionally in ordinary discourse, although I think the evidence that there is such use is strong. But there is also reason to think that classical conditionals are sometimes used in ordinary discourse. For this reason, I will eventually examine such logics and try to determine which best represent ordinary usages.

2.2. THE CASE FOR NON-CLASSICAL LOGIC

The reason for rejecting RCEA is not so much because there is something terribly wrong about RCEA, as that there is something terribly right about certain competing principles. The principles in question are simplification theses for antecedents, intuitively valid argument forms which involve substituting less complex antecedents for more complex ones. These principles compete with RCEA because any □-normal extension of W which contains these simplification theses and is closed under RCEA will also contain Triviality. Since nearly everyone rejects Triviality, we can say that these simplification principles are intuitively incompatible with RCEA. In this section we will look at these simplification theses and consider arguments for and against accepting them and rejecting RCEA.

Consider the following:

(1)   If the Reds had won ten more games or the Dodgers had lost ten more games, the Reds would have won the pennant.

(2)   So if the Reds had won ten more games, they would have won the pennant.

(3)   The Reds would also have won the pennant if the Dodgers had lost ten more games.

This argument certainly appears to be valid. Such examples give us reason to think that the following simplification thesis for disjunctive antecedents should be contained by any adequate conditional logic:

(SDA) $((A \vee B) > C) \rightarrow ((A > C) \,\&\, (B > C))$

SDA is also involved in arguments which have a negative conclusion. Consider, for example, the following two sentences:

(4)   If Ford or Maddox had won in the last election, we would have a Republican in the White House.

(5)   If Maddox had won the last election, we would have a Republican in the White House.

Since (5) is false, (4) is also false. Rejecting (4) on the basis of a rejection of (5) would seem to depend upon the use of SDA and *modus tollens*. SDA has had considerable intuitive appeal to various philosophers. It was suggested by Fine (1975) and Creary and Hill (1975) as well as in my (1975a).

Semantically, SDA has the following result: in evaluating a conditional with antecedent A ∨ B, we consider both some reasonable situations in which A is true (if there are any) and some reasonable situations in which B is true (again, if there are any). Axiomatically, we note that SDA is just the converse of (A7). We could incorporate SDA into our conditional logic very simply. The price that must be paid, though, is that our conditional logic must then be non-classical. If we accept both SDA and RCEA, we will have

(6) $(A > B) \rightarrow (((A \& C) \vee (A \& \sim C)) > B)$

by RCEA, and then have Weakening Antecedents by SDA. Since Weakening Antecedents is equivalent to Triviality in □-normal extensions of W, we cannot have an acceptable classical conditional logic containing SDA. We must reject either SDA or RCEA.

Consider another argument:

(7)   If Nixon and Agnew had not both resigned, Ford would never have become President.

(8)   So if Agnew had not resigned, Ford would never have become President.

This argument and others like it appear to be valid and suggest an additional simplification thesis for antecedents:

(S*) $(\sim(A \& B) > C) \rightarrow ((\sim A > C) \& (\sim B > C))$

S* follows from SDA and the following substitution thesis for antecedents:

(9) $(\sim(A \& B) > C) \rightarrow ((\sim A \vee \sim B) > C)$

Of course, we may not want to link S* to SDA too closely. If we decide that non-classicality is too high a price to pay for SDA and that the evidence for SDA can be explained in some other way, we might want to keep open the possibility of accepting both RCEA and S* while rejecting SDA. It turns out, though, that S* and RCEA are also intuitively incompatible. By RCEA we have

(10) $(A > B) \rightarrow (\sim(\sim(A \& C) \& \sim(A \& \sim C)) > B),$

by S* we have

(11) $(A > B) \rightarrow (\sim\sim(A \& C) > B),$

and by RCEA we have Weakening Antecedents. So we must also reject either S* or RCEA.

So we have two simplification principles, SDA and S*, both of which appear to be intuitively valid and both of which are intuitively incompatible with RCEA. We must choose. But before we choose, is there any independent evidence against RCEA? I think not. There are arguments that could be given, but those of which I am aware all involve one or the other of SDA or S* in some way. For example, consider the following argument:

(12)   If Thurston had watched the road, he would not have crashed.

(13)   So if Thurston had watched the road or he had watched the road and his brakes had failed, he would not have crashed.

This argument is surely invalid, yet it appears to involve no more than an application of RCEA since A and A ∨ (A & B) are truth-functionally equivalent and hence provably equivalent. The problem with this example is that rejection of (13) seems to depend upon a use of SDA.

If we accept SDA and S*, and hence accept a non-classical conditional logic, we must respond to Stalnaker's suggestion that the semantic content of an expression is always a function of the semantic content of its parts. In the writings of Stalnaker and others, the semantic content of a wff has come to be identified with the set of hypothetical situations in which the wff would be true. This view has become codified into the intensionalist dogma that a proposition is a set of possible worlds. What we now need to consider is the possibility that the proposition is more and that to identify the set of worlds at which a wff is true does not fully exhaust the semantic content of the wff. Let us call the set of hypothetical situations in which a wff A is true the *intensional content* of A. Where ⟨W, f⟩ is a BCS-model we have W/A as a formal counterpart to the intensional content of A. But the wff A has a further semantical content which we can call the *hypothetical content* of A. This is also a set of hypothetical situations, namely the set of situations which it is reasonable to consider in looking for counter-examples to conditionals which have A as antecedents. As the notion of reasonableness changes from occasion to occasion, so too will the hypothetical content of A change. Further, since the hypothetical content of a wff depends upon the way things actually are, hypothetical content is relative to the hypothetical situation from the viewpoint of which the hypothetical deliberation is to be conducted. The set f(A, w) is the formal counterpart of the hypothetical content of A from the point of view of a hypothetical situation which corresponds to the possible world w. It is clear that in general the intensional and the hypothetical content of any given wff A are distinct and that in general W/A ≠ f(A, w) for any w. What an intensionalist like Stalnaker would have us believe, though, is that the hypothetical content of a wff is itself simply a function of the intensional content. If this were true, then whenever A and B were true in the same hypothetical situations, then the hypothetical contents of A and B would be identical. Since provably equivalent wffs must be true in the same hypothetical situations, we have RCEA. It is this assumption that identity of intensional content entails identity of hypothetical content that we are questioning. Surely A and (A & B) ∨ (A & ~B) are true in exactly the same hypothetical situations, but we may consider rather different sets of situations in evaluating conditionals which have antecedents of these forms. Our standard of reasonableness may advise us to consider only situations in which B is true when we evaluate a conditional with A as antecedent, but we are forced to consider some situations where B is not true when our antecedent is (A & B) ∨ (A & ~B). We can reject RCEA and still accept the Stalnakerian principle that the semantic content of a complex expression is a function of the semantic contents of its parts, but in doing so we recognize a richness of semantic content which Stalnaker does not. The proposition is at least the combination of the intensional and hypothetical contents of the wff which expresses it, and it may be that the latter is not simply a function of the former.

Now we must ask ourselves why so many authors have accepted RCEA and rejected both SDA and S* if theses are so obviously correct and RCEA is so obviously mistaken. The answer, of course, is that matters do not so obviously favor the adoption of SDA and S* as we have so far made them out to do. In order to reject SDA, proponents must first explain away the evidence in support of SDA. Fine (1975), Loewer (1976), and McKay and van Inwagen (1977) suggest that the arguments from ordinary language which have been used here in support of SDA have been wrongly interpreted. Our error is supposed to lie in the claim that ordinary language sentences like (1) are properly symbolized by wffs like (2). The 'or' in (1), it is claimed, represents wide-scope conjunction rather than narrow-scope disjunction. Hence, (1) should be symbolized as

(14) $(A > C) \& (B > C)$

If we symbolize such English sentences in this way to begin with, we have no need for a simplification principle like SDA. A similar suggestion is made for the case of 'indicative' conditionals by Adams (1975). How shall we respond to this argument?

The defenders of RCEA are suggesting a set of rules for symbolizing ordinary English sentences according to which the English 'or' is sometimes symbolized as '∨' and sometimes as '&'. As McKay and van Inwagen put it in their (1977):

For every regimented idiom, there is a body, of "lore" concerning the translation of natural-language sentences into it. The discovery of sentences like [(1)] is a contribution not to the problem of assigning truth-conditions to sentences expressed in the regimented counterfactual idiom, but rather to the translation-lore of that idiom.

In general, I prefer to keep our hidden 'translation-lore' as small as possible. I choose an explicit richness in the complexity of the formalization itself rather than a complicated procedure for translating ordinary language into formal language. So far as possible, the subtleties of the natural-language idiom should be mirrored in the 'regimented idiom' if our goal is primarily descriptive. Of course the bit of translation lore being proposed is not particularly noxious and might easily be tolerated if that would put an end to our problem. But before accepting event this complication of our translation rules, I think we should ask what advantages, other than that it would allow us to preserve RCEA, would follow from this move?

There would be an obvious advantage to translating (1) as (14) if, for example, there were some other English sentence which might plausibly be translated as SDA and which has a content different from that of (1). But there does not appear to be such a sentence. Furthermore, it seems to me, at least, that whatever the natural-language counterpart of $(A \vee B) > C$ might be, it should imply both $A > C$ and $B > C$. But perhaps $(A \vee B) > C$ is one of those peculiar wffs which we sometimes run across in formal languages for which no comfortable ordinary counterpart exists. Other examples would include $(\exists x) (Fx \rightarrow Gx)$ in the predicate calculus. But this does not seem likely. After all, SDA is nothing more than the converse of (A7), and (A7) is almost universally accepted as a valid principle of conditional logic. In fact, some authors such as Pollock (1976) draw special attention to (A7) by including it as an explicit axiom of their conditional logics as we have done here. However we are to understand $(A \vee B) > C$, it would seem that we would want the converse of (A7). Ultimately, if we confine our attention to SDA, it seems we have two choices: we can symbolize 'or' one way when it occurs in the antecedent of an ordinary language conditional and another way in all other occurrences, or we can symbolize 'or' the same way in all of its occurrences but recognize that wffs of the form $A \vee B$ have a richer semantic content than has heretofore been recognized.

But we have been ignoring S*. If the proponents of RCEA are to use the same ploy in responding to S* that they have used in the case of SDA, then they must insist that (7) be symbolized as

(15) $(\sim A > C) \& (\sim B > C)$

This suggestion distorts what is going on in the natural language even more than did the suggested alternative symbolization of (1). Our innocent-seeming translation-lore threatens to grow into a monster. Now we have two *ad hoc* translation rules to which adoption of RCEA commits us. This still may not be too great a price to pay if compensation is forthcoming, but the only compensation appears to be RCEA. Should we cling to an admittedly elegant feature of formal systems which does not fit well with the most straightforward procedure for representing the logical structure of ordinary language conditionals? Probably not if our primary goal is to fully capture the logical structure of those conditionals as they are actually used rather than to subtly reform that usage.

Another reason for rejecting SDA and S*, of course, would be if there were examples of English sentences of the form $(A \vee B) > C$ which clearly did not imply both sentences of the corresponding forms $A > C$ and $B > C$. Actually, there are English sentences like (1) which do not satisfy SDA. McKay and van Inwagen (1977) suggest

(16)   If Spain had fought on one side or the other in World War II, it would have been the Axis side.

Michael Dunn has suggested in conversation

(17)   If Gladhand were to run for Congress, he would run for the Senate.

McKay and van Inwagen claim that (16) does not imply

(18)   If Spain had fought for the Allies, she would have fought for the Axis.

and Dunn claims that (17) does not imply

(19)   If Gladhand were to run for the House of Representatives, he would run for the Senate.

The example supplied by (16) and (18) seems unimpeachable, while there seems to be one way of reading (17) which would not allow us to infer (19). The antecedent of (17) is, of course, supposed to be equivalent to the disjunctive antecedent, 'If Gladhand were to run for the House or the Senate'. These examples require careful consideration.

First, we notice that the examples we are considering are surely not of the most general form $(A \vee B) > C$; at best, they are of the form $(A \vee B) > A$. Second, we notice that the two disjuncts included in the antecedent of (16) are mutually exclusive — not logically incompatible, I suppose, but practically so. Third, the disjuncts in the antecedent of (17) are also mutually exclusive in some sense, although we are probably less inclined to think of them as being mutually exclusive than we are in the case of (16). It would be difficult either to fight on both sides in a war or to run at the same time for two different offices, but it would be more difficult to do the former. Fourth, (16) seems to imply the following:

(20)   If Spain had fought on one side or the other in World War II, it would *not* have been on the Allied side.

Fifth, reading (17) in the sense which makes it peculiar to infer (19), (17) seems to imply

(21)   If Gladhand were to run for Congress, he would *not* run for the House of Representatives.

Taking this data together, we can devise an analysis of (16) and (17) which preserves SDA. Simply put, the 'or' in (16) and (17) is an exclusive 'or' and each of these English sentences is really of the form

(22) $((A \vee B) \mathbin{\&} \sim(A \mathbin{\&} B)) > A$

Since the antecedent of neither (16) nor (17) is a simple disjunction, SDA cannot be used to infer either (18) or (19) from them. This solution requires a 'translation-lore' of our own, but it is well known that 'or' is sometimes inclusive and sometimes exclusive. Another advantage of this analysis, and one which should make us feel more comfortable with it, comes from the fact that W contains the following:

(23) $(((A \vee B) \mathbin{\&} \sim(A \mathbin{\&} B)) > A) \rightarrow (((A \vee B) \mathbin{\&} \sim(A \mathbin{\&} B)) > \sim B)$

So we have an explanation for the fact that (20) and (21) follow, respectively, from (16) and (17).

A difficulty with this proposal was pointed out to me by Alan Gibbard. There are, of course, many ways to symbolize the exclusive 'or'. What happens if we use some method other than that represented by the antecedent of (22)? In particular, what happens if we symbolize (16) as

(24) $((A \mathbin{\&} \sim B) \vee (\sim A \mathbin{\&} B)) > A$

Our weak logic W also contains

(25) $(((A \mathbin{\&} \sim B) \vee (\sim A \mathbin{\&} B)) > A) \rightarrow (B > A)$

But if we do this, we are once again commited to inferring (18) from (16).

At least three responses are available to us. First, we simply reject Gibbard's suggestion and insist that (16) be symbolized by (22) and not by (24). This suggestion makes more sense if we consider that the two different wffs occurring as antecedents are assumed to have different hypothetical contents. In (22) we are required to consider all reasonable situations in which A ∨ B and ~(A & B) are both true. In cases like that of (16), we could justifiably say that there aren't any situations reasonable enough to consider in which Spain fought for the Allies in World War II if we are allowed the alternative of supposing that Spain fought for the Axis. In the case of (24), on the other hand, we are required to consider all reasonable situations in which A & ~B is true and all reasonable situations in which ~A & B are true. Since both these are possible, we are required to come up with situations for both. But in the case of (22), we may only be required to consider situations in which A & ~B is true, or situations in which ~A & B is true. Second, we can admit that Gibbard's argument is effective and reject the solution based upon treating the 'or' in (16) as exclusive. But in this case we can still draw attention to (20) and (21), and to the fact that all of the putative counterexamples to SDA are not of the most general form treated by SDA and have implications which conditionals with disjunctive antecedents do not usually have. We can then maintain that conditionals of the sort represented by (16) and (17) are of a different and less common sort than those for which SDA is acceptable. In this case, we consider (22) to represent one possible analysis of this kind of conditional.

The second response to Gibbard's argument would be more persuasive if we could find English sentences like (16) which did not imply other sentences like (20). Such examples are not difficult to find. Suppose Olive Oyl knows Wimpy is being offered a hamburger and a frankfurter. Olive believes the following:

(26)   If Wimpy takes either, he will take the hamburger.

Olive is quite sure of (26) since Wimpy's love of hamburgers is famous and phenomenal. His taking a frankfurter while leaving a hamburger is unthinkable. However, Olive does not believe the following:

(27)   If Wimpy takes either, he will not take the frankfurter.

So far as Olive knows, Wimpy might take both. She is, however, sure of the following:

(28)   If Wimpy takes the frankfurter, he will (also) take the hamburger.

It looks, then, as if we have the conditional construction performing two different roles. If we accept SDA for '$>$', then we might symbolize (26) as $(A \lor B) > A$ and (16) as $(A \lor B) \geqslant A$. Then '$>$' and '$\geqslant$' have different logics. Actually, '$\geqslant$' might not occur in any other constructions than those of the form $(A \lor B) \geqslant A$. If that is true, then the occurrence of '$\lor$' is really superfluous and we might as well represent (16) as being of the form $A \# B$ for some new operator '$\#$'. We might read $A \# B$ as 'A is more possible than B' (Lewis, (1973)) or 'A is more *nearly* possible than B' (colloquial). Then (22) would be one possible analysis of $A \# B$. But even if we do not accept this particular analysis of $A \# B$, the difference in the logical consequences of (16) and (26) still seem to dictate that we analyze these two sentences differently.

The third response to Gibbard's objection was suggested to me by Dan Turner. According to Turner, (16) really says the same thing as

(29)   If Spain had chosen between fighting for the Allies and fighting for the Axis in World War II, she would have chosen to fight for the Axis.

while (17) really says the same thing as

(30)   If Gladhand were to choose between running for the Senate and running for the House of Representatives, he would choose to run for the Senate.

Understood in this way, neither (29) nor (30) is really of a form to which SDA can even be applied. This response is very similar, at least in spirit, to the second response.

We have now amassed a number of examples from ordinary discourse to aid us in our choice between RCEA and the two simplification principles SDA and S*. I do not think this evidence conclusively establishes that conditionals are always used in a way that would validate SDA and S*, but I do think the evidence very strongly supports the position that ordinary language conditionals are frequently used non-classically.

There is one other principle which is intuitively incompatible with SDA and which has found considerable support. This is the thesis

CS: $(A \,\&\, B) \rightarrow (A > B)$.

It turns out that any $\square$-normal extension of W which contains both SDA and

CS will also contain Triviality. This has until now been overlooked, primarily, I think, because most of those writers who have suggested SDA have not actually tried to formulate a conditional logic containing SDA. While I have developed logics containing SDA in earlier papers, I was committed as well in those papers to the rejection of CS. The reasoning behind my rejection of CS has been confused, since it involved conflating necessitation conditionals with conditionals which do not require a connection between antecedent and consequent. But whatever the reasons, I have in the past rejected CS and hence the question of the intuitive compatibility of SDA and CS did not arise in those writings. Now that I no longer reject CS on the mistaken notion that all conditionals are necessitation conditionals, I yet find in SDA a reason for rejecting CS. In the last chapter, I offered examples of conditionals with disjunctive antecedents which appeared to be counterexamples to CS. My rejection of CS depends at least in part, then, on my commitment to SDA.

I will not compare the advantages of SDA and CS as thoroughly as I did in the case of SDA and RCEA. One reason for this is that CS does not enjoy as good a reputation as does RCEA: CS has already come under fire in such writings as Bennett (1974) and Bigelow (1976). But a few remarks are in order, remarks which at least in part echo the discussion of the last chapter. The *prima facie* case for accepting CS for conditionals which do not require a connection between antecedents and consequent seems to depend upon the claim that if B is true, then $A > B$ is true unless A's being true would interfere with B's being true. If A is in fact true, then clearly A's being true *does* not interfere with B's being true, so $A > B$ must be true. But this line of reasoning is less persuasive in the case where A is a disjunction. If C is true and D is false, then $C \vee D$ is true. Suppose B is true and D's being true would definitely interfere with B's being true. Then even though $C \vee D$ and B are both true, we are inclined to reject $(C \vee D) > B$. We do not treat $C \vee D$ as a simple proposition whose truth either would or would not interfere with the truth of B. When we consider $C \vee D$, we view the two disjuncts separately and consider whether the truth of either separately would interfere with the truth of B. Of course, to offer this argument is but to indicate that one finds the *prima facie* case for SDA more persuasive than the *prima facie* case for CS. Where the two principles do not come into conflict, CS may be acceptable. Since, however, they sometimes do come into conflict, CS can not be accepted as a general principle so long as we accept SDA.

Our next step is to develop a non-classical conditional logic which contains a sufficiently strong set of substitution principles to satisfy our intuitions on that score.

2.3. THE NON-CLASSICAL LOGIC H

We have seen that any □-normal extension of **W** which contains either SDA or S* and is closed under RCEA also contains Triviality. But is RCEA really the culprit? Perhaps any □-normal extension of **W** containing either SDA or S* is already too strong and already contains Triviality. This is not the case, and we can show that it is not by constructing a BCS-model in which both SDA and S* are valid but in which Triviality is not valid.

We begin by simultaneously defining two functions w_1 and w_2 from CL into $\{T, F\}$ and a function f from CL $\times \{w_1, w_2\}$ into $\mathscr{P}(\{w_1, w_2\})$ as follows. Where $P_1, P_2, \ldots$ are our proposition letters, let $w_1(P_1) = T$, $w_2(P_1) = F$, and for all $n > 1$, let $w_1(P_n) = w_2(P_n) = T$. Let $f(P_1, w_1) = f(P_2, w_1) = \{w_1\}$, and for all $n > 2$, let $f(P_n, w_1) = \{w_1, w_2\}$. Let $f(P_1, w_2) = \emptyset$, and for all $n > 1$, let $f(P_n, w_2) = \{w_2\}$. For A, B $\in$ CL and $n \in \{1, 2\}$, let

(c1) $w_n(\sim A) = \begin{cases} T \text{ if } w_n(A) = F \\ F \text{ otherwise} \end{cases}$,

(c2) $w_n(A \mathbin{\&} B) = \begin{cases} T \text{ if } w_n(A) = T \text{ and } w_n(B) = T \\ F \text{ otherwise} \end{cases}$,

(c3) $w_n(A \vee B) = \begin{cases} T \text{ if } w_n(A) = T \text{ or } w_n(B) = T \\ F \text{ otherwise} \end{cases}$,

(c4) $w_n(A > B) = \begin{cases} T \text{ if } w(B) = T \text{ for all } w \in f(A, w_n) \\ F \text{ otherwise} \end{cases}$,

(c5) $f(\sim A, w_1) = \begin{cases} f(B, w_1) \text{ if } A = \sim B \\ \{w \in \{w_1, w_2\}: w(\sim A) = T\} \text{ if there is no } B \in CL \\ \text{such that } A = \sim B \end{cases}$,

(c6) $f(A \mathbin{\&} B, w_1) = \{w \in \{w_1, w_2\}: w(A \mathbin{\&} B) = T\}$,

(c7) $f(A \vee B, w_1) = f(A, w_1) \cup f(B, w_1)$,

(c8) $f(A > B, w_1) = \{w \in \{w_1, w_2\}: w(A > B) = T\}$, and

(c9) $f(A, w_2) = \begin{cases} \{w_2\} \text{ if } w_2(A) = T \\ F \text{ otherwise} \end{cases}$.

We can show that $\mathscr{M}$ is a BCS-model. We can also show that every instance of either SDA or S* is true in $\mathscr{M}$. Let **L** be the smallest □-normal extension of **W** which contains both SDA and S*. Then every member of **L** is valid in $\mathscr{M}$. But $w_1((P_2 > P_1) \to \square(P_2 \to P_1)) = F$, so Triviality is not valid in $\mathscr{M}$ and hence **L** does not contain Triviality. This establishes that there are □-normal extensions of **W** which contain both SDA and S* but which do not contain Triviality.

Not only is $\mathscr{M}$ a 'nice' BCS-model in which SDA and S* hold but Triviality does not; there is also a rather lengthy list of substitution theses which hold in $\mathscr{M}$. It is easier to show that these theses hold in $\mathscr{M}$ if one first proves the following result, where 'Sub(A, B, C, D)' means D is the result of replacing one or more occurrences of A by B in C:

LEMMA 2.3.1. If A ↔ B is a tautology, $f(A, w_1) = f(B, w_1)$, and Sub(A, B, C, D), then W/C = W/D.

Given this result, we can show that each of the following holds in $\mathscr{M}$, where 'A :: B' abbreviates the rule 'infer C ↔ D, if Sub(A, B, C, D)':

ST1: A ∨ B :: B ∨ A

ST2: A ∨ (B ∨ C) :: (A ∨ B) ∨ C

ST3: A ∨ A :: A

ST4: A & B :: B & A

ST5: A & (B & C) :: (A & B) & C

ST6: ∼(A & B) :: ∼A ∨ ∼B

ST7: ∼(A ∨ B) :: ∼A & ∼B

ST8: A & B :: ∼(∼A ∨ ∼B)

ST9: A & (B ∨ C) :: (A & B) ∨ (A & C)

If we replace the double-colon by '↔' in each of ST1–ST9, the resulting wffs are tautologous. Using the definition of $\mathscr{M}$, it can be shown that for each pair of wffs A and B which are instances of one of ST1–ST9 that $f(A, w_1) = f(B, w_1)$. Hence, by Lemma 2.3.1, each of the rules ST1–ST9 preserves validity in $\mathscr{M}$. Finally, we have a weak double negation thesis which holds in $\mathscr{M}$:

ST10: (A > B) ↔ (∼∼A > B)

Let **H** be the smallest □-normal extension of **W** containing all of SDA and ST1–ST10. By ST6 and SDA, **H** also contains S*. We know that all the axioms of **H** are valid in $\mathscr{M}$ and that the rules of **H** preserve BCS-validity, so every member of **H** must be valid in $\mathscr{M}$. But not every instance of Triviality is valid in $\mathscr{M}$. We will not concern ourselves with the question whether the axioms of **H** are independent since our primary goal is descriptive adequacy rather than formal elegance.

I do not know whether **H** is the strongest (or even *a* strongest) conditional logic which contains both SDA and S*. I suspect that it is not. **H** contains the following formula:

(31) $[(A \& A) > B] \to (A > B)$

In fact, (31) is contained in **W**. But **H** does not contain the converse of (31):

(32) $(A > B) \to [(A \& A) > B]$

We know this because every member of **H** is valid in $\mathscr{M}$, but $w_1(P_2 > P_1) = T$ while $w_1((P_2 \& P_2) > P_1) = F$. Among other things, this means that **H** is not closed under an &-counterpart to rule ST3:

ST11: $A \& A :: A$

My intuitions strongly support ST11, but I am not yet in a position to accept it. Let **H11** be the smallest □-normal extension of **H** which is closed under all of ST1–ST9 and ST11. I have not yet managed to show that Triviality either is or is not contained in **H11**, that is, whether **H11** is *trivial*. I suspect, however, that **H11** does not contain Triviality, and if this were so then **H11** would be preferable to **H**.

There is another very important question about **H** which remains unanswered. This question concerns the two formulae (22) and (24) of the previous section. These formulae need to be distinguished if we have any hope of handling certain putative counterexamples to SDA through the ploy of treating the disjunctive antecedents of these alleged counterexamples as really involving exclusive disjunction. But these two formulae are equivalent in **H**, i.e., **H** contains the following:

(33) $(((A \vee B) \& \sim(A \& B)) > C) \leftrightarrow (((A \& \sim B) \vee (\sim A \& B)) > C)$

If we adopt **H**, we must give up on one possibility for solving the problem presented by putative counterexamples to SDA of the sort presented by Dunn, and by McKay and van Inwagen.

As extensive as our list of substitution principles for **H** is, we still do not have a system which is closed under RCEA. Ideally, we should be able to provide an ordinary language justification for the rejection of substitutions of those provable equivalents not countenanced by our substitution principles. This, of course, would be a Herculean task. We will consider one case to see what such an attempt would involve. Consider the following substitution rule:

ST12: $A \vee (B \& C) :: (A \vee B) \& (A \vee C)$

ST9 and ST12 are familiar to us as the laws of distribution for the classical propositional calculus. We can show that every □-normal extension of **H** closed under all of ST1–ST9 and ST12 also contains Triviality.

In proving this we use ST9 itself as well as other more 'innocent' substitution principles in our argument *contra* ST12. So what we have actually shown is that we can not include *all* of these principles in a non-trivial logic. The possibility remains open that we might have a non-trivial logic containing both SDA and S* which is closed under ST12 if we choose our other substitution principles differently. At this point, our justification for preferring ST9 and ST12 is that we *can* show that **H** does not contain Triviality.

Through an examination of both hypothetical deliberation and conditional inference, we have developed a very powerful formal system. The logic **H**, because it contains both SDA and S*, can make a claim on descriptive adequacy that many other recently developed conditional logics cannot make. Of course, if the proponents of RCEA are correct, then **H** is actually less adequate than some of these other logics. And the price we have to pay for SDA and S* in terms of complicating our formal system is very high. What is worse, we cannot even be sure that **H** is complete in the sense that it is a strongest non-trivial logic containing both SDA and S*. **H** is a not entirely satisfying result of one attempt to allow a careful examination of our use of the conditional construction in English to dictate completely the direction in which the development of a conditional logic will go.

Finally we note some formal results for **H**.

THEOREM 2.3.2. **H** is consistent.
The consistency of **H** follows from Lemma 1.4.2 and the observation that the trivialization of each axiom of **H** is tautologous and that each rule of **H** preserves tautologous trivializations.

DEFINITION 2.3.3. A *descriptive class-selection model* (*DCS-model*) is a BCS-model $\mathscr{M} = \langle W, f \rangle$ which satisfies the following three conditions:

c1. $f(a, w) \cup f(B, w) \subseteq f(A \vee B, w)$;

c2. $f(C,w) = f(D,w)$ provided that one of the following conditions is satisfied:

(a) Sub(A ∨ B, B ∨ A, C, D),
(b) Sub(A ∨ (B ∨ E), (A ∨ B) ∨ E, C, D),
(c) Sub(A ∨ A, A, C, D),
(d) Sub(A & B, B & A, C, D),

(e) Sub(A & (B & E), (A & B) & E, C, D),
(f) Sub($\sim$(A & B), $\sim$A $\lor$ $\sim$B, C, D),
(g) Sub($\sim$(A $\lor$ B), $\sim$A & $\sim$B, C, D),
(h) Sub(A & B, $\sim$($\sim$A $\lor$ $\sim$B), C, D), or
(i) Sub(A & (B $\lor$ E), (A & B) $\lor$ (A & E), C, D); and

c3. $f(A, w) = f(\sim\sim A, w)$.

We say a wff A is *DCS-valid* if and only if A is valid in every DCS-model.

THEOREM 2.3.4 (Soundness for **H**). Every member of **H** is DCS-valid.

THEOREM 2.3.5 (Completeness for **H**). Every DCS-valid wff is in **H**.

By Theorems 2.3.4 and 2.3.5, **H** is determined by the class of all DCS-models.

2.4. AN EVALUATION OF H

The non-classical conditional logic **H** was developed with particular goals in mind. Primarily, we wanted a logic which properly took into account the natural language evidence for SDA and S*. Let's now consider how well **H** performs in this role.

First, recall that certain putative counterexamples were offered against SDA. These included the English sentences (16) and (17). Our response to these examples was to point out that they had other unique logical features besides their apparent failure to support SDA, and to suggest that these examples actually involved a different use of the conditional construction than that more common use which was under investigation. We further suggested that this new use of 'If A or B were true, A would be true' might depend upon reading the English 'or' as an exclusive disjunction while interpreting the conditional construction exactly as we had been interpreting it. This latter suggestion, if we could carry it off, is more attractive. Symbolizing (16) as (22) seemed to do the trick, but then we noted that (22) did not represent the only way to symbolize exclusive disjunction. Another way is given in (24), and this leads once again to counterintuitive results. We then suggested that we might insist on the symbolization given by (22). After all, we have already committed ourselves at this point to non-classicality so we shouldn't balk at preferring one of two-functionally equivalent wffs over the other, as the proper symbolization of some particular English sentence.

Unfortunately, our logic **H** offers us no aid in such a program. (22) and

(24) are provably equivalent in **H**. Since **H** does not make the right kind of distinction between these two wffs, we can't very well both adopt **H** as an adequate logic of conditionals and also use this particular method in arguing away the evidence against SDA.

We also noticed another puzzling feature of **H**: It lacked 'A & A : : A' as a substitution rule. Adding this rule to form the logic **H11** resulted in a logic which may or may not be trivial. These considerations suggest the direction in which further research should go. First, we want a non-trivial logic containing both SDA and S*. (We have seen that such a logic must be non-classical.) Second, we want this logic to distinguish between (22) and (24). Third, we want this logic to preserve as many of the substitution rules ST1–ST9 as possible. In fact, we should have reasons for our choices among substitution rules. Fourth, we want this logic to contain ST10. Finally, we want this logic to in some sense be a strongest non-trivial logic which satisfies these conditions.

Is there any reason at all to think that these conditions might be satisfiable? For example, is there any reason to think that we should want to distinguish between (22) and (24) other than that this would allow us to reject the putative counterexamples to SDA? And if we are to make this distinction, we must give up some of the substitution principles we have included in **H**. Are any of these more suspect on intuitive grounds than any others? I think the answer is a careful 'yes'.

Consider first the pair of wffs (22) and (24). What we seek is an example from ordinary discourse in which we would normally distinguish between the English equivalents of these two wffs. How about

(34)   If Ford or Maddox had won the last Presidential election, it
         ʻwould have been Ford.

I think most people who followed the election would accept (34). But then we also have

(35)   If Ford had won and Maddox lost, or Maddox won and Ford lost,
         then Ford would have won.

My limited experience, trying (34) and (35) on different people, has been that (34) is almost always accepted while (35) is usually not accepted. However, people seem to be more inclined to accept (35) if they have first accepted (34). And you can't ask an individual subject more than a couple of questions concerning such examples or the subject starts comparing the conditionals and quits giving the kind of immediate, intuitive response you seek.

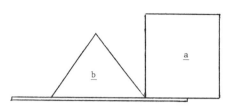

Fig. 2.4.1.

One more example concerns Figure 2.4.1. Here we see two objects, *a* and *b*, sitting on a shelf. Suppose that an earthquake in fact cause both objects to fall from the shelf. But what would have happened if the earthquake had caused only one of the objects to fall? The usual answer is that *a* would have fallen. Now what if the earthquake had caused *a* to fall but not *b*, or *b* to fall but not *a*? Presented in this way, it is not so clear that *a* would fall. Once again, we are distinguishing between sentences of the forms (22) and (24).

The examples of the previous paragraph exactly represent the kind of consideration I suggested when we first discussed (22) and (24). We consider situations when $(A \mathbin{\&} {\sim}B) \vee ({\sim}A \mathbin{\&} B)$ is the antecedent which we do not consider when the antecedent is $(A \vee B) \mathbin{\&} {\sim}(A \mathbin{\&} B)$. In the first case we consider all reasonable situations in which either disjunct is true, while in the second case we consider only the most reasonable situations in which the entire antecedent is true.

We also considered the two different versions of the substitution rule known as distribution in the last section. **H** is closed under ST9 but not under ST12. No ordinary language argument was given to justify this choice, but an argument of some persuasive value is available. Consider Figure 2.4.2. In the diagram, *a*, *b*, and *c* are switches which are either open or closed. We assume that the switches are actually in the open position. But suppose they were in a different position. What if *a* were closed, or *b* and *c* were closed? In that

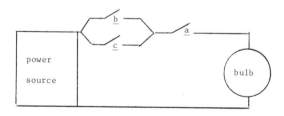

Fig. 2.4.2.

case, I think we would conclude that the bulb would not be lit, i.e., we accept a statement of the form

(36) $(A \vee (B \ \& \ C)) > \sim L$

But then what if *a* or *b* were closed, and also *a* or *c* were closed? Everyone I have tried this example on has replied that in this case, the bulb might be lit or it might not. They are accepting, then, a statement of the form

(37) $\sim(((A \vee B) \ \& \ (A \vee C)) > \sim L)$

These choices amount to a rejection of ST12. I must note, however, that acceptance of (36) is almost immediate while acceptance of (37) needs no prompting but is slow in coming. I think this is because it is much more difficult to decide what situations are to be considered in evaluating (37) than it is in evaluating (36).

Getting back again to the two different ways of symbolizing exclusive disjunction, we recall that (22) and (24) are provably equivalent in **H**. If these wffs should not be equivalent, then some of the substitution principles in **H** must also be unacceptable. After examining the list carefully, the most likely culprit seems to me to be ST6. Consider Figure 2.4.1 once again. Recall that an earthquake is supposed to have caused both *a* and *b* to fall from the shelf. But suppose that it hadn't caused them both to fall. It seems reasonable to say that if they hadn't both fallen, *a* would have still fallen, i.e., to accept

(38) $\sim(A \ \& \ B) > A$

But what would have happened if *a* hadn't fallen or *b* hadn't fallen? With this antecedent, it is not so clear that *a* would still have fallen. The inclination here is to accept

·(39) $\sim((\sim A \vee \sim B) > A)$

And this amounts to a rejection of ST6.

It is rather unfortunate for our program that ST6 has drawn suspicion since **H** contains S* only because it contains SDA and is closed under ST6. Perhaps we should begin our repair of **H** by deleting ST6 from the list of substitution rules and adding S* to the list of axioms. But this won't solve our problem since we will still be able, in the resulting logic, to infer (39) from (38) using only S* and (A7). In the English sentence with which (38) and (39) were associated in the text, we may have found an apparent counterexample to S* of the sort which corresponds to (16) and (17) with respect to SDA. It begins more and more to look as if our only response to such examples is to insist that the conditional construction is being used in these examples to play a quite different role from its more usual role. Where sentences of the apparent form of (38) cause problems for our analysis, such sentences are really of the form 'If A and B were not both to happen, A would *still* happen'. They tell us that ~B is more possible than ~A, and we should be able to infer from such a claim that 'If A and B were not both to happen, then B would not happen' is also true.

The initial evidence favoring SDA and S* is very persuasive. When we consider counterarguments based upon ordinary language examples, it seems likely that there are ways of circumventing those arguments. So we begin the process of developing a non-classical conditional logic. In doing this, we find that the task of providing adequate substitution principles for such a logic is monumental. The arguments favoring one substitution rule rather than another become more and more complicated, more and more subtle. In fact, this difficulty may be the overriding consideration.

So what is our situation now? I think the evidence is clear that we frequently use both SDA and S* as valid inference patterns in ordinary discourse. I have tried to explain this use by the most direct means, incorporating both SDA and S* into a conditional logic. The result of this attempt is far from being entirely satisfactory. I do not admit that such an attempt can not be completed successfully, but I do admit that the intuitive support for such an effort seems flimsier as difficulties mount.

It may be the case that our intuitions concerning conditionals are not fully developed for conditionals with complicated antecedents. This would mean that the conventions governing the use of conditionals only cover conditionals with antecedents of fairly simple logical form. When we try to formalize these conventions and thereby to extend them to cases of conditionals with antecedents of complicated logical form, we run into difficulties. There does not appear to be any way to extend our conventions governing conditionals with simple antecedents to an exhaustive set of conventions governing all conditionals, which is not either intuitively incompatible, or extremely complicated. We may be forced to reform our intuitions, at least to the extent that we must extend them to cover conditionals with complicated antecedents. Are we also forced to reform our intuitions in another way? The most direct way to formalize the intuitions we actually have about relatively simply conditionals seems to be to accept SDA. But this makes our other reform, the one forming new intuitions to cover complicated cases, much more difficult. Perhaps it is preferable to reform our intuitions from the ground up. If the fat lady finds her portrait unattractive, she should not try to persuade the painter to alter it so that it no longer resembles her; instead, she should lose weight and sit for another portrait. And this is the point at which I will leave the controversy for now.

CHAPTER 3

ALTERNATIVE MODEL THEORIES

3.1. INTRODUCTION

The analysis of conditionals presented so far is far from unique. In fact, many authors have suggested some sort of 'possible worlds' analysis of conditionals. These include Chellas (1975), Hansson and Gärdenfors (1973), Lewis (1973), Pollock (1976), and Stalnaker (1968). We can view such analyses as involving two distinct but related parts: the formal semantics or model theory itself and the informal account or intended interpretation which undergirds the model theory. Ultimately, I want to examine the informal or philosophical foundations of the analyses of a number of authors, comparing these attempts with my own, but this task will be made easier if we first summarize the formal part of each author's work. In this chapter I will define several possible worlds model theories for conditional logics and explore the formal, mathematical relationships between them. Some of these model theories will have actually been offered as part of an analysis of ordinary language conditionals, while others are primarily of technical interest only. For the moment, we will not be concerned with the philosophical merits of these theories, but only with their formal properties. In the next chapter we will consider the adequacy of some of these theories as representations of the conceptual structure lying behind our use of conditionals. Some readers may wish to omit this chapter, referring back to it as necessary in reading later chapters.

The (conditional) logics to be discussed here will be defined in terms of the following rules and wffs:

RCEA: from $A \leftrightarrow B$, to infer $(A > C) \leftrightarrow (B > C)$

RCEC: from $A \leftrightarrow B$, to infer $(C > A) \leftrightarrow (C > B)$

RCK: from $(A_1 \& \ldots \& A_n) \to B$, to infer $[(C > A_1) \& \ldots \& (C > A_n)] \to (C > B), n \geqslant 0$

RCE: from $A \to B$, to infer $A > B$.

ID: $A > A$

MP: $(A > B) \to (A \to B)$

MOD: $(\sim A > A) \to (B > A)$ (or $\Box A \to (B > A)$)

CSO: $[(A > B) \& (B > A)] \to [(A > C) \leftrightarrow (B > C)]$

CV: $[(A > B) \& \sim(A > \sim C)] \rightarrow [(A \& C) > B]$
CEM: $(A > B) \vee (A > \sim B)$

Much of the terminology used here and in the rest of this chapter is due to Chellas (1975) and Lewis (1973). ID is an identity thesis for conditionals, MP supplies a detachment principle for conditionals, and CEM is the conditional excluded middle thesis. A logic which is closed under both RCEA and RCEC is said to be *classical* and a logic which is closed under both RCEA and RCK is said to be *normal*. A classical logic which is closed under RCE is said to be *entailment preserving*. A logic which is closed under RCEC is *half-classical* and a logic closed under RCK is *half-normal*. Every normal logic is classical and every half-normal logic is half-classical. A normal logic which contains ID, MOD, CSO, and CV is called *variably strict*, and a variably strict logic which contains MP and CEM is called *singular*. Let **Ce** be the smallest half-classical logic, **Ck** the smallest half-normal logic, **CE** the smallest classical logic, **G** the smallest entailment preserving logic, **CK** the smallest normal logic, **V** the smallest variably strict logic, and **C2** the smallest singular logic. These definitions of **Ce**, **CE**, **Ck**, and **CK** are taken from Chellas (1975), Gabbay proposes a non-normal entailment preserving logic in his (1972), an alternative axiomatization of **V** is found in Lewis (1973), and an axiomatization of **C2** first appeared in Stalnaker (1968).

A *model* is an ordered pair ⟨W, X⟩ such that W is a non-empty set of possible worlds. A wff A is *valid* in a model ⟨W, X⟩ if and only if W/A = W. Two models ⟨W, X⟩ and ⟨U, Y⟩ are *equivalent* iff W = U. Different model theories are distinguished by the different natures of the second components of the models they define. A class Γ of models *determines* a logic **L** just in case for every sentence A, A $\in$ **L** iff for every model $\mathcal{M} \in \Gamma$, A is valid in $\mathcal{M}$. The *width* of the theory of α-models is the logic **L** which is determined by the class of all α-models. The *depth* of the theory of α-models is the class Γ of logics such that each member of Γ is determined by some class of α-models. A model theory has *maximal* depth iff every logic **L** which contains the width of the theory is a member of the depth of the theory. (Cf. Hansson and Gärdenfors (1973)).

The simplified notion of a model developed here will allow us to compare various model theories more easily. In fact, the original formulations of the model theories considered are more complicated than the formulations we will give them. I leave it to the reader to determine that our formulations are merely simplifications of the original formulations.

54   CHAPTER 3

3.2. WORLD-SELECTION-FUNCTION MODELS

Possible worlds semantics for conditionals were developed prior to Stalnaker (1968), but these earlier semantics ultimately treated conditionals as reducible to truth functions and a monadic modal operator with a logic at least as strong as that of the modal system **M**. Stalnaker provided the first possible worlds analysis of conditionals which lacked such features as Transitivity and Weakening Antecedents. Stalnaker's semantics, which involves the notion of a world-selection-function, is developed in more detail in Stalnaker (1968), and semantics for a quantified logic of conditionals is found in Stalnaker and Thomason (1970).

DEFINITION 3.2.1. A *world-selection-function model* (*WS-model*) is a model $\langle W, \langle \alpha, R, s \rangle \rangle$ such that:

(1) α is the constant T-function on the set of wffs;
(2)   R is a reflexive binary relation on $W \cup \{\alpha\}$;
(3)   for all $w \in W$, $\langle w, \alpha \rangle \notin R$ and $\langle \alpha, w \rangle \notin R$;
(4)   s assigns to each wff A and each $w \in W$ a member $s(A, w)$ of $W \cup \{\alpha\}$ such that $s(A, w)(A) = T$;
(5)   if $s(A, w) \neq \alpha$, then $\langle w, s(A, w) \rangle \in R$;
(6)   if $s(A, w) = \alpha$, then for all $w' \in W$, either $w'(A) = F$ or $\langle w, w' \rangle \notin R$;
(7)   if $w(A) = T$, then $s(A, w) = w$;
(8)   if $s(A, w)(B) = T$ and $s(B, w)(A) = T$, then $s(A, w) = s(B,w)$;
(9) $W/A > B = \{w \in W: s(A, w)(B) = T\}$.

R is to be interpreted as an *accessibility relation* on the set of possible worlds W, a notion borrowed from the now-familiar semantics for model logics. s is a function which selects for each sentence A and world w, the world most like w at which A is true. α is the *absurd world* at which everything is true; we let $s(A, w) = \alpha$ just in case there is no possible world accessible from w at which A is true.

THEOREM 3.2.2. **C2** is determined by the class of all WS-models. This theorem is proved in Stalnaker and Thomason (1970).

3.3. SYSTEM-OF-SPHERES MODELS

DEFINITION 3.3.1. A *system-of-spheres model* (*SOS-model*) is a model $\langle W, \$ \rangle$ such that:

(1) $ assigns to each $w \in W$ a nested set $\$_w$ of subsets of W which is closed under unions and finite intersections;

(2) $W/A > B = \{w \in W: \bigcup \$_w \cap W/A = \emptyset$ or there exists an $S \in \$_w$ such that $\emptyset \neq S \cap W/A \subseteq W/B\}$.

This type of model is due to Lewis (1971), (1973). A system-of-spheres around a world tells us the relative similarity of other worlds to that world. If $S \in \$_w, w' \in S$ and $w'' \notin S$, then w' is more similar to w than is w''

THEOREM 3.3.2. **V** is determined by the class of all SOS models. **V** is equivalent to the logic **CO** defined in Lewis (1971) where it is shown that **CO** is determined by the class of all SOS-models.

THEOREM 3.3.3. Each WS-model is equivalent to some SOS-model.
Theorem 3.3.3 is proved in Sections 2.7 and 3.4 of Lewis (1973).

3.4. RELATIONAL MODELS

We can think of '>' as a modal functor rather than a sentence connective. Then '>' assigns to each sentence A a model operator 'A >'. Something of this sort is suggested by Lewis (1971), when he says that any logic weaker than **V** (including all non-classical logics) might be called a logic of "sententially indexed modalities" rather than a logic of conditionals. The corresponding suggestion for semantics is that we supply a separate accessibility relation for each modal operator 'A >'.

DEFINITION 3.4.1. A *relational model* (*R-model*) is a model $\langle W, R \rangle$ such that:

(1)   R assigns to each sentence A a binary relation R_A on W;

(2) $W/A > B = \{w \in W:$ for all $w' \in W$, if $\langle w, w' \rangle \in R_A$ then $w'(B) = T\}$.

THEOREM 3.4.2. **Ck** is determined by the class of all R-models.
    The proof of Theorem 3.4.2 and similar theorems will be omitted. The techniques involved are exactly those used in Chapters 1 and 2 to provide similar results for the logics **W** and **H**.

Rather than sententially indexed modalities, we can also think of conditionals as involving propositionally indexed modalities. This gives rise to the notion of a 'propositional' relational model. As was mentioned in Chapter 2, possible worlds semanticists frequently suggest that propositions should be conceived as sets of possible worlds.

DEFINITION 3.4.3. A *propositional relational model* (*PR-model*) is a model $\langle W, R \rangle$ such that:

(1)   R assigns to each subset S of W a binary relation R_S on W;

(2) $W/A > B = \{w \in W:$ for all $w' \in W$, if $\langle w, w' \rangle \in R_{W/A}$ then $w'(B) = T\}$.

THEOREM 3.4.4. **CK** is determined by the class of all PR-models.

THEOREM 3.4.5. Each WS-model is equivalent to some PR-model.
    Proof. Let $\langle W, \langle \alpha, R, s \rangle \rangle$ be a WS-model. For each sentence A, let $T_{W/A} = \{\langle w, w' \rangle \in W^2: s(A, w) = w'\}$. If $S \subseteq W$ and there is no sentence A such that $S = W/A$, let $T_S = \emptyset$. Since **C2** is classical and **C2** is determined by the class of all WS-models, T_S is well-defined for such $S \subseteq W$; in particular, there do not exist sentences A and B such that $W/A = W/B$ and yet $s(A, w) \neq s(B, w)$ for some $w \in W$. Let $w \in W$. Suppose $w(A > B) = T$ and $\langle w, w' \rangle \in T_{W/A}$. Then $s(A, w) = w'$ and $w'(B) = T$. Conversely, suppose for all $w' \in W$, if $\langle w, w' \rangle \in T_{W/A}$ then $w'(B) = T$. Then either $\langle w, s(A, w) \rangle \in T_{W/A}$ or $s(A, w) = \alpha$; in either case, $s(A, w)(B) = T$ and, $w(A > B) = T$. Hence, $W/A > B = \{w \in W:$ for all $w' \in W$, if $\langle w, w' \rangle \in T_{W/A}$ then $w'(B) = T\}$. So $\langle W, T \rangle$ is a PR-model and our theorem is established.

THEOREM 3.4.6. Each PR-model is equivalent to some R-model.
    Proof. For PR-model $\langle W, R \rangle$, we let $T_A = R_{W/A}$ for each sentence A. It is then obvious that $\langle W, T \rangle$ is an R-model.

Gabbay (1972) proposes that conditionals should be viewed as propositionally indexed modalities, but he makes the additional suggestion that both the antecedent and the consequent of the conditional should serve as indices for the accessibility relation. This gives rise to an interesting variation on the notion of a relational model for conditionals

DEFINITION 3.4.7. A *dual propositional relational model* (*DPR-model*) is a model $\langle W, R \rangle$ such that:

(1)   R assigns to each pair of subsets S and T of W a binary relation $R_{S,T}$ on W;

(2) $W/A > B = \{w \in w: \text{ for all } w' \in W, \text{ if } \langle w, w' \rangle \in R_{W/A, W/B} \text{ then } w'(A \to B) = T\}$.

THEOREM 3.4.8. **G** is determined by the class of all DPR-models.

THEOREM 3.4.9. Each SOS-model is equivalent to some DPR-model.
  Proof. Let $\langle W, S \rangle$ be an SOS-model. For each $T, U \subseteq W$ and $w \in W$, let

$$\mathscr{S}_{T,U,w} = \left\{ \begin{array}{l} \{S_i \in \$_w: \emptyset \neq S_i \cap T \subseteq U\} \text{ if} \\ \{S_i \in \$_w: \emptyset \neq S_i \cap T \subseteq U\} \neq \emptyset \\ \{\bigcup \$_w\} \text{ otherwise} \end{array} \right\}.$$

For each $w \in W$, we pick an $S_w \in \mathscr{S}_{T,U,w}$ and set $\langle w, w' \rangle \in R_{T,U}$ iff $w' \in S_w$. Then $\langle W, R \rangle$ is a DPR-model.

THEOREM 3.4.10. Each PCS-model is equivalent to some DPR-model.
  Proof. Let $\langle W, f \rangle$ be a PCS-model. For each $S, T \subseteq W$, let $R_{S,T} = \{\langle w, w' \rangle: w' \in f(S, w)\}$. Then $\langle W, R \rangle$ is a DPR-model.

3.5. CLASS-SELECTION-FUNCTION MODELS

A *class-selection-function model* (*CS-model*) is a model $\langle W, f \rangle$ such that:

(1)   f assigns to each sentence A and each $w \in W$ a subset $f(A, w)$ of W;

(2) $W/A > B = \{w \in W: f(A, w) \subseteq W/B\}$.

The notion of a CS-model is developed in Chapter 1 of this volume, in Lewis (1971), and in Nute (1975).

THEOREM 3.5.1. There is a one-to-one correspondence between CS-models and equivalent R-models.
  Proof. Let $\langle W, f \rangle$ be a CS-model. For each sentence A, let $R_A = \{\langle w, w' \rangle \in W^2: w' \in f(A, w)\}$. Then for all $w \in W$, $f(A, w) = \{w' \in W: \langle w, w' \rangle \in R_A\}$; so $W/A > B = \{w \in W: \text{ for all } w' \in W, \text{ if } \langle w, w' \rangle \in R_A \text{ then } w'(B) = T\}$ and $\langle W, R \rangle$ is an R-model. Now let $\langle W, R \rangle$ be an R model. For each sentence A and each $w \in W$, let $f(A, w) = \{w' \in W: \langle w, w' \rangle \in R_A\}$. Clearly, $\langle W, f \rangle$ is a CS-model.

THEOREM 3.5.2. **Ck** is determined by the class of all CS-models. Theorem 3.5.2 follows immediately from Theorems 3.4.2 and 3.5.1.

Class-selection function models also have their propositional counterparts.

DEFINITION 3.5.3. A *propositional class-selection-function model (PCS-model)* is a model $\langle W, f \rangle$ such that:

(1)   f assigns to each $S \subseteq W$ and $w \in W$ a subset $f(S, w)$ of W;

(2) $W/A > B = \{w \in W: f(W/A, w) \subseteq W/B\}$.

PCS-models are developed in Chellas (1975) where they are called *standard* models.

THEOREM 3.5.4. There is a one-to-one correspondence between PCS-models and equivalent PR-models.
    Proof. The proof of this theorem is very similar to the proof for Theorem 3.5.1. Let $\langle W, f \rangle$ be a PCS-model. For each $S \subseteq W$, let $R_S = \{\langle w, w' \rangle \in W^2:$ $w' \in f(S, w)\}$. Then it can easily be shown that $\langle W, R \rangle$ is a PR-model. Conversely, let $\langle W, R \rangle$ be a PR-model. For each $S \subseteq W$ and each $w \in W$, let $f(S, w) = \{w' \in W: \langle w, w' \rangle \in R_S\}$. Then $\langle W, f \rangle$ is a PCS-model.

THEOREM 3.5.5. **CK** is determined by the class of all PCS-models.

THEOREM 3.5.6. Each PCS-model is equivalent to some CS-model.

Theorem 3.5.5 is proved in Chellas (1975). We did not provide a proof for Theorem 3.4.4; Chellas's proof of Theorem 3.5.5 and our proof of Theorem 3.5.4 together provide such a proof.

3.6. NEIGHBORHOOD MODELS

In section 3.4 we saw how the relational model theory for modal systems could be adapted to produce a model theory for conditionals. A similar adaptation of the neighborhood model theory for modal systems discussed in Montague (1970) and Scott (1970) also can be produced.

DEFINITION 3.6.1. A *neighborhood model (N-model)* is a model $\langle W, N \rangle$ such that:

(1)   N assigns to each sentence A and each $w \in W$ a set $N(A, w)$ of subsets of W;

(2) $W/A > B = \{w \in W: W/B \in N(A, w)\}$

Chellas (1975) alludes to neighborhood models in a footnote.

THEOREM 3.6.2. **Ce** is determined by the class of all N-models.

THEOREM 3.6.3. Each R-model is equivalent to some N-model.

Proof. Let $\langle W, R \rangle$ be an R-model. For each sentence A and each $w \in W$, let $N(A, w) = \{S \subseteq W:$ for all $w' \in W$, if $\langle w, w' \rangle \in R_A$ then $w' \in S\}$. Let $w \in W$. Suppose $w(A > B) = T$. Then for all $w' \in W$, if $\langle w, w' \rangle \in R_A$ then $w'(B) = T$. So $W/B \in N(A, w)$. Now suppose $W/B \in N(A, w)$ and $\langle w, w' \rangle \in R_A$. Then $w' \in W/B$ and hence $w'(B) = T$. Thus, $W/A > B = \{w \in W: W/B \in N(A, w)\}$ and $\langle W, N \rangle$ is an N-model.

As in the case of both relational and class-selection-function models, the theory of neighborhood models admits of a propositional version.

DEFINITION 3.6.4. A *propositional neighborhood model (PN-model)* is a model $\langle W, N \rangle$ such that:

(1)   N assigns to each $S \subseteq W$ and each $w \in W$ a set $N(S, w)$ of subsets of W;

(2) $W/A > B = \{w \in W: W/B \in N(W/A, w)\}$

PN-models are developed in Chellas (1975) where they are called *minimal models*.

THEOREM 3.6.5. **CE** is determined by the class of all PN-models.

Theorem 3.6.5 is proved in Chellas (1975).

THEOREM 3.6.6. Each PN-model is equivalent to some N-model.

Proof. Let $\langle W, N \rangle$ be a PN-model. For each sentence A and each $w \in W$, let $M(A, w) = N(W/A, w)$. Then $\langle W, M \rangle$ is an N-model.

THEOREM 3.6.7. Each SOS-model is equivalent to some PN-model.

Proof. Let $\langle W, \$ \rangle$ be an SOS-model. For each $S \subseteq W$ and each $w \in W$, let

$$N(S, w) = \left\{ \begin{array}{l} \{U \subseteq W:\ \text{there exists } V \in \$_w \text{ such that} \\ \emptyset = V \cap S \subseteq U\} \\ \text{if} \bigcup \$_w \cap S \neq \emptyset \\ \mathscr{P}(W) \text{ otherwise} \end{array} \right\}$$

Let $w \in W$. Suppose $w(A > B) = T$. Then $\bigcup \$_w \cap W/A = \emptyset$ or there exists $U \in \$_w$ such that $\emptyset \neq U \cap W/A \subseteq W/B$. In either case, $W/B \in N(W/A, w)$. Suppose conversely that $W/B \in N(W/A, w)$. If $\bigcup \$_w \cap W/A = \emptyset$ then $w(A > B) = T$, so suppose $\bigcup \$_w \cap W/A \neq \emptyset$. Then there exists $U \in S_w$ such that $\emptyset \neq U \cap W/A \subseteq W/B$. So $w(A > B) = T$. Thus, $W/A > B = \{w \in W: W/B \in N(W/A, w)\}$ and $\langle W, N \rangle$ is a PN-model.

THEOREM 3.6.8. Each PR-model is equivalent to some PN-model.

Proof. Let $\langle W, R \rangle$ be a PR-model. For each $S \subseteq W$ and each $w \in W$, let $N(S, w) = \{U \subseteq W: $ for all $w' \in W$, if $\langle w, w' \rangle \in R_S$ then $w' \in U\}$ proof that $\langle W, N \rangle$ is a PN-model parallels the proof for Theorem 3.6.3.

THEOREM 3.6.9. Each DPR-model is equivalent to some PN-model.

Proof. Let $\langle W, f \rangle$ be a DPR-model. For each $S \subseteq W$ and $w \in W$, let $N_w(S) = \{T \subseteq W: $ if $\langle w, w' \rangle \in R_{ST}$, then $w' \in (W - S) \cup T\}$. Then $\langle W, N \rangle$ is a PN-model.

3.7. EXTENSIONAL MODELS

DEFINITION 3.7.1. An *extensional model* (*E-model*) is a model $\langle W, f \rangle$ such that:

(1)   f assigns to each $S, S' \subseteq W$ a subset $f(S, S')$ of W;

(2) $W/A > B = f(W/A, W/B)$.

Extensional models are suggested in Hansson and Gärdenfors (1973). These models are called *extensional* because they treat wffs as having sets of worlds as extensions and give truth conditions for all complex wffs strictly in terms of the extensions of their subformulas. We noted in Chapter 2 that Stalnaker says all so-called intensional semantics are extensional in this sense. Hansson and Gärdenfors, however, suggest that we should reserve the term 'intensional' for logics and semantics which are not extensional in this sense. Thus, Hansson and Gärdenfors use 'extensional' and 'intensional', respectively, as Stalnaker uses 'intensional' and 'hyperintensional'.

THEOREM 3.7.3. There is a one-to-one correspondence between E-models and equivalent PN-models.

Proof. The simple proof of Theorem 3.7.3 is left to the reader.

3.8. SUMMARY OF EQUIVALENCE RESULTS

Letting $\alpha \to \beta$ indicates that each α-model is equivalent to some β-model we can summarize our results in Figure 3.8.1. The width of each model theory is displayed in parentheses. We note that the relationship represented by the arrows in the diagram is transitive.

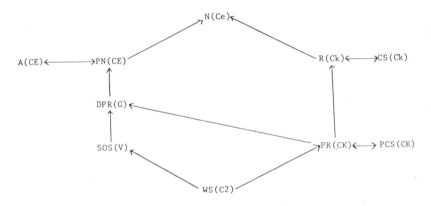

Fig. 3.8.1.

It remains to be shown that this diagram is complete. In Nute (1978a) a CS-model is constructed in which RCEA does not hold. Since **CE** and **CK** are both closed under RCEA, we conclude that for any α and β such that $\beta \to$ PN or $\beta \to$ PR, and CS $\to \alpha$, we have not $-\alpha \to \beta$. Lewis (1971) shows that we can construct an SOS-model for which there exists no equivalent CS-model. From this we conclude that for all α and β such that SOS $\to \alpha$ and $\beta \to$ CS, we have not $-\alpha \to \beta$. To see that DPR is properly located, we need to show that **CE** is not closed under RCE and that **G** is not closed under RCK. Both of these results are proved in Section 7.4. It is also proved in Section 7.4 that (CS) $[(A > B) \& \sim(A > \sim C)] \to [(A \& C) > B]$ is not contained in the □-normal extension **SS** of **CK**, and hence is not contained in **CK**. Since CS is contained in **V**, we have not $-$PCS $\to$ SOS. For the remaining cases, we need to show that **CK** does not contain MP. Let w be any possible world such that for all A, $B \in$ CL, $w(A > B) = T$. Clearly, every member of **CK** is true in the model $\langle \{w\}, \emptyset \rangle$, but $[(A \lor \sim A) > (A \& \sim A)] \to [(A \lor \sim A) \to (A \& \sim A)]$ a substitution instance of MP, is not. Since **CK** does not contain MP, neither does **CE**. Since **C2** contains MP while **CK** does not, we have not $-$PR $\to$ WS and not $-$PCS $\to$ WS. Since **V** contains MP while **CE** does not, we have not $-$E $\to$ SOS and not $-$PN $\to$ SOS. Thus, we justify the omission of the arrows which are

3.9. DEPTH

missing in our diagram. In my (1978) I adapted results by Fine (1974) and Thomason (1974) to show that the SOS-model theory lacks maximal depth. We can also adapt a result from Gerson (1975) to show that *all* of the model theories explored in this chapter lack maximal depth.

We call any logic which contains MOD *modally proper*. Examples of modally proper logics are **V** and **C2**. We define a unary modal operator as suggested in Chapter 1:

$$\Box A =_{df} \sim A > A.$$

Let $\langle W, N \rangle$ be any N-model in which every substitution instance of MOD is true. Then we can show that $W/\Box A = \{w \in W: W/A \in \bigcap_B N(B, w)\}$. For each $w \in W$, let $M(w) = \bigcap_B N(B, w)$. Then $\langle W, M \rangle$ is a *neighborhood model for modal systems* of the sort developed in Montague (1970) and Scott (1970).

Gerson (1975) shows that there is an extension **L** of the modal system **S4** which is not determined by any class of Scott-Montague neighborhood models. The logic of the modal operator '$\Box$' in the conditional logic **C2**, the strongest logic we need consider, is **M**. Since **S4** is an extension of **M** and Gerson's **L** is an extension of **S4**, we can strengthen **C2** to produce a logic **C2L** for which the logic of the modal operator '$\Box$' is **L**. Then **C2L** is determined by some class of N-models only if **L** is determined by some class of Scott-Montague models, which it is not. Since every other logic we have explored is equivalent to some N-model, it is obvious that none of the examined model theories has maximal depth.

CHAPTER 4

CLASSICAL ANALYSES OF CONDITIONALS

4.1. INTRODUCTION

In Chapter 2, we reviewed the evidence favoring each of SDA and RCEA, and we tentatively accepted SDA. In Chapter 3, we considered the formal properties of various possible worlds model theories for conditional logics. Now we will consider the question of the *philosophical adequacy* of several semantics for subjunctive conditionals, tentatively accepting RCEA.

Starting with our weak conditional logic **W**, we can form a classical logic simply by adding the rule RCEA. However, once we admit classicality, the thesis CSO becomes attractive. Provided that we accept classicality at all, I propose that we also accept CSO. Let **WC** be the smallest □-normal extension of **W** which contains CSO. It can easily be shown that WC is closed under RCEA and RCEC and is therefore classical. **WC** is determined by the class of all BCS-models $\langle W, f \rangle$ such that for all $w \in W$ and $A, B \in CL$, if $f(A, w) \subseteq W/B$ and $f(B, w) \subseteq W/A$, then $f(A, w) = f(B, w)$.

In this chapter, we will consider various suggestions for strengthening **WC**. The force of these suggestions is that we require a stronger logic than **WC** to adequately represent the way in which conditionals are used in ordinary discourse. We will also look at proposals for weakening our conditional logic. All of these suggestions are linked more or less firmly with alternative semantics for conditionals. We will, then, be examining the descriptive adequacy of possible worlds semantics which may be viewed as alternatives to the theory of CS-models.

4.2. STALNAKER AND THE UNIQUENESS ASSUMPTION

In his (1968), Stalnaker describes a thought experiment to be used in evaluating conditionals which is similar to the procedure described in Chapter 1:

Consider a possible world in which A is true, and which otherwise differs minimally from the actual world. '*If A, then B' is true (false) just in case B is true (false) in that possible world* (p. 169).

This proposal seems to leave open the possibility that there might be several possible worlds in which A is true (A-worlds) and which differ minimally from

63

the actual world, and that any one of these may be used in determining the truth value of $A > B$. But this interpretation of Stalnaker must be rejected if possible worlds satisfy a reasonable identity condition and Stalnaker's truth condition for counterfactuals is to be well defined. For suppose w_1 and w_2 are distinct A-worlds which differ minimally from the actual world. We assume that since w_1 and w_2 are distinct, there is some sentence B which is true in w_1 and false in w_2. (We are assured of this identity condition for the possible worlds of Chapter 1.) Then performing Stalnaker's thought experiment will result in different truth values for $A > B$ depending on which minimally different A-world we consider. So Stalnaker is committed to the view that there is for each sentence A at most one A-world which differs minimally from the actual world.

A difficulty with Stalnaker's account concerns impossible antecedents. We have assumed that impossible sentences or wffs are not true in any possible world. Stalnaker takes a different approach, postulating an absurd world in which every sentence is true. Then the A-world least different from the actual world is the absurd world just in case A is impossible. Hence, Stalnaker actually assumes that for each sentence A there is *exactly* one A-world which differs minimally from the actual world. This is *Stalnaker's uniqueness assumption*.

The WS-models defined in Chapter 3 were developed by Stalnaker as the formal expression of his analysis of conditionals. In a WS-model, α is the absurd world and R is an accessibility relation used to interpret modal sentences. In fact, we get the familiar truth condition for modal sentences of Kripke (1963): $w(\Box A) = T$ if and only if $w'(A) = T$ for all w' such that $\langle w, w' \rangle \in R$. The function f in a Stalnaker model is very much like a CS-function that satisfies the assumption that for each wff A and world w, $f(A, w)$ has at most one member. The logic proposed by Stalnaker is **C2** which contains the thesis CEM and CEM is true in any WS-model.

We saw in Chapter 3 that **C2** is determined by the class of all WS-models and that every WS-model is equivalent to some CS-model. Thus, **C2** must be determined by some class of CS-models. We might, then, prefer CS-models to WS-models, even if we judge **C2** to be adequate, simply because CS-models avoid the notion of an absurd world. However, we shall see that both CEM and Stalnaker's uniqueness assumption must be rejected. The logic **C2** is too strong to be the logic of conditionals which we are seeking.

Difficulties begin to show up when we try to incorporate Stalnaker's proposal into our account of hypothetical deliberation. The evaluation of conditionals, we said, involves a search for counterexamples. According to the uniqueness assumption, there is only one situation which *can* be a legitimate counterexample. The situation we examine is *the* situation most like the actual situation in which the antecedent of the conditional being evaluated is true. Determining which situation this is, will not in general be easy. Consider the sentence

(1)   If Carter had never served as Governor of Georgia, he would never have been President of the United States.

According to Stalnaker, we evaluate (1) by considering the situation in which Carter never serves as Governor, which is most like the actual situation. Which situation is this? Do we simply kill Carter off before he becomes Governor? Implicit in the conditional seems to be the assumption that Carter lives but *fails* to become Governor. Perhaps we should keep Carter in Plains raising peanuts, but this would require rather drastic changes in Carter's personality. A situation more similar to the actual one might be a situation in which Carter seeks to be elected Governor, but loses the election. Then again, this would require changing the minds of a goodly number of voters in Georgia. It might change the world less if Carter were to change his mind about the way he will pursue his political ambitions rather than to change the minds of so many people about the way they will vote. Carter might, for example, decide to run for U.S. Senator instead of Governor. If he runs for the Senate, does he win or lose? If he wins, does the resultantly greater national exposure concerning his views on national and international issues enhance or detract from his appeal to the voters? In short, which of the myriad situations which come to mind, is the situation most like the actual situation in which Carter never serves as Governor? I, at least, find myself unable to decide. Notice that we are only considering what seem to be relevant features of the situations which come to mind. Ideally, we would have to know everything about the actual situation in order to pick the situation we will consider in our hypothetical deliberations, but this requirement is one which would apply to the idealized instructions for hypothetical deliberation developed in Chapter 1 as well as it applies to Stalnaker's proposal. Even lumping together those situations which are alike with regard to those features we take to be relevant and treating them as a single situation, which we must do in actual practice, we are still required to accomplish a selection from among the many alternative situations that come to mind which we are in general unable to accomplish. But even making the grand assumption that we could pick out this unique world, this is not the procedure we actually use in our hypothetical deliberations. Even if we decide that a situation in which Carter never served as Governor because he instead ran for the Senate is more like what actually happened than is any situation in which Carter never won either of the two gubernatorial contests he entered, we might still consider this latter kind of situation, an appropriate kind of situation to consider in evaluating (1). More generally, even if we could determine the situation in which A is true which differs least from the actual situation, we clearly do not in general confine our hypothetical deliberation to a consideration of that situation, for we nearly always consider a number of possibilities in evaluating conditionals.

Besides the practical difficulties involved in trying to follow Stalnaker's instructions, Lewis in his (1973) argues persuasively that there are sentences such that there can be no 'closest' worlds in which those sentences are true.

Suppose we entertain the counterfactual supposition that at this point——— there appears a line more than an inch long. (Actually, it is just under an inch.) There are worlds with a line 2″ long; worlds presumably closer to ours with a line 1-1/2″ long; worlds presumably still closer . . . But how long is the line in the *closest* worlds with a line more than an inch long? If it is $1 + x''$ for any x however small, why are there not worlds still closer to ours in which it is $1 + 1/2x''$, a length still closer to its actual length? The shorter we make the line (above 1″), the closer we come to the actual length; so the closer we come, presumably, to our actual world. Just as there is no shortest possible length above 1″, so there is no closest world to ours among the worlds with lines more than an inch long . . . (p. 20).

We conclude, then, that for many sentences there exist no worlds in which those sentences are true and which differ minimally from the actual world. The uniqueness assumption is intuitively false and the corresponding singularity condition for CS-models is unacceptable. Lewis's example also shows that we must reject CEM, for the two sentences 'If the line were longer than 1″, it would be 2″ long' and 'If the line were longer than 1″, it would not be 2″ long' are both false.

Stalnaker's analysis of conditionals is based on the false assumption that for every wff A, there is a unique A-world most like the actual world. Even were Stalnaker's assumption adopted, it is unlikely that we would in general be able to pick out for a given sentence A the A-world most like the actual world. And even if we *could* always pick out the A-world most like the actual world, we certainly do not actually confine our attention to such a world in evaluating conditionals with A as antecedent, and we do not in general accept the validity of the counterfactual thesis CEM. C2 and WS-models are not an attractive alternative to WC and CS-models.

4.3. LEWIS AND SYSTEMS OF SPHERES

The opening statement in Lewis (1973) is strongly reminiscent of Stalnaker:

'If Kangaroos had no tails, they would topple over' seems to me to mean something like this: In any possible state of affairs in which kangaroos have no tails, and which resembles our actual state of affairs as much as kangaroos having no tails permits it to, the kangaroos topple over (p. 1).

Although his analysis depends upon the similarity of worlds just as Stalnaker's does, Lewis explicitly rejects Stalnaker's uniqueness assumption and offers a much more complex account. Since we are not always able to determine a *closest* world in which some antecedent A is true, we must find some other way of evaluating our conditionals. $A > C$ is true, says Lewis, just in case A is impossible or there is at least one world in which A & C is true that is nearer (more similar to) the actual world than is any world in which A & $\sim$C is true. To verify $A > C$ (in the non-vacuous case where A is possible), we do not need to determine that C is true in the *nearest* A-world as Stalnaker suggests; we only need to determine that some confirming situation is more like the actual situation than is any disconfirming situation.

Lewis's formal semantics makes use of the notion of a system-of-spheres model. A system-of-spheres on a set W of possible worlds is the formal counterpart of the intuitive notion of similarity of worlds. For $w_1, w_2, w_3 \in$ W, we say w_1 is *closer, nearer,* or *more similar* to w_2 than is w_3 if there is a sphere about w_2 which contains w_1 but does not contain w_3. The conditional logic which Lewis actually endorses is **VC**. **VC** is the smallest □-normal extension of **V** containing both MP and the following thesis:

(CS) $(A \& B) \rightarrow (A > B)$

The logic **VC** is determined by the class of all SOS-models $\langle W, \$ \rangle$ such that for each $w \in W$, $\{w\} \in \$_w$.

In Chapter 1, I offered reasons for rejecting CS, reasons involving conditionals with disjunctive antecedents. This seemed a good enough justification for omitting CS at the time since we were trying to develop as uncontroversial a basis as possible upon which we could build more satisfactory logics. Since SDA was one of the theses I wished to consider for inclusion in our conditional logic, implicitly relying upon SDA in an argument to reject CS, at least initially, made good sense. Then we could consider separately the question which of the two competing theses CS or SDA we wished to adopt, if indeed we wished to adopt either. But now we have provisionally rejected SDA, so we will need a new reason to reject CS if that continues to be our position. In fact, I think that is probably what we should do.

The *prima facie* case for accepting CS was discussed in Chapter 1. If B is true and our conditional does not require a connection between A and B, then A > B is true unless there is an *antagonistic* connection between A and B. So A > B is true, in other words, if B is true and the truth of A *would not* interfere with the truth of B. But if A is also true, then clearly the truth of A *does not* interfere with the truth of B. Yet this does not insure that there is no antagonistic connection between A and B. I draw an example from Bennett (1974):

> Suppose that I believe (perhaps on hearsay) that Caspar didn't come to the party and that the party was a bad one, and I say "If Caspar had come, the party would have been a good one". You hear me say this, and you know that Caspar did attend the party and that it was a good party; but you also know that Caspar ruins most parties he attends, and that he nearly ruined this one. It was a good party *despite* the fact that Caspar came to it. Everyone on whom I have tried this example insists that the statement "If Caspar had come, the party would have been a good one" is *not true*; most say it is *false*; and none will allow that the statement is true but "odd" [as Lewis suggest] (pp. 287–388).

By making an appeal to a survey of opinion as he does, Bennett is explicitly charging that Lewis's analysis of conditionals is descriptively inadequate. Lewis's method of evaluating conditionals, as well as any other method which validates CS, leads to results which are intuitively objectionable. Nor does the source of the objection appear to be some assumed requirement that there must be a positive connection between the antecedent and the consequent in order for the conditional to be true. If Caspar were an innocuous little fellow whom nobody ever noticed, and if the party was in fact a good one, then the party would have been a good one if Caspar had come. The reason the conditional is objectionable is that there is such a strong *negative* connection between the antecedent and the consequent. In the case of Bennett's example, the negative connection is so strong that we reject the conditional, even though its antecedent and consequent are both true. There is good reason for rejecting CS even for conditionals which are not necessitation conditionals.

A rejection of CS does not commit us to a complete rejection of Lewis's semantics. We can give up CS and retreat to the more solid ground of the weaker logic **VW**, the smallest □-normal extension of **V** containing the thesis ID. But there is another thesis contained by both **VW** and **V** which causes concern. This is

CV: $[(A > B) \, \& \sim(A > \sim C)] \rightarrow [(A \, \& \, C) > B]$

Pollock, for one, rejects CV ((1976), p. 43). As he notes, any classical conditional logic containing CV will also contain

CV*: $(\sim[(A \vee B) > A]$ & $\sim\{[(A$ & $C) \vee B] > B\}) \rightarrow \sim[(A \vee B) > \sim C]$

Let A be 'The Rams won Super Bowl X', let B be 'The Forty-Niners won Super Bowl X', and let C be 'Three River Stadium is in California'. Surely it is false that if the Rams or the Forty-Niners had won Super Bowl X, then the Rams would have won. Since neither of these teams won, and in fact neither played in Super Bowl X, assuming that one of them won does not commit us to either in particular. As Pollock says, disjunctions whose disjuncts are not related do not necessitate either disjunct. Here, of course, the disjuncts are related since both could not be true, but either disjunct is still as likely as the other. And the same is true of 'The Rams won Super Bowl X and Three River Stadium is in California, or the Forty-Niners won Super Bowl X'. So the antecedent of CV*, with these substitutions, is true. But Three River Stadium would remain in Pittsburgh regardless of who won Super Bowl X, so the consequent is false. The only way I can see to avoid this counterexample is to deny that the second conjunct of the antecedent is true, on the grounds that the Forty-Niners would win Super Bowl X rather than Three River Stadium be in California. But I do not find this response very satisfying.

Pollock points out one more formal inadequacy of Lewis's semantics ((1976), p. 19). This latest indictment does not concern any theses which are or are not true in all SOS-models. Instead, it concerns a class of deductions which we would expect to be valid but which do not hold in all SOS-models. Pollock proposes that we should want a *Generalized Consequence Principle* to hold for conditional logic:

GCP: If Γ is a set of sentences, and for each $B \in \Gamma$, $A > B$ is true, and $\Gamma \vdash C$, then $A > C$ is true.

Unfortunately, SOS-models can be constructed in which GCP does not hold. We note, by the way, that GCP does hold in all CS-models.

Suppose for a moment, though, that we are prepared to accept CV and that we feel GCP is unnecessary (which is Lewis's actual response to Pollock's criticism). I think we still have good reason to question the adequacy of the informal semantics formally captured in the notion of an SOS-model. Even if such an informal semantics made the right sentences *valid* and validated all the right deductions, it still does not make exactly the right sentences *true*. The problem with Lewis's analysis, is the way in which he suggests the similarity of worlds is involved in the truth conditions for conditionals. Surely, the actual world is more similar to itself than is any other world; otherwise, the notion of the similarity of worlds would be incomprehensible. Once we accept Lewis's truth conditions, then, we are in principle committed to CS. We may try to avoid CS, but this amounts to accepting the questionable thesis that two distinct worlds might be as similar to each other as either is to itself. Yet even this implausible tactic (which Lewis himself does not propose) will not save the Lewis analysis of conditionals. An example to which Lewis's semantics may give the wrong truth value was suggested to me by George Schumm. Suppose due to the peculiar effects of a rare compound of kryptonite, Superman is rendered incapable of lifting any object weighing more than 100 pounds and less than 10 000 pounds. He can, however, still lift all objects he could previously lift which weigh less than 100 pounds or more than 10 000 pounds. Since his exposure, Superman has not had occasion to try to lift anything weighing over 10 000 pounds, but he has attempted to lift several objects weighing between 100 and 10 000 pounds. After lifting an object weighing just under 100 pounds, Superman tells Lois Lane, "If that had been heavier, I wouldn't have been able to lift it". Lewis's semantics would verify Superman's claim since worlds in which the object is heavier and weighs between 100 and 10 000 pounds are more similar than is any world in which the object weighs over 10 000 pounds. Yet intuitively Superman is mistaken. If the object were *much* heavier, Superman *would* be able to lift it.

Less whimsical examples of this sort can be constructed. Suppose a chemistry professor knows that a certain substance melts at 23°C but does not know that the substance boils at 24°C. He might well tell a graduate student on a cool day, "If the lab became warm today, this substance would be a liquid rather than a powder". Lewis's semantics would verify this intuitively false conditional.

Lewis has responded to such examples (in conversation) by saying that the *coarseness* of the comparative similarity relation may vary. In the case of the chemist, for example, we might consider all worlds in which the temperature in the lab is between, say, 23°C and 30° as being *equally similar* to the actual situation. This accounts for the falseness of the putative counterexample. This response is not very satisfying. To find a counterexample, we now only have to suppose that the substance in question melts at 23°C and boils at 31°C. However fine or coarse we make our similarity relation, we could find propositions which had one truth value in situations very much like or very much unlike the actual situation and which have a different truth value in situations of intermediate similarity.

Even if Lewis's view led to a correct determination of both the class of logically true wffs and the class of true wffs, there would be good reason to reject it as an analysis of conditionals. As in Stalnaker's case, difficulties arise when we try to incorporate Lewis's suggestions into an adequate account of hypothetical deliberation. According to Lewis, we can't reject a conditional on the basis of a single counterexample; instead, we must find a counterexample for each confirming example. In some cases, the same counterexample may work for every confirming example, but this will not be true in general. Consider once again the conditional 'If Carter had never served as Governor of Georgia, he would never have been President of the United States'. Suppose we decide the following situations are fairly similar to what actually happened:

w_1 in which Carter loses two bids for Governor and never becomes President

w_2 in which Carter runs for the Senate instead of Governor, is elected, establishes a good legislative record, and becomes President

w_3 in which Carter runs for the Senate instead of Governor, is defeated, and never becomes President

w_4 in which Carter runs for the Senate instead of Governor, is elected, establishes a reputation for radicalism, and never becomes President

If these are the only situations we need consider, we may still have a very difficult time on Lewis's view. We will judge the conditional to be true if any of w_1, w_3, or w_4 is closer to what actually happened than is w_2. While we are prepared to say that all of w_1–w_4 should be considered, since all are reasonable situations in which Carter never served as Governor of Georgia, we are at a loss when it comes to deciding which of these is closer to the actual situation than which others. What is more important, I don't think we even try to rank these situations when we try to evaluate the sentence with which we began. We would say that w_2 is a counterexample to the conditional with which we began, and the conditional is false. If we must first be able to rank w_1–w_4, then we will never arrive at a conclusion about the sentence. It is difficult enough to decide which situations are similar enough to the actual situation to consider *at all* without also trying to rank these in order of similarity to the actual situation.

Because the theory of SOS-models is committed to the thesis CV, because it does not validate the deduction principle GCP, because it makes true certain conditionals which are not true, and because it does not adequately capture the processes involved in hypothetical deliberation, we prefer CS-models in our attempt to provide truth conditions for ordinary language conditionals.

In his (1973), Lewis shows how we can construct CS-models by beginning with certain kinds of SOS-models. This suggests that, after all, the theory of CS-models, or at least of PCS-models, is simply a notational variation of a part of the theory of SOS-models. Before closing our discussion of Lewis, this possibility needs our attention.

Lewis's derivation of what he calls a set-selection function involves the Limit Assumption. An SOS-model $\langle W, \$ \rangle$ satisfies the Limit Assumption iff for each $w \in W$ and $A \in CL$, if $W/A \cap \bigcup \$_w \neq \emptyset$, then $\bigcap \{S \in \$_w : W/A \cap S \neq \emptyset\} \in \$_w$. The Limit Assumption assures us that for each $w \in W$ and $A \in CL$, there is a *smallest* A-permitting sphere around w if there is *any* A-permitting sphere around w. If $\langle W, \$ \rangle$ is an SOS-model satisfying the Limit Assumption, then $\langle W, f \rangle$ is an equivalent CS-model where for each $w \in W$ and $W \in CL$,

$$f(A, w) = \begin{cases} W/A \cap \bigcap \{S \in \$_w : S \cap W/A \neq \emptyset\} \text{ if } \bigcup \$_w \cap W/A \neq \emptyset \\ \emptyset \text{ otherwise} \end{cases}.$$

Thus, every SOS-model satisfying the Limit Assumption is equivalent to some CS-model.

We should first note that not every CS-model can be constructed in this manner. In Section 7.4 it is shown that an extension **SS** of our weak classical logic **WC** does not contain CV. Since CV is true in every SOS-model, it follows that there exist CS-models for which there are not equivalent SOS-models.

Interestingly, GCP holds in every SOS-model satisfying the Limit Assumption. Lewis notes on p. 121 of his (1973) that there is no characteristic axiom corresponding to the Limit Assumption. Although adoption of the Limit Assumption within the theory of SOS-models does not change the set of sentences which are valid, it does change the set of acceptable deductions.

Even if we were to accept CV, the version of the theory of CS-models which can be derived from the theory of SOS-models is not adequate. The problem is that some conditionals come out true which should not, and that we get a distorted view of hypothetical deliberation if we accept the informal semantics which this theory formalizes. First, since the actual situation must be more similar to itself than is any other situation, such a theory implicitly commits us to CS. Second, such a theory verifies even some *counterfactual* conditionals which it should not. At the moment, there are eight keys on my key ring. Any situation in which I had nine keys on my key ring would be more similar to the actual situation than would be any situation in which I have more than nine keys on my key ring. So if we adopt Lewis's version of the theory of CS-models, we must conclude that 'If I had more keys on my key ring, I would have exactly nine keys on my key ring' is true. But this is surely false. And this last example also shows in exactly what way the informal semantics upon which this specialized theory of CS-models is predicted fails to accurately represent hypothetical deliberations.

4.4. GABBAY AND THE ROLE OF CONSEQUENTS

Looking more carefully at the semantics discussed so far, we notice a distinction that has not yet been mentioned. SOS-models involve functions which take only possible worlds as arguments, while both CS-models and WS-models involve functions which take both possible worlds and sentences-qua-antecedents as arguments. We could say that CS-models and WS-models take account of the antecedents in a way that SOS-models do not. It is noteworthy that none of these accounts takes similar notice of sentences-qua-consequents. We will now examine a semantics which pays special attention to both antecedents and consequents.

Dov M. Gabbay in his (1972) develops an account of conditionals which depends upon a search for counterexamples as does the account developed in Chapter 1. There is an important difference in Gabbay's view, however, which can be seen in the following passage:

Generally, whenever a statement $A > B$ is uttered at a world t, the speaker has in mind a certain set of statements Δ (A, B, t) (concerning the political situation or geographical situation, etc.) which is supposed to remain true, and the speaker wants to express that in all worlds in which all statements of Δ retain their truth $(A \supset B)$ must hold.

What is Δ (A, B, t)? Well, one can perhaps find out what Δ is from A, B and the general knowledge and the particular circumstances at the time of utterance in the world of utterance (i.e., t). The following examples show that Δ depends on both A and B. Consider the statements:

(1)   If I were the Pope, I would have allowed the use of the pill in India.

(2)   If I were the Pope, I would have dressed more humbly.

Clearly, in the first statement, we must assume that India remains overpopulated and poor in resources, while in the second example nothing of the sort is required (p. 98).

Thus, the set of worlds we consider in evaluating $A > B$ is determined by both A and B.

A similar view is held by Daniels and Freeman in their (1977). Where Δ (A, B) is the conjunction of the set of sentences held to remain true in evaluating $A > B$, Daniels and Freeman suggest that $A > B$ is elliptical for $\Delta(A, B) \& \Box[(\Delta(A, B) \& A) \rightarrow B]$. The modal system T provides the logical features of $\Box$. Gabbay considers completing his analysis in this way but rejects it because "we do not want to deal with (possibly) infinite conjuctions" (p. 99).

The formal problem of infinite conjunctions has a natural counterpart within the discussion of hypothetical deliberation: the Daniels–Freeman suggestion becomes problematical in actual practice since it may be impossible to explicate Δ(A, B) for a given A and B. Jonathan Bennett in his (1974) makes the difficulty clear with an example. Consider the following sentences, all of which we may accept as true:

(2)   If I walked on the ice, it would remain firm.

(3)   If I walked on the ice and you walked on the ice, it would not remain firm.

(4)   If I walked on the ice and wore 60 lb boots, it would not remain firm.

From (3) and (4), we conclude that 'you do not walk on the ice', and 'I do not wear 60 lb boots' are both conjuncts of Δ ('I walk on the ice', 'the ice remains firm'). But as Bennett points out, there are plenty more where (3) and (4) came from. Listing, or even entertaining, all the conjuncts of Δ(A, B) will, in the general case, be impossible. Another problem with this account is that we may not even know exactly which sentences we are holding constant, paradoxical as that may sound. They usually, for example, include stipulations to the effect that the laws of nature do not change. Such a stipulation seems perfectly reasonable even though we do not know exactly what the laws of nature are. In fact, many disputes about the truth values of conditionals can also be construed as disputes about the nomological relations holding in the actual situation. This feature of conditionals should not be expected to change simply because we give additional consideration to the consequent in our hypothetical deliberations. In short, although the Daniels–Freeman suggestion certainly captures the spirit of the Gabbay hypothesis, it is very unlikely that the Gabbay hypothesis can in day-to-day usage be captured syntactically.

Rejecting the syntactical approach, Gabbay develops his views within the framework of a formal semantics for a *ternary* modal operator '$\Vdash$'. Roughly, A, B $\Vdash$ C is true at a world w, if and only if, C is true at every world accessible from w in which every member of Δ (A, B, w) is true. Then A > B is treated as being equivalent to A, B $\Vdash$ (A → B). We will let G^* be the formal system developed by Gabbay in his (1972). The language GL of G^* is obtained by adding the ternary operator '$\Vdash$' to the language of the propositional calculus. We then define A > B as A, B $\Vdash$ A → B. Gabbay suggests that the proper logic for conditionals is the CL-fragment **G2** of G^*, i.e., the set of theorems of $\mathbf{G}^*$ in which all occurrences of '$\Vdash$' can be replaced by occurrences of '$>$'. The conditional semantics corresponding to Gabbay's semantics for '$\Vdash$' is the theory of DPR-models. Gabbay claims that $\mathbf{G2}$ is the smallest conditional logic which is closed under the inference rule

RCE: from $A \rightarrow B$, infer $A > B$

and contains the theses MP and

CG: $[(A > B) \& (A > \sim B)] \leftrightarrow [A > (B \& \sim B)]$.

However, G2 is not determined by the class of all DPR-models. In the first place, the two rules RCEA and RCEC both hold in all DPR-models. Omission of these two rules is, I think, an oversight, and we should consider Gabbay to mean that G2 is closed under these rules. More importantly, CG is not true in every DPR-model.

We begin to define two possible worlds a and b by specifying the values they take for all sentence letters. Let $a(P_1) = b(P_0) = T$, $a(P_0) = b(P_1) = F$, and $a(Pn) = b(Pn) = T$ for all $n > 0$. We let $W = \{a, b\}$. Let G be a function which assigns to each pair of subsets S, $T \leqslant W$ the smallest reflexive binary relation $R_{S,T}$ on W such that for all S, $T \leqslant W$

$$R_{S,T} = \begin{cases} \{\langle a, a\rangle, \langle a, b\rangle, \langle b, b\rangle\} \text{ if } S = \{b\} \text{ and } T = \emptyset \\ \{\langle a, a\rangle, \langle b, b\rangle\} \text{ otherwise} \end{cases}$$

We complete our definitions of a and b by stipulating that $\langle W, R\rangle$ is a DPR-model. Since $W/P_0 = \{b\}$, $W/P_1 = \{a\}$, $R_{\{b\},\{a\}} = \{\langle a, a\rangle, \langle b, b\rangle\}$, and a $(P_0 \rightarrow P_1) = T$, $a(P_0 > P_1) = T$. Since $W/\sim P_1 = \{b\}$, $R_{\{b\},\{b\}} = \{\langle a, a\rangle, \langle b, b\rangle\}$, and $a(P_0 \rightarrow \sim P_1) = T$, $a(P_0 > \sim P_1) = T$. Hence $a((P_0 > P_1) \& (P_0 > \sim P_1)) = T$. But since $w/P_1 \& \sim P_1 = \emptyset$, $R_{\{b\},\emptyset} = \{\langle a, a\rangle, \langle a, b\rangle, \langle b, b\rangle\}$, and $b(P_0 \rightarrow (P_1 \& \sim P_1)) = F$, $a(P_0 > (P_1 \& \sim P_1)) = F$. Hence, we have a substitution instance of CG which is not true in the DPR-model $\langle W, R\rangle$. This result also shows that the logic $\mathbf{G}$ defined in Section 3.4 is not identical to $\mathbf{G2}$.

To get $\mathbf{G2}$, we must add a restriction onto our theory of DPR-models. The restriction we need is that for any DPR-model $\langle W, R\rangle$, and every $A, B \in CL$, $R_{W/A,W/B} = R_{W/A,W/\sim B}$. We generalize this by insisting that for every DPR-model $\langle W, R\rangle$ and every S, $T \subseteq W$, $R_{S,T} = R_{S,W-T}$. In fact, Gabbay prefers the stronger requirement that $R_{W-S,T} = R_{S,T} = R_{S,W-T}$. The first identity in this requirement does not affect the set of theorems. Gabbay adopts this restriction because he thinks that we should have $\Delta(\sim A, B) = \Delta(A, B) = \Delta(A, \sim B)$.

Gabbay's analysis of conditionals has one apparent advantage that other analyses we've examined lack: it offers a semantic counterpart for the fact, which we have observed, that the evaluation of two conditionals with the same antecedent may require consideration of different sets of situations. Any semantics which takes into account only the antecedent of the conditional and the situation of the speaker in determining the situations to be considered in hypothetical deliberation does not explicitly recognize this fact. Gabbay's analysis takes antecedent, world, *and consequent* into account in determining the set of worlds which determine the truth value of a conditional. However, the apparent superiority of Gabbay's account is only apparent since it does not provide a *sufficient* semantical counterpart for the kind of ambiguity we have in mind and it invalidates certain very plausible conditional inference patterns.

Recall our earlier example, 'If Caesar had commanded the UN forces in Korea, he would have used catapults'. According to Gabbay, we should assent to this conditional if Caesar uses catapults in every situation in which he commands the UN forces and certain other states of affairs also obtain. The additional requirements are determined by the antecedent and consequent of the conditional and would probably amount to Caesar's having the same weapons systems available to him that he actually had available historically. Given all this, the conditional is probably true. It doesn't really matter whether we have actually determined the correct set of worlds to look at in the case of this particular example, for difficulties arise whether in using Gabbay's approach we judge the conditional to be true or false. The problem is that Gabbay's analysis, just like the other analyses we have examined, will give a single, determinate truth value to the conditional, regardless of the circumstances under which the conditional is evaluated. The formal semantics does not explicitly make provisions for the conditional being accepted on one occasion and rejected on another due to the different circumstances of those occasions. Gabbay's analysis can at best account for a relevant difference in occasions by appeal to a difference in the consequents associated with the same antecedent on the two occasions, but there may be a relevant difference in the occasions of evaluation, as in our example, even when *both* the antecedent and the consequent of the conditional remain the same. The only other factor Gabbay considers is the time of utterance, which should not affect our example so long as the time is post-Korean-conflict.

While failing to fulfill a certain promise that it at first seems to hold, Gabbay's view also has certain very definite disadvantages: if fails to validate certain very reasonable inference patterns such as that represented by the inference rule RCK. The reason for the failure of RCK (and similar principles) on Gabbay's account is that the conditionals involved in RCK, all of which share a common antecedent, are to be evaluated through consideration of possibly different sets of worlds. As we have seen, this may certainly be the case when the conditionals are evaluated on different occasions and under different circumstances, but it seems very likely that on a single *extended* occasion of thought or utterance, a *constant* set of reasonableness conditions will be maintained and a single set of worlds will be considered in evaluating all conditionals with the same antecedent. Any change in the reasonableness condition should be construed as a change from one occasion of discourse to another. In a certain practical sense, Gabbay's suggestion is certainly well-taken. We certainly don't think much about whether there is famine in India when we are trying to decide what we would wear if we were Pope, and we certainly aren't concerned with dress codes when we are trying to decide whether as Pope, we would allow use of the pill in India. This is because in actual practice we have to 'lump' vast classes of worlds together in our deliberations according to the properties relevant to determining whether the consequent of a conditional is true in all those worlds. A difference in consequent will certainly result in different 'equivalence classes' of worlds being consciously considered, but the intuitive acceptability of rules like RCK strongly support the view that only a change of antecedent can, on a single occasion of discourse, justify a change in the set of worlds which are ideally to be considered, a change in the set of worlds which make up the members of the 'equivalence classes' of worlds which are actually considered in hypothetical deliberation. Gabbay has concentrated on one feature of hypothetical deliberation to the detriment of an adequate account of conditional inference.

4.5. POLLOCK AND JUSTIFICATION CONDITIONS

The possible worlds semantics John Pollock endorses for conditionals in his (1976), is a notational variant of the theory of PR-models, and is therefore equivalent to the theory of PCS-models. The conditional logic **SS** which Pollock endorses is just the smallest □-normal extension of **WC** containing CS. Since we have already endorsed the theory of CS-models and discussed CS, there is little left to say about Pollock's choice of possible worlds semantics or conditional logic. However, Pollock has a great deal to say about the nature of the propositionally indexed accessibility relation (PR-model theory) or the class-selection function (PCS-model theory) involved in this semantics. His analysis is intended to give justification conditions for conditionals rather than truth conditions. He does not recognize any ontologically irreducible class of counterfactual situations corresponding to possible worlds as we have done. In his (1976), possible worlds simply are maximally consistent sets of propositions or, equivalently, the kind of function from propositions to truth values which we have here taken the notion of a possible world to intend. The way in which Pollock attempts to elucidate these suggestions is extremely interesting.

Pollock rests justification for subjunctive conditionals upon inductive confirmation of another class of subjunctive statements, those which he calls *basic subjunctive generalizations*. These are statements of the form 'Any A would be a B'. To symbolize these statements, Pollock introduces two new logical constants '$\Rrightarrow$' and '$\Rightarrow$'. Where P and Q are open sentences sharing the same free variables, both $P \Rrightarrow Q$ and $P \Rightarrow Q$ are *closed* sentences; these new logical constants not only *connect* open sentences but also *bind* their free variables. Pollock gives an account in his (1974) of how certain basic subjunctive generalizations are to be confirmed inductively. The rest are derived from these basic ones. The difference between *strong* subjunctive generalizations (symbolized using '$\Rrightarrow$') and *weak* subjunctive generalizations (symbolized using '$\Rightarrow$') lies in the kinds of statements that may be used to defeat the generalization. As an example, Pollock supposes we have confirmed inductively that the 9.14 train from Boston is always late. We believe the reason this is so is because of the worn-out equipment used. If the equipment were replaced, the train wouldn't be late. Since it is possible to replace the equipment, the truth of the subjunctive generalization depends upon contingent facts, and the generalization is therefore weak. If the possibility of equipment replacement, or some similar defeater, were not available, the subjunctive generalization would be strong.

Let N be the set of basic strong subjunctive generalizations and let W be the set of basic weak subjunctive generalizations. As mentioned before, members of $N \cup W$ are to be confirmed inductively. Now Pollock must explain how other subjunctive generalizations are to be derived from these. For any open sentence P, let $\forall P$ be the universal closure of P. Then let $\forall N = \{\forall(P \rightarrow Q) : P \Rrightarrow Q \in N\}$, and similarly for $\forall W$. Pollock says $(P \Rrightarrow Q)$ is 'true' (scare quotes mine) just in case every largest subset of $\forall N$ which is consistent with $\exists P$ entails $\forall(P \rightarrow Q)$. Weak subjunctive generalizations have a more complicated analysis since preservation of strong subjunctive generalizations is to be preferred over that of weak. To determine whether $(P \Rightarrow Q)$ is 'true', we first consider all largest subsets N_P of $\forall N$ consistent with $\exists P$. Then for each such N_P, we consider each largest subset W_P of $\forall W$ consistent with $\{\exists P\} \cup N_P$. Finally, $(P \Rightarrow Q)$ is 'true' just in case each such $\{\exists P\} \cup N_P \cup W_P$ entails $\forall(P \rightarrow Q)$.

Pollock next introduces the notion of a simple proposition. P is simple, if it is logically possible for one to 'know the truth' of P non-inductively without first 'knowing the truth' of each proposition in some set Γ which entails P. Pollock's intention is to eliminate all propositions which are *epistemologically* complex. This is not *prima facie* unreasonable given that Pollock's analysis in terms of justification conditions is basically an epistemological analysis. If we allow him the notion of a simple proposition, Pollock is prepared to provide an analysis of subjunctive conditionals. Where a and b are possible worlds, Pollock writes 'bM_aP' for 'If a were the actual world, then b would be a world that might be actual if P were true'. We have bM_aP just in case b is obtained by making a minimal change on a which suffices to make P true. To see what a minimal P-change on a amounts to, first let S_a be the set of simple propositions in a, let N_a be the set of strong basic subjunctive generalizations in a, and let W_a be the set of weak basic subjunctive generalizations in a. After performing cut-downs on $\forall N_a$ and $\forall W_a$ after the manner previously described in order to get a set $\{P\} \cup N_P \cup W_P$ of propositions, we take a largest subset S_P of S_a which is consistent with $\{P\} \cup N_P \cup W_P$. If and only if b is the product of such a construction do we have bM_aP. Then $(P > Q)$ is 'true' at a just in case Q is true in every world b such that bM_aP.

This summary of Pollock's analysis is certainly oversimplified, but space will not allow a complete summary. Yet at least one additional detail must be included here. Occasionally we have a subjunctive antecedent which is incompatible with the conjunction of two sentences without being incompatible with either of the sentences individually. For example, 'If Churchill and Stalin had not both survived the war' is compatible with both 'Churchill survived the war', and 'Stalin survived the war', but it is not compatible with their conjunction. Pollock offers a Requirement of Temporal Priority (RTP) to help us decide which if either of such pairs of sentences is to be preferred in our construction of alternative worlds. First Pollock says that some simple propositions (perhaps all) have dates, times at which they become true. Where S_a is the set of simple propositions in a possible world a and t is a time, let $S_a(t)$ be the members of S_a which become true at times no later than t. Then RTP demands not only that we make minimal P-changes on S_a, but also that we make minimal P-changes on each $S_a(t)$ for each time t.

To see how RTP works, consider an example. Let P be the proposition that there are massive glacial deposits in my backyard. In fact, P is false. What would a minimal P-change on the set of true propositions contain? First, it seems likely that we would change fewer propositions if we made our supposed glacial deposits the product of one of the ice ages which have actually occurred, rather than suppose a new ice age for the task. Now consider any ice age other than the last one. It is certainly compatible with there being glacial deposits in my backyard, that they were not left by *that* ice age. So RTP would seem to dictate that these deposits were not left by that ice age. Thus, we seem to be forced to conclude that if there were massive glacial deposits in my back yard, they would have been left there by the *last* ice age. But this is counterintuitive; we are inclined to say that if there were such deposits, they might have been the product of *any* of the recent ice ages. Pollock would resolve this problem by pointing out that each of the ice ages has historical antecedents extending indefinitely far back into time. At the time of the next-to-last ice age, for example, there already existed circumstances which insured that the last ice age would occur. In making our minimal P-change on the simple propositions true by this time, we would either have to make the next-to-last ice age produce our deposits, or we would have to alter the antecedents of the last ice age in such a way as to result in the leaving of the deposits by the last ice age. And similar conclusions apply to the times of all of the ice ages. If it required no greater change to alter a particular ice age than to alter the contemporaneous antecedents of some later ice age, then RTP does not dictate that the deposits be left by the last ice age. Instead, we get the intuitive result that the deposits might have been left by *any* recent ice age.

This appeal to historical antecedents will not save RTP in those cases in which the relevant events either lack historical antecedents altogether, or are not completely determined by their historical antecedents. Suppose ours is a probabilistic universe. Suppose that in a certain region of space during a certain period of time there exists nothing but two unstable atoms. At time t the first atom emits a particle from a certain location traveling in a certain direction at a certain speed. Let Q be the proposition that this happens. At a slightly later time the second atom also emits a particle from a certain location in a certain direction at a certain speed giving us proposition R. At an even later time these two particles collide. This collision, complete with location, etc., is reported in proposition P. I assume that the events reported by Q and R are of the sort which are not entirely determined by their antecedents. Now $\sim$P is incompatible with Q & R, but intuitively either Q or R could still be true if $\sim$P were true. Let's look at what happens when we apply RTP. Since the events reported in R are not completely determined by their antecedents, *nothing* which is true by time t is incompatible with $\sim$P. As a result, we change none of the propositions which are true by t and in particular we do not negate Q. But then we have it that $\sim$P $>$ $\sim$R is true, contrary to intuition. Such examples make RTP highly suspect.

John Post offers additional reasons for rejecting, or at least reformulating and restricting, RTP in his (1979). These objections involve Pollock's implicit assumption of a certain kind of spacetime and his failure to consider the way in which relatively affects RTP. Post proposes that RTP be made more precise by taking one event to be temporally prior to the other if the location of the first is in the backward light cone of the second. When we consider alternatives involving bizarre spacetime, it becomes impossible to determine which *events* are prior. Problems may even arise given 'normal' spacetime for events at space-like separation, such that none of the the antecedents of one is in the backward light cone of any other. Since we have already found less exotic cases which cast doubt upon RTP, I will not rehearse Post's examples further. I do, however, recommend them to the attention of the reader.

Another problem with Pollock's account of subjunctive conditionals concerns the relation between the sets of propositions N, W and S. If N and S are really complete, then together they should ential all members of W. This would seem to make mention of W superfluous. More importantly, mention of W may lead to error. Suppose N contains the proposition 'Strychnine is poisonous' and W contains 'Anyone who drank from this bottle would be poisoned'. I assume that both of these propositions can be confirmed directly by induction. Suppose, though, that the reason anyone who drinks from the bottle will be poisoned, is because the bottle's contents include strychnine. Now consider the conditional 'If it were the case that people frequently ingested strychnine without harm and I were to drink from this bottle, I would be poisoned'. Intuitively, this counterlegal conditional is false. However, the antecedent of the conditional contradicts 'Strychnine is poisonous' but does not contradict 'Anyone who drank from this bottle would be poisoned'. So in applying Pollock's analysis, we delete 'Strychnine is poisonous' from N but we do not delete 'Anyone who drank from this bottle would be poisoned' from W. Hence, our odd counterlegal would appear to be true on Pollock's account.

Pollock defines three other subjunctive conditionals in terms of the simple subjunctive conditional. The first of these, 'Q might be the case if P were', in symbols (QMP), he defines as $\sim(P > \sim Q)$. 'Q would be the case even if P were the case', in symbols (QEP), is defined as $Q \,\&\, (P > Q)$. Finally, 'If it were true that P, it couldn't be false that Q', a *necessitation* conditional which is symbolized as $(P \gg Q)$, is defined as $(P > Q) \,E\, (\sim P \,\&\, \sim Q)$. We might object to Pollock's analysis of (QMP) and (QEP) because we suspect CS; but even if we reject CS, QMP and QEP appear to bear the same relations to $P > Q$ as those Pollock suggests.

We have noted certain difficulties Pollock's account of subjunctive conditionals encounters, but there is another problem which Pollock himself
raises: the account is incomplete if there are probabilistic laws. Probabilistic
laws for Pollock are indefinite probability statements, i.e., statements to the
effect that the probability of an A being a B is n. Pollock gives a measure-
theoretic analysis of indefinite probabilities, but this analysis does not meet
Pollock's own criterion of adequacy since it does not provide justification
criteria for such statements. In fact, Pollock admits that he is not presently
able to provide such justification conditions. He favors a frequency analysis,
but he also holds that indefinite probabilities are subjunctive. Hence, the
probability of an A being a B (or that an A *would be* a B) is not in general the
same as the ratio of actual A's which are B's to all actual A's. Our judgements
concerning indefinite probabilities must be based upon observed frequencies,
but Pollock cannot explain this dependence. Pollock defines what can be
called *logical* indefinite probabilities as those which would obtain even if
all laws were deterministic. Definite probabilities, i.e., the probability that Q
would be the case if P were, are defined in terms of indefinite probabilities.
Then Pollock says P is *positively relevant* to Q, roughly, if the *actual* probability that Q would be the case if P were, is greater than the logical probability
that Q would be the case if P were. Finally, Pollock says that whenever P is
positively relevant to Q (at world a), then there must be a world b such that
$Q \in b$ and bM_aP. Althought the notion of a logical probability is problematic,
the restraints probabilistic laws place upon the relation M_a must surely be
taken into account somehow. If Pollock cannot provide justification conditions for indefinite probabilities, then this analysis of conditionals must
remain incomplete.

With all its problems, I find Pollock's analysis of conditionals very attractive. I think this analysis is essentially complementary rather than antithetical
to the approach I have myself taken in this work. What Pollock has tried to
do is to tie the analysis of conditionals and related bits of language to such
epistemological notions as inductive confirmation and justification in a way
that no other author has managed to do and in a way that scientists and
philosophers of science are most particularly likely to appreciate.

Formally, Pollock proposes what amounts to a PCS-model theory for *subjunctive* conditionals (i.e., conditionals in which the main verb of both antecedent and consequent are in the subjunctive mood). Where w is a world and
A is a wff, Pollock interprets f(A, w) as the set of all *minimal A-changes on w*.
In fact, I think this interpretation of the class-selection function is better
suited for a semantics for *indicative* conditionals (i.e., conditionals in which

the main verb of both antecedent and consequent are in the indicative mood) than for a semantics for subjunctive conditionals. My reasons for making this suggestion concern once again the thesis CS and the case of conditionals with true consequents. Where B is true, we evaluate the conditional 'If A were true, B would be true' by considering whether the truth of A *would* or *could* interfere with the truth of B; but in evaluating the conditional 'If A is true, B is true' we try to determine only whether the truth of A *does* interfere with the truth of B. If A & B is true, we might still reject the subjunctive conditional if there is a strong negative or antagonistic connection between A and B, and we will do the same thing in the case of the indicative conditional if ~A & B is true and there is an antagonistic connection. But if A & B is true, then clearly the truth of A *does* not interfere with the truth of B and hence the indicative conditional is true. Even the sorts of examples offered against CS earlier do not seem persuasive when they are reformulated in the indicative mood. For example, both 'If Carter or Ford won the last Presidential election, then Amy Carter lives in the White House' and 'If Caspar attended the party, then it was a great party' seem true despite the antagonistic connections involved. Since CS seems unobjectionable for indicative conditionals and since **SS** is the smallest □-normal extension of **WC** containing CS, I propose that **SS** is the proper logic for indicative conditionals. Since CS is intuitively incompatible with SDA, I also unequivocally reject SDA and accept RCEA for indicative conditionals.

4.6. ADAMS AND PROBABILISTIC ENTAILMENT

Stalnaker, Lewis, and Gabbay all offer truth conditional accounts of conditionals involving possible worlds semantics, accounts which are based upon fundamental assumptions shared by the analysis of the present author. Pollock, while attempting to give justification conditions rather than truth conditions, nevertheless offers a possible worlds account which is compatible, in spirit if not in detail, with other formal accounts. Ernest W. Adams departs from this general camp and offers an innovative, probabilistic account of conditionals. I think, though, that the innovations of Adams (1975) constitute no real advantage.

Adams reasonably claims that we do not usually assert a proposition unless the subjective probability of the proposition is high. In particular, we assert an indicative conditional of the form 'If A is the case, then B is the case' only when the conditional subjective probability $p(B/A) = p(A \& B)/p(A)$ is high. Even in assessing arguments, it is not argument forms which preserve truth but those which guarantee the high probability of the conclusion when the premises are probable which we are concerned to identify. Adams even suggests that conditionals lack truth value altogether. As a consequence, compounds of conditionals lack both truth values and probabilities.

Though usually the case, we do not always refrain from asserting conditionals of low probability. Imagine a terminally ill legislator sponsoring tax reform legislation. A television commentator might reasonably say, "Despite his illness, the Senator keeps on fighting. If his own bill is killed in committee, he will support the legislation of the administration". The subjective probability of this last statement must be low since the commentator realizes that the Senator likely will not survive committee action on his bill. Yet these remarks, heard on the evening news, would hardly cause an eyebrow to be raised.

At the base of this example is a distinction between indicative and subjunctive or counterfactual conditionals which Adams maintains but which should be denied. The scope of antecedent restrictability of a conditional is the set of propositions that may be added to the antecedent of the conditional without changing the acceptability of the conditional. Adams says the scope of an indicative conditional includes all known propositions while the scope of a counterfactual may not. The scope of 'If Germany had won World War II, Hitler would not have committed suicide' does not include the known proposition 'Hitler committed suicide'. Adams is right about counterfactuals but errs in supposing that indicative conditionals cannot also exclude known propositions from their scopes. In our earlier example, the likelihood that the Senator will not survive committee action on his bill is excluded from the scope of the conditional asserted by the television commentator.

Adams dismisses the suggestion that the inapplicability of his analysis to compounds of conditionals is a handicap, with the response that we do not really understand such compounds in any case. He lists several intuitively invalid argument forms involving such compounds which are valid if we interpret conditionals as material implications. These examples actually show that one who interprets conditionals truth functionally understands neither compounds of conditionals nor simple conditionals. But Adams pays too high a price to avoid the invalid argument forms. The theory of CS-models, to name but one, is a formalization of a truth conditional analysis of conditionals which is applicable to compounds of conditionals and which avoids all the argument forms that Adams lists. Furthermore, there is no intuitive problem in understanding compounds of conditionals. Even complicated constructions like 'If the vase will break if it is dropped on the sofa, then it will break if it is dropped on the floor' are quite normal. Accounts of conditionals which apply to compounds must enjoy an advantage over Adams' account.

The central notion in Adams's book is that of probabilistic entailment. Roughly, a set Γ of premises *probabilistically entails* a conclusion B iff for every $\epsilon > 0$ there exists $\delta > 0$ such that for every probability assignment p, if $p(A) \geqslant 1 - \delta$ for each $A \in \Gamma$, then $p(B) \geqslant 1 - \epsilon$. The arguments from ordinary language involving conditional premises and/or conclusions which withstand our most careful scrutiny are claimed to be exactly those in which the conclusion is probabilistically entailed by the premises.

There would be no particular advantage to the probabilistic analysis of conditionals, says Adams, if it coincides with some truth conditional analysis. He further offers that such coincidence is very likely if the probability associated with a conditional is the probability that the conditional is true, a suggestion we find less obvious than Adams apparently does. But this, he says, is not the case. Triviality results presented by David Lewis (1976a), by Robert Stalnaker (1976), and by Adams himself show the implausibility of assuming that the probability that a conditional is true is equal to the conditional probability when this assumption is conjoined with various other assumptions varying from author to author. The implicit claim is that the probabilistic account does not coincide with any truth conditional account of conditionals. (The only truth conditional account Adams examines is the truth *functional* account.) If the logics derived from the probabilistic approach and the truth conditional approach differ, we must look for reasons for preferring one over the other.

A primary reason for accepting a probabilistic account of indicative conditionals, Adams implies, is that such an account validates exactly the *right* argument forms, while truth conditional accounts all validate argument forms which intuitively are invalid. Examples of argument forms rejected by the probabilistic interpretation include Transitivity, Contraposition, Weakening Antecedents, and others which we have already discussed and rejected. If we can find a truth conditional account which validates all the argument forms Adams accepts while rejecting all those Adams rejects, then Adams will be left with a very weak case for this radical proposal. In fact, Pollock's conditional logic **SS** rejects every argument form explicitly rejected by Adams, while every argument form such that the premises probabilistically entail the conclusion corresponds to a valid derivation in **SS**, and all argument forms containing no compounds of conditionals and corresponding to inference rules or theses of **SS** appear to be probabilistically sound. For example, the argument form $A > B$, $B > A$, $A > C \vdash B > C$, which corresponds to the thesis CSO, is probabilistically sound. Although I will not attempt to prove it, it looks very much like Adams's probabilistic logic may simply be the non-compound fragment of Pollock's **SS**.

Counterfactual conditionals are also given a probabilistic interpretation. (To distinguish, I will use '$\gg$' for indicative conditionals and '$>$' for subjunctive or counterfactual conditionals in the remainder of this section.) Adams suggests that the probability of a counterfactual is the same as the probability of the corresponding indicative conditional on some previous occasion. For example, we hear a bird in the bush and say 'If that is a canary, it is yellow'. Then the bird flies from the bush and is seen to be a blue jay. Now we find the indicative conditional inappropriate. We replace it with the counterfactual 'If that had been a canary, it would have been yellow'. This counterfactual has the same probability that the indicative conditional had before the bird could be seen. Adams suggests that the two conditionals express different propositions although we reaffirm the indicative conditional by asserting the counterfactual.

Since Adams offers strong criticisms of his 'epistemic past' analysis of counterfactuals, I will offer only a few additional comments. Adams leaves the conditional probability corresponding to $A > B$ undefined in cases where A has probability 0. The alternative, he says, is to make the conditional probability 1 in such cases. Neither of these alternatives is helpful when we try to apply his account of counterfactuals. Consier the two indicative conditionals 'If I jump off Pike's Peak, I will land in Colorado' and 'If I jump off Pike's Peak, I will land in Georgia'. Since the probability of my jumping off Pike's Peak is 0, the probability Adams associates with these two conditionals is either undefined or equal to 1. Yet we would claim that the probability that I *would* land in Colorado if I *were* to jump off Pike's Peak is 1 while the probability that I *would* land in Georgia is 0. Adams's theory of counterfactuals runs into extreme difficulty in the case of counterfactuals with antecedents having probability equal to 0.

Since there are truth conditional analyses of conditionals (such as the theory of CS-models) which can support a logic (probably **SS**) having the properties Adams insists upon, I suggest we reject Adams' probabilistic analysis. Although Adams's views have a certain plausibility and attraction, accepting the claims that conditionals lack truth value and that we cannot understand even the simplest compounds of conditionals, is far too high a price to pay for the luxury of accepting these views.

CHAPTER 5

CAUSATION AND THE TEMPORAL REGULARITY OF SUBJUNCTIVE CONDITIONALS

5.1. INTRODUCTION

Many counterfactual subjunctive conditionals are true because of a causal relationship which holds between events mentioned in their antecedents and consequents. In fact, our understanding of causation, subjunctive conditionals, and laws or law statements are inextricably intertwined. Because of this, we might expect that we could use an analysis of subjunctive conditionals to explicate certain causal notions or the notion of a physical law. Certain authors have attempted this recently, two of these being David Lewis and Marshall Swain. Both of these attempts make use of an account of subjunctive conditionals in explaining what are the conditions for one event to be a cause of another. Of the two, Lewis includes the unanalysed notion of a law in his analysis of causation as well. Both of these very similar accounts fail, I think, for reasons which make it very unlikely that any such explication of causation will succeed. To show this will be the primary task for the next section of this chapter.

Closely connected to the fact that many subjunctive conditionals are true because of causal relations, is the temporal regularity of subjunctive conditionals. Time, as we all know, is asymmetrical; it has a direction. The asymmetry of time is reflected in our use of subjunctive conditionals. It turns out that most of the conditionals we actually assert, in which both antecedent and consequent are entirely about states of affairs which obtain at particular times display a certain relationship between these times. Suppose for example that A is a statement about states of affairs obtaining during an interval of time t_A, and B is a statement about states of affairs obtaining during an interval of time t_B. Let $A > B$ be the conditional 'If A were true, then B would be true'. In most cases in which we assert a subjunctive conditional which has all the properties I have ascribed to $A > B$, or which is a more colloquial paraphrase of such a conditional, t_A is *no later than* and usually *earlier than* t_B.

True conditionals which lack this feature certainly do exist, but they tend to be simple instantiations of some law and to be less informative than those conditionals which comply with the noted temporal regularity. Take for example 'If deer were to gnaw away the bark, then the tree would die'. This conditional exhibits the temporal relationship between antecedent and consequent which I indicated. Consider some corresponding conditionals which do not exhibit this temporal relationship. One is 'If the tree were to die, then the deer would have gnawed away the bark *or* the tree would have been infested with parasites *or* there would have been a drought *or* . . .'. Here the consequent is disjunctive and nearly impossible to complete. Another is 'If the tree were to survive, then the deer would not have gnawed away the bark *or* someone would have grafted on some new bark *or* the tree would have dropped down a branch from above the injury to establish a new root system *or* . . .'. Just these few examples should indicate the kind of temporal regularity which subjunctive conditionals exhibit.

An obvious but also incomplete explanation of the temporal regularity of subjunctive conditionals would be that many of these conditionals depend for their truth on causal relationships and causation itself is temporally regular. But the difficulty, of course, is to give an account of the way in which causation is involved in our use of conditionals, an account which at the same time dictates the temporal regularity for subjunctive conditionals which we have noted. David Lewis has attempted such an account, utilizing the notion of a miracle. In the final two sections of this chapter, I will try to show how such a miraculous account subverts the very reliance of subjunctive conditionals upon causal relations while it uses this dependence, that such an account ultimately fails to explain the temporal regularity of subjunctive conditionals in certain hard cases, and that it is possible to explain the temporal regularity of subjunctive conditionals without resorting to the notion of a miracle.

I fear that I must leave unanswered many questions about the relationships between temporal and causal relationships on the one hand, and our use of subjunctive conditionals on the other. Yet we will see where certain interesting and clever attempts to answer such questions go astray and we will accomplish, hopefully, at least a better, if not a complete understanding of these relationships.

5.2. THE COUNTERFACTUAL ANALYSIS OF EVENT CAUSATION

David Lewis (1973b) and Marshall Swain (1978) use counterfactual conditionals in the analysis of event causation. Where 'c' and 'e' are names of events, Lewis and Swain attempt to explicate expressions of the form 'c causes e' or 'c is a cause of e'. The starting point for their analysis is the intuitive claim that if c causes e, then e would not have occurred if c had not. The analysis achieves considerable sophistication at Lewis's hands and becomes even more elaborate in Swain's treatment. It is a very attractive account in many ways. I shall try to show, however, that it is still inadequate, at least in the versions produced to date.

For any event e, we let $0e$ be the proposition which is true if and only if e occurs. Lewis proposes that a possible event e is *causally dependent* upon a distinct possible event c just in case both $0c > 0e$ and $\sim 0c > \sim 0e$ are true. Following Lewis, Swain suggests that an *occurrent* event e is causally dependent upon a distinct occurrent event c if and only if $\sim 0c > \sim 0e$ is true. This suggestion of Swain's comes to the same thing as Lewis's proposal when we realize that both Lewis and Swain accept the conditional thesis CS. This guarantees that $0c > 0e$ is true when c and e are occurrent events. Swain also offers a definition of the notion of distinctness of events: two events c and e are distinct if and only if $c \neq e$ and neither event is a constituent of the other.

Jaegwon Kim (1973) argues that the causal dependence defined by Lewis (and adopted by Swain) is really too broad a notion to be properly called causal. There are, he maintains, many examples of events which satisfy the criteria for causal dependence but which are not really connected in a manner which we would normally call causal. Examples offered by Kim involve the following conditionals:

(1)   If I had not written 'r' twice in succession, I would not have written 'Larry'.

(2)   If I had not turned the knob, I would not have raised the window.

(3)   If George had not been born in 1950, he would not have reached the age of 21 in 1971.

(4)   If my sister had not given birth at t, I would not have become an uncle at t.

Swain's elaboration of Lewis's account is intended in part as a reply to Kim's objections. His clarification of the notion of the distinctness of events eliminates both (1) and (2) as counterexamples to the analysis. As for (3), he has said in conversation that he thinks George's birth in 1950 is in fact a cause of his reaching the age of 21 in 1971. This example, then, is not a counterexample because it is not *counter*. Although he does not respond explicitly to (4), it seems that Swain might offer either of these two kinds of answer in this case. He might suggest that the event of the sister giving birth and the event of the speaker becoming an uncle are actually the same event. This, of course, would involve us in an analysis of the notion of an event, a topic which Swain chooses to avoid. Alternatively, Swain might recognize the distinctness of the events but simply accept that the one is after all a cause of the other. This latter seems the more likely approach. In any case, there is good reason for thinking that the counterfactual analysis of event causation is not done serious damage by the kinds of considerations Kim puts forth.

Lewis proceeds to define causation in terms of causal dependence. First, a *causal chain* is a finite sequence of events $c, d, e, \ldots$ such that d depends causally upon c, e depends causally upon d, etc. Then Lewis says c is a cause of e just in case there exist events $d_1, \ldots, d_n$ such that $c, d_1, \ldots, d_n, e$ is a causal chain. But why do we need the notion of a causal chain to capture causation? Why can't we simply say that c is a cause of e if and only if e depends causally upon c? Both Lewis and Swain accept the view that causation is transitive while causal dependence is not. An immediate reason for thinking that causal dependence might not be transitive is the fact that subjunctive conditionals (or counterfactuals in particular) are not transitive. For example both 'If the match had not been scratched, it would not have burned' and 'If the match had not been scratched and had been thrown in the fire, it would not have been scratched' might be true and yet 'If the match had not been scratched and had been thrown in the fire, it would not have burned' is surely false. But this example should not persuade us that causal dependence is not transitive, for at least one of the conditionals involved does not support a claim of causal dependence. If 'the match is not scratched and is thrown into the fire' can be construed as being of the form Oe in the first place, then the event e which it reports to occur surely is not distinct in Swain's sense from the event reported to occur by 'the match is not scratched'. Indeed, I confess that I am unable to construct a legitimate causal chain in which the last member of the chain is not causally dependent upon the first member. Although both Lewis and Swain apparently assume that such chains are possible, neither offers examples. Even though subjunctive conditionals are not in general transitive, I suspect that transitivity may well hold for that class of conditionals which support claims of causal dependence.

Lewis's attempts to explain causal asymmetry, epiphenomena and preemption involve the liberal use of the concept of a miracle, i.e., a violation of physical law. I argue against the use of the notion of a miracle in the analysis of subjunctive conditionals in section 5.4; I am not inclined to think that that method is any more appropriate in the context of an analysis of event causation. Swain offers additional reasons for rejecting this approach if any additional reasons are needed. In particular, Swain argues that the very same kinds of considerations Lewis gives for saying that the effect does not cause the cause, can also be used to support the claim that the cause does not cause the effect. The too-liberal use of miracles destroys causal symmetry at the expense of destroying the causal connection altogether.

Swain prefers a more complex, non-miraculous solution to the problem of causal asymmetry. His penultimate analysis of event causation, which incorporates this solution, runs like this:

SWAIN 1: Where c and e are specific events that occurred, c is a cause of e iff:

(i)   there is a causal chain of occurrent events from c to e;

(ii)   where w_1 is a world in which c occurs and e does not occur, and w is the actual world, w_1 would only have to have been different from w in the following respect: some event a (other than c) which occurs in w and upon which e depends causally in w fails to occur in w_1;

(iii)   where w_2 is a world in which e occurs and c does not occur, and w is the actual world, w_2 would have to be different from w in at least the following respects: (1) some event f (other than e) which occurs in w and upon which c depends causally in w fails to occur in w_2; and (2) some event g occurs in w_2 such that e is not causally dependent upon g in w but e is causally dependent upon g in w_2.

To see how this solves the problem of causal asymmetry, we must first note that Swain is at least tentatively accepting Lewis's analysis of subjunctive conditionals. Lewis's analysis, we will recall, uses the theory of SOS-models. What Swain needs to accomplish causal asymmetry, then, is some way of insuring that worlds in which the cause occurs but the effect does not, are more similar to the actual world than are worlds in which the effect occurs but the cause does not. Given the theory of SOS-models, this will allow $\sim 0c > \sim 0e$ to be true while $\sim 0e > \sim 0c$ is false. In effect, Swain accomplishes asymmetry by *fiat*, building it directly into his analysis by insisting that one kind of world requires only the deletion of some occurrent event, while the other kind of world requires both the deletion of some occurent event and the addition of some non-occurrent event. The latter worlds are then supposed to be less similar to the actual world than are the former.

The problems of preemption and overdetermination raise new problems that require additional refinement of the analysis. Swain holds that preempted causes are not really causes at all while in cases of true overdetermination all of those events which were sufficient to cause the effect are to be considered causes. As an example of preemption, the shooting of a dead horse cannot be the cause of the horse's death even though it would have caused the horse's death had it not already been dead. As an example of actual overdetermination, if two people were to simultaneously shoot a living horse through the head, then both shootings would be causes of the horse's death. This informal solution to the problems of preemption and overdetermination seem correct. The question is then one of including these intuitively acceptable results in the counterfactual analysis of event causation. Swain attempts to do this in the following, final analysis:

SWAIN 2: Where c and e are specific events that occurred, c was a cause of e iff:
Either (A) (i), (ii) and (iii), as above in SWAIN 1;
Or   (B) some set of events $D = \{d_1, d_2, \ldots, d_n\}$ occurred (possibly having only one member) such that

(a)   If c had not occurred, and if any member d_i of D had occurred, but no other members of D had occurred, and if e had occurred anyway, then there would have been a causal chain from d_i to e consisting wholly of occurrent events, and d_i to e would have satisfied (ii) and (iii) of SWAIN 1; and

(b)   If no member of D had occurred, and if c and e had occurred anyway, then there would have been a causal chain from c to e consisting wholly of occurrent events, and c and e would have satisfied (ii) and (iii) of SWAIN 1.

SWAIN 2 offers the most careful formulation of a counterfactual analysis of event causation that is known to me, yet I think it suffers from a number of rather serious shortcomings. Indeed I think that the problems with this analysis are so dire as to throw into doubt the outcome for the entire enterprise.

The first problem I wish to raise concerns the possibility of closed causal loops. This charge is in part an *ad hominem* directed against Swain. In the beginning of his (1978), Swain says that he is, so far as he can tell, developing an account which is completely neutral with respect to a number of perplex-ing questions about causation, including the question of the possibility of closed causal loops. I admit that my intuitions are vague about causal loops and I certainly do not wish to argue for their possibility, but one of Swain's goals seems to be to leave this question open. Yet we find that his final analysis rules out closed causal loops on two different counts. First, he stipulates that c causes e only if c and e are distinct. Since causation is supposed to be transitive, this rules out causal loops immediately. This particular difficulty, however, may be easily remedied. We might allow that c is a cause of c *provided* that there is some sequence of events $d_1, \ldots, d_n$ such that at least one of the d_i is distinct from c and the sequence of events $c, d_1, \ldots, d_n, c$ comprises a causal chain. This move would allow an event to be a cause of itself, although it still would rule out the possibility that an event could be the *sole immediate* cause of itself. The second difficulty for causal loops concerns conditions (ii) and (iii) of SWAIN 1. These conditions simply will not be applicable in cases where $c = e$. Of course the purpose of these two conditions is to guarantee causal asymmetry, and we don't have to worry about asymmetry when cause and effect are identical. But this response is a bit too quick. If we can have closed causal loops at all, I don't see any reason why we can't have very short ones. In fact, why shouldn't we have distinct events a and b such that each is an immediate cause of the other, i.e., such that both a, b and b, a comprise causal chains? This seems as plausible as does the whole notion of a closed causal loop. But conditions (ii) and (iii) can't be satisfied by such an example. Indeed, this conclusion can be drawn about causal loops in general. Let a and b be separated by ever so many events and we still cannot have a a cause of b, and b a cause of a. Lewis's solution to the problem of asymmetry failed because it allowed us to discount all causal claims. Swain's solution fails, at least if we wish to keep alive the possibility of closed causal loops, because it guarantees asymmetry in every case. Of course, this is always a danger when we try to make our analysis fit a certain requirement by *fiat*. If the requirement is only occasional, the solution by *fiat* will always be too strong.

Another problem with this analysis is the one raised by Kim. One event may be counterfactually dependent upon another without the dependence being the kind that we would call causal. The particular examples Kim offers may be handled by appeal to the requirement for the distinctness of cause and effect (although this then gives rise to the difficulties of the previous paragraph), but there are other examples which I think are immune to this tactic. Let us consider some of these.

One kind of example concerns deontic or axiological connections between events. The clearest cases are those in which some act of judging or valuing is involved. These acts may depend upon other events in a non-causal way. Suppose that George once became very ill after eating liver. As a result, he has become conditioned to dislike the taste of liver. He attends a dinner and tastes a particular dish. The dish tastes like liver to him and he finds the dish unpleasant. He would not have found the dish unpleasant if it had not tasted like liver to him. However, the connection between his seeing that the dish tastes like liver and his finding the dish unpleasant does not seem to be a causal connection. The *cause* of his finding the dish unpleasant is his previous bad experience with liver. It might be objected that George's seeing that the dish tastes like liver and his finding the dish unpleasant are in fact the same event. But consider another similar case. Suppose George tastes some new and unfamiliar taste for the first time. First he sees what the taste is like. Then he ponders whether or not the taste is pleasant or unpleasant. He decides that it is unpleasant, which is unusual for George. Let us suppose that this is the only taste that George would ever find unpleasant. Then he would not have decided that the dish was unpleasant if it had not tasted as it did. Are we now to say that George's determining what the taste is like and his deciding that the taste is unpleasant are the same event? I think such a claim goes contrary to experience. I have myself found that I must eat a fair portion of some dishes before I can decide whether or not I find the taste pleasant.

If we can agree that an act of lying and an act of truth-telling, an act of murder and an act of justifiable homicide, and other pairs of acts which are distinguished by some moral quality, cannot through their commissions constitute the same event, then we have another kind of potential counter-example to the Lewis—Swain analysis. Suppose George's friend Alvin drops by for a visit and George wishes to persuade Alvin to stay for dinner. Let's also say that it was raining very hard when Alvin arrived, that Alvin was walking, and that one reason Alvin stopped in was to get out of the rain. Looking out the window, George sees that the rain has stopped. Nevertheless, he says to Alvin, "It's still raining cats and dogs, Old Boy. You had better stay for dinner." George lied because he wanted Alvin to stay. Of course, George would have said exactly the same thing if it had not stopped raining, but then he would not have lied. His lying depends upon its having stopped raining, but is his lying caused by its having stopped raining? I think not. George's lying is counterfactually, but not causally, dependent upon its having stopped raining. In this example, the two events are clearly distinct.

Another example concerns 'preventers', events whose non-occurrence would have prevented other events but which would not normally be said to be causes of those other events. Suppose a mother is watching her two children at play. One child takes a toy away from the other, an argument ensues, and a shoving match is the final result. It would certainly be peculiar to say that any particular act of the mother caused the fight, yet the fight would not have occurred if the mother had not done what she did. The mother's immediate reaction, when the quarrel began, was to interfere. However, she was one of those mothers who believes that children should in most cases be left to work out their own problems. So she *refrained* from interfering. If she had not refrained from interfering, the fight would not have occurred. Yet it would be odd to say that anything she did caused the fight. Of course, one might object that *refraining* constitutes neither an act nor an event, but this would surely have to be supported by some account of events which is missing from the accounts of both Lewis and Swain.

Let's consider another case of a 'preventer'. Suppose an exit ramp on a freeway is being repaired. To stop traffic from entering the ramp, barricades have been set up. Now the repairs have been completed and the barricades have just been removed. Some driver now becomes confused, thinks the exit ramp is an approach ramp, drives onto the freeway going the wrong direction, and has a head-on collision with another car. The accident would not have happened if the barricade had not been removed, but the removal of the barricade would surely not be considered a cause of the accident.

Not only is counterfactual dependence too broad a notion to capture causation, but there are cases where one event depends causally upon another even though it does not depend counterfactually upon the other event. A good example is a pinball machine. Once a ball is in play, it must exit from the playing area through one of several openings. Consider a pinball machine wired in such a way that a certain light flashes when the ball goes through any of these openings. A particular ball goes through a particular opening, causing the light to flash. But it is not true that the light would not have flashed if the ball had not gone through the opening it in fact went through. Lewis or Swain might object that causation is not simply the same thing as causal dependence. There is, they would have to say, a complex causal chain of occurrent events connecting the exit of the ball through a particular opening and the flashing light. If the ball had exited through a different opening, some of these events would not have occurred. This might even be thought to constitute a counterexample to my suggestion that causal dependence is transitive. The kinds of events Swain mentions in this sort of example include the passage of electric current through different lengths of wire, etc. Yet some of these events would surely be the same regardless of exactly which particular circuit in the machine is activated. At the very least, what goes on in the light bulb will be the same. Where c is the event of the ball going through the particular opening and e is the flashing of the light, let $c, d_1, \ldots, d_n, e$ be the causal chain connecting c and e. Then let $d_i, \ldots, d_n, e$ be those events which would have occurred even if the ball had gone through some other opening, so long as its exit occurred at an appropriate time. Then for c, $d_1, \ldots, d_n, e$ to *be* a causal chain, $\sim Od_{i-1} > \sim Od_i$ would have to be true. But it isn't. So c causes e even though there is no causal chain connecting c and e.

This point might be made more forcefully if we consider a case in which the supposed causal chain is shorter. Let's suppose we have a weight suspended by a cord from a rigid support. (Sam Hall will do for those familiar with the classic folksong.) Let c be the cutting of the cord at a particular point and let e be the falling of the weight. If c and e both occur, then we should say that c causes e. Furthermore, c appears to be an immediate cause of e with no intervening events in the 'causal chain'. Then according to Lewis and Swain, it should be the case that e would not have occurred if c had not occurred. This, however, is simply false. I am assuming, of course, that if the cord had been cut at any point other than the point at which it was actually cut, then c would not have occurred. Furthermore, if the cord had been cut at any other point, the weight would still have fallen, i.e., e would still have occurred. Finally, we simply need to observe that the worlds most similar to the actual world in which c does not occur would very likely be worlds in which the cord was still cut, but at a different point. Even accepting the Lewis analysis of subjunctive conditionals, then, we have a case where c causes e even though there is no 'causal chain' connecting c and e.

I think that these arguments probably cannot be countered. The problem of getting causal asymmetry in exactly the cases we want it is a particularly difficult one for this or any other analysis of causation. Perhaps a way can be found to patch up the counterfactual analysis of event causation on this particular point. But I think I have shown a far more fundamental flaw in this approach. There are cases of counterfactual dependence which do not involve causation, and there are cases of causal dependence which do not support the kinds of counterfactuals upon which the analysis depends. Counterfactual dependence is both too large and too small a hook from which to suspend an analysis of causation.

5.3. A MIRACULOUS ANALYSIS AND A
NON-MIRACULOUS ANALYSIS

In his unpublished (1976), David Lewis suggests first that we might try to account for the temporal regularity of subjunctive conditionals by fiat, that is, by explicitly mentioning times in giving the truth conditions for conditionals. In formulating an analysis by fiat, Lewis utilizes the notion of a miracle, of the laws of one world being violated in another world. If we incorporate Lewis's most sophisticated version of this suggestion into the interpretation of the theory of CS-models, we have the following:

Miraculous Analysis: where A is a statement which is entirely about the state of affairs at a stretch of time t_A and w is any possible world, let $f(A, w)$ contain exactly those worlds w' such that:

(1)   A is true in w';

(2) w' is exactly like w at all times before a transition period beginning shortly before t_A;

(3) w' conforms to the natural laws of w at all times after t_A; and

(4)   during t_A and the preceeding transition period, w' differs no more from w than it must to permit A to hold.

To understand the Miraculous Analysis, we must first understand what it is for one world to conform to the natural laws of another. Lewis suggests that we simplify our discussion by assuming some form of determinism, and I will follow this suggestion. In particular, I will assume that no laws are probabilistic. Then we can associate with the system of laws of a world w a set of universal generalizations which these laws imply. We will say of a world w' and a stretch of time t that w' conforms to the laws of w during t if, and only if, all of the generalizations corresponding to laws of w are true when we restrict the quantifiers to particulars which exist in w' during t.

In his (1976), Lewis assumes complete determinism, at least for the purposes of this discussion. Two deterministic worlds sharing the same set of laws cannot differ at any time unless they differ at every time, according to Lewis. Given complete determinism, any change in the present would determine a completely different past and a completely different future. Lewis seems implicitly to assume that complete determinism should result in something quite different from the temporal regularity we actually observe for subjunctive conditionals unless we resort to miracles in our analysis. The argument that complete determinism together with a non-miraculous analysis of conditionals leads to the symmetry of temporal regularity, an argument which Lewis does not offer, might go something like this. If we change the present to accommodate some counterfactual antecedent, then we must also alter the past. Since there are likely to be many different ways of accomplishing the truth of the antecedent, there will be many different alternative pasts to consider. For this reason we undermine past-directed conditionals. But the various changes in the past will each of them have consequences in the present, above and beyond the desired goal of making the antecedent true. Some of the resulting changes in the present are likely to affect the future consequences of the antecedent's having become true. So we also undermine many future-oriented conditionals. This being the case, there is no reason to think that we should be, as we actually are, more inclined to accept future-directed conditionals than to accept past-directed conditionals. I think it is some argument of this sort which Lewis does not articulate but which prompts him to resort to the notion of miracles in his attempt to explain the usual temporal regularity under the assumption of complete determinism.

A great many writers who have dealt with subjunctive conditionals have insisted upon the preservation of natural law except in the case of 'counterlegals', conditionals in which the antecedent contradicts some law. The casual acceptance of miracles as being commonly involved in the truth conditions for conditionals whose antecedents are not counterlegal provides an excellent *prima facie* reason for rejecting the Miraculous Analysis.

Lewis also rejects the Miraculous Analysis, but for quite different reasons. First, Lewis says that such an analysis is too strong. It will not allow us to avoid temporal regularity in those unusual cases where we might want to avoid it. It would make statements about time travel, clairvoyance, and tachyons necessarily false. Second, this analysis cannot be applied to conditionals whose antecedents are not confined to states of affairs which obtain during a particular stretch of time, for example, 'If kangaroos had no tails, . . .' But the lack of generality of the Miraculous Analysis does not present a problem so long as we recognize that it is to be taken as providing one way of resolving the vagueness of subjunctive conditionals within the framework of a general account of conditionals such as the theory of CS-models. We realize that there may be many conditionals, including counterlegals, to which the analysis will be inapplicable. We also realize that even in cases where the analysis is applicable, we may on occasion require that the vagueness of the conditional be resolved differently. But this is just to repeat our assumption that conditionals are vague and that in particular cases this vagueness may be resolved in different ways. If we are to reject the Miraculous Analysis, it should be because it is *miraculous* rather than because it is not universally applicable.

I don't think Lewis is being entirely honest with us. I shall argue in Section 5.4 that the real reason Lewis rejects the Miraculous Analysis is because it does not fit well with the general semantics for conditionals which he has developed, even though he thinks it gives the correct result in all those cases to which it applies. A proper analysis, then, meaning an analysis which fits into Lewis's general schema, should agree with the Miraculous Analysis in all those cases to which both are applicable.

Finding miracles objectionable, I offer an analysis which does not require them:

Non-Miraculous Analysis: where A is a statement which is entirely about the state of affairs at a stretch of time t_A and w is any possible world, let $f(A, w)$ contain exactly those worlds w' such that:

(1)   A is true at w';

(2) w' conforms to the laws of w at all times; and

(3)   during t_A, w' differs no more from w than it must to permit A to hold.

The difference between this and the Miraculous Analysis is that here we reject miracles and instead allow the 'transition' period leading up to t_A to be indefinitely, even infinitely, long. Condition (3) is stronger than we really wish. In practice we require only that the differences between w' and w during t_A be *reasonably* small.

The Miraculous Analysis gives history a privileged role while the Non-Miraculous Analysis gives physics a privileged role. It would be very difficult to explain the temporal regularity which actually obtains without miracles *if* we assumed complete determinism.[1] This conclusion applies equally well to complete determinism with respect to the past. The easiest way to reject miracles and let physics play the privileged role it plays in the Non-Miraculous Analysis, is to accept at most, complete determinism with respect to the future. If we assume that our system of natural laws allows branching in the past, we undermine conditionals whose antecedents concern later times than do their consequents. Although we know that changing the present must result in many changes in the past, we may also believe that the present does not completely *determine* the past. Perhaps there could have been many pasts, each of which differs from the actual past, which would have led up to the alternative present we are considering. With so many alternative pasts available to us, we have no principle which allows us to choose one over the others. Hence, we can't say *exactly* how the past would be different if the present were changed.

I would like to consider some instructive examples of very simple universes. The universes I want to consider contain nothing but a 'clock' and a 'counter'. Both the clock and the counter are nothing more than displays upon which appear integers. Assume that we can distinguish the clock from the counter; perhaps the figures upon the clock appear in red, while those upon the counter appear in blue. The integers on the clock change, appearing in the normal numerical order from minus infinity to plus infinity. The integers on the counter may appear in any order, but the counter can't display two different integers while the clock displays a single integer. Times in such a universe simply correspond to readings on the clock. So for such a universe, time is discrete. Given any such universe, we can let $f(t)$ be the reading the counter displays at time t. Thus we can think of these universes simply as functions from the set of integers into the set of integers.

Consider a universe in which the counter reads 0 at all times. Call this the ZERO universe. We can suppose the ZERO universe to be bound by certain laws. Let one of these correspond to our own law that no signal can travel faster than the speed of light. This law says that from one time to the next, the reading of the counter can't change by more than 1. We can express this law in terms of absolute values of the function mapping times to counter readings as follows:

Law 1. $(t) (| f(t) - f(t-1) | \leqslant 1)$.

The second law is a law of 'inertia' which says that f decreases steadily, increases steadily, or remains constant. This law is mitigated by a boundary condition which says that the counter can't ever read less than 0. This law of 'inertia' together with its boundary condition can be expressed as follows:

Law 2. $(t) (f(t) = \max \{0, f(t-1) - (f(t-2) - f(t-1))\})$.

Suppose that the laws governing the ZERO universe are *exactly* laws 1 and 2. These two laws comprise a system which is deterministic with respect to the future in the sense that if we know what the universe 'reads' at any two consecutive times, then we know what it reads at any times later than these two. But this system of laws is not *totally* deterministic since we cannot tell exactly what the counter reads at any time earlier than t if we know only that the counter reads 0 at both t and t + 1. In a universe conforming to Laws 1 and 2 the counter either must read the same thing at all times, or must count down from infinity until it reaches 0 and then read 0 ever after.

Assuming that the ZERO universe is actual and given Laws 1 and 2, what would the counter have read at time 2 if it had read 1 at time 1? According to the Miraculous Analysis, we need to look at all universes in which the counter reads 0 for all times before time 1, in which it reads 1 at time 1, and which conform to Laws 1 and 2 for all times after time 1. But there is exactly one such universe, and in it the counter reads 0 for all times before time 1, and t for all times t after time 0. Since in this universe the counter reads 2 at time 2, we conclude that if the counter in the ZERO universe had read 1 at time 1, then it would have read 2 at time 2. We get a quite different result if we apply the Non-Miraculous Analysis. Then we must look at all universes in which the counter read 1 at time 1 and which conform to Laws 1 and 2 at *all* times. There are two such universes. In the first, which I will call the ONE universe the counter reads 1 at all times. In the second, which I will call the COUNT-DOWN universe the counter reads the greater of 0 and 2 − t at all times t. The counter in the COUNT-DOWN universe thus counts down from infinity, first reaching 0 at time 2. Since the counter in the ONE universe reads 1 at time 2 and the counter in the COUNT-DOWN universe reads 0 at time 2, we must conclude in the ZERO universe that if the counter had read 1 at time 1, then it would have read either 0 or 1 at time 2.

Which of these conclusions is correct? It depends, for conditionals are vague. We can decide to preserve law in our hypothetical deliberation at the expense of history, or we can decide to preserve history at the expense of law. But if we give history preference, our conditional is not merely *counterfactual*, but *counterlegal* as well.

What these examples point out is that the Miraculous Analysis treats a large class of conditionals as counterlegals which are not explicitly counterlegals at all. But they also point out that there are two different kinds of counterlegals which should be distinguished. One kind of counterlegal conditional might be called a *global* counterlegal since such conditionals suppose that some law is deprived of its status as a law throughout spacetime. An example of a global counterlegal antecedent would be 'If the force of attraction between two bodies were inversely proportional to the *cube* of the

distance between their centers of mass . . .'. Another kind of counterlegal
conditional might be called a *local* counterlegal since such conditionals
suppose that some law is deprived of its force only within some specified part
of space-time. An example of a local counterlegal antecedent might be 'If
Jones had hit the ground harder when he fell from the ten foot roof . . .'.
Local counterlegals ask us to consider what would happen if a miracle were to
occur and the Miraculous Analysis treats conditionals which we wouldn't
normally classify as counterlegals as if they were *local* counterlegals. Where
we actually are dealing with a local counterlegal, the Miraculous Analysis may
be entirely proper.

5.4. LEWIS'S MIRACULOUS ANALYSIS

I have suggested that the real reason Lewis finds the Miraculous Analysis so
unattractive is because he prefers a general semantics for subjunctive conditionals which is quite different from the theory of CS-models, a semantics
into which neither the Miraculous nor the Non-Miraculous Analysis fits very
well. Recall that the central notion of Lewis's theory of SOS-models is that
of the comparative similarity of worlds. According to Lewis, a counterfactual
$A > B$ is (non-vacuously) true at a world w just in case there is a world w' at
which both A and B are true which is more like w than is any world at which
A is true and B is false.

Corresponding to the vagueness of conditionals are various ways of determining the relative similarity of worlds. There is one way of resolving vagueness which Lewis considers to be standard, and corresponding to it is a
standard set of guidelines for determining the relative similarity of worlds.
These guidelines are as follows:

(1) It is of the first importance to avoid big, complicated, varied, wide-
spread violations of law.

(2) It is of the second importance to maximize the spatio-temporal
region throughout which perfect match of particular fact prevails.

(3) It is of the third importance to avoid even small, simple, localized
violations of law.

(4) It is of little or no importance to secure approximate similarity of
particular fact, even in matters that concern us greatly.

In countenancing violations of law, Lewis's account is clearly of the
'miraculous' variety.

Besides his general semantics and his standard guidelines for determining the similarity of worlds, Lewis also makes some very strong assumptions about the actual world. These assumptions concern the way in which the states of affairs obtaining at one time determine those obtaining at another time. Lewis says

> Any particular fact about a deterministic world is predetermined throughout the past and postdetermined throughout the future. At any time, past or future, it has at least one *determinant*; a minimal set of conditions jointly sufficient, given the laws of nature, for the fact in question. The fact may have only one determinant at a given time . . . Or it may have two or more essentially different determinants at a given time, each sufficient by itself; if so, it is *overdetermined* at that time (1976).

Lewis holds that events in the actual world are for the most part overdetermined by later events to a far greater degree than they are overdetermined by earlier events. To put it another way, most events or facts about particular times have more postdeterminants than they do predeterminants.

The laws of a world cannot be violated *within that world*; otherwise, they would not be laws of that world. However, the laws of one world can be violated in another world with different laws. Whenever the laws of a world w are violated in a world w', we say that a *miracle* occurs in w' relative to the laws of w. All miracles involve two worlds in this way for Lewis. Furthermore, some miracles relative to the laws of w may be bigger than others. This notion of bigger and smaller miracles is at base primitive for Lewis, but he gives examples of the sort of thing he has in mind. Most important is his claim about *divergence* miracles and *convergence* miracles. Suppose two deterministic worlds share a common history up until time t, at which point their histories begin to diverge. Then in each of these worlds a divergence miracle must occur at time t relative to the laws of the other world. At a later time, say t', the histories of these two worlds might converge once again. If they do, then a *convergence* miracle must occur in each relative to the laws of the other. In worlds like the actual world, Lewis claims, convergence miracles tend to be much larger than divergence miracles. This is just another way of saying that the past is overdetermined to a greater extent than is the future. This means that we can cause divergence from a deterministic world by means of a relatively small miracle without changing much of the past, but once we have diverged from a deterministic world it takes a very large miracle to converge with it once again. Fit this into Lewis's general semantics together with his standard similarity relation for worlds, and Lewis claims we have temporal regularity of the usual kind.

I don't think Lewis's analysis gives us the usual temporal regularity for conditionals. To see this, consider an example suggested to me by John Pollock. Suppose I left my coat in a classroom yesterday and was surprised to find it right where I left it today. Consider the antecedent, 'If my coat had been missing when I returned . . .'. What true conditionals might have this antecedent? According to Lewis, we first rule out large miracles. Since many people were in the room between the time I left the coat and the time I returned, we should probably consider worlds in which one of these people removed the coat. This would seem to be about the smallest miracle we could get by with. Next, Lewis proposes that we should maximize the spatio-temporal region of exact match of particular fact. Since no one actually removed my coat yesterday, and since people had an opportunity to remove it today, we should consider worlds in which the coat was not removed yesterday in order to maximize the common history of the worlds involved. So one conditional which would seem to be true on Lewis's account is 'If my coat had been missing when I returned, it would have been here if I had returned yesterday evening'. But surely we would reject this conditional. The coat might have been removed anytime between the time I left and the time I returned. In fact, my experience is that when things are left unattended they tend to be removed earlier rather than later. It looks as though Lewis's account doesn't after all produce the temporal regularity that actually obtains.

The same criticism might also be leveled against the Miraculous Analysis if we interpret the requirement that the transition period which leads up to the time t_A at which the state of affairs mentioned in the antecedent obtains 'shortly before' t_A to mean that this transition period should be as short as possible. Without this interpretation we might take the transition period in our example to begin as early as the time at which I deserted my coat. If the transition period can begin this early, then Lewis's account fails to coincide with the Miraculous Analysis as he claims. If these two accounts don't coincide, then we can consider the question which of these offers the best treatment of local counterlegal conditionals.

To compare Lewis's account and the Miraculous Analysis for the case of a local counterlegal, let us consider the ZERO universe once again. This time, however, we will assume total determinism just as Lewis does. One totally deterministic system of laws for the ZERO universe would consist of the following:

Law 3. $(t)(f(t) = f(t-1))$.

Now, assuming the ZERO universe is actual, let us ask what would happen if the counter had read 0 at time 0 and 1 at time 1.

The Miraculous Analysis would require us to consider only one universe which I will call the ZERO-ONE universe. In this universe the counter reads 0 for all times before time 1 and reads 1 for all times after time 0. Since in the ZERO-ONE universe the counter reads 1 at time 2, the Miraculous Analysis tells us that the *counterlegal* 'If the counter had read 0 at time 0 and 1 at time 1, then it would have read 1 at time 2' is true in the ZERO universe. And this seems to be the intuitively correct result. We can think of Law 3 as stating a kind of principle of 'inertia'. The reading stays put. Miraculously, it is jarred from 0 to 1 at time 0. But after the miracle, our law of 'inertia' becomes effective once again and the reading stays put at its new value.

To see what result we get when we apply Lewis's analysis, I am going to consider the second of his guidelines for determining the similarity of worlds first. This guideline says that it is of the second importance to maximize the spatio-temporal region of exact match of particular fact. Let the BUMP universe be the universe in which the counter reads 1 at time 1 and reads 0 at all times other than time 1. Surely this universe maximizes the 'spatio' temporal region of agreement with the ZERO universe; no other universe in which the counter reads 1 at time 1 could possibly agree more with the ZERO universe. So no other universe can satisfy Lewis's second guideline better than the BUMP universe. But now we must consider the first guideline, which says it is of the first importance to avoid big, complicated, varied, widespread violations of law. The ZERO-ONE universe violates Law 3 during the period from time 0 to time 1, while the BUMP universe violates Law 3 during the period from time 0 to time 2, so the BUMP universe certainly involves a bigger 'miracle' than does the ZERO-ONE universe. But in neither case does the miracle seem to be very large, complicated, etc. So it would seem that the BUMP universe is more similar to the ZERO universe than is any other universe in which the counter reads 1 at time 1. According to Lewis's general semantics, then, since in the BUMP universe the counter reads 0 at time 2, the *counterlegal* 'If the counter had read 0 at time 0 and 1 at time 1, then it would have read 0 at time 2' is true in the ZERO universe. But this is contrary to intuition. It seems the Miraculous Analysis handles local counterlegals better than does Lewis's analysis.[2]

Lewis anticipated simple examples like these, for he explicitly says his analysis is not intended to deal with worlds which have suffered heat death, worlds which contain a single atom in the void, and so on. But Lewis also thinks that this analysis agrees with the Miraculous Analysis where both apply in the case of complicated worlds like the actual world. The disappearing coat example, however, suggests that this is not the case. So we are forced to try to simplify our worlds in order to determine which of these analyses best captures ordinary intuition concerning the local counterlegal conditionals which seem most appropriate for a 'miraculous' treatment. In the case of the disappearing coat, it depends upon how we restrict the length of the transition period in applying the Miraculous Analysis whether or not the two analyses coincide. But we need make no assumptions about how to interpret this requirement in the case of the ZERO universe to see that the two analyses do not coincide and that the Miraculous Analysis better reflects intuition.[3]

Can we draw any simple conclusions from this discussion? I think we can. First, we have noted that it is difficult to accommodate the normal temporal regularity of the subjunctive conditionals unless we either accept a miraculous analysis of some sort or reject total determinism. We have seen that adoption of both a non-miraculous analysis and total determinism would result in the past and future both being totally determined by an alternative present we might consider. But then we must choose our alternatives very carefully if we are to avoid a complete symmetry of temporal regularity, contrary to what we actually observe. Lewis opts for miracles and assumes total determinism, at least for the sake of argument. But it is not clear that this will solve the problem. We have considered two different analyses which involve miracles. Lewis's analysis gives history such a privileged role that we again appear to be stuck with a great many conditionals whose antecedents concern later times than their consequents, conditionals which we don't want and which violate the observed temporal regularity of subjunctive conditionals. The Miraculous Analysis might avoid this problem if we interpret it a certain way, but it nevertheless asks us to treat many conditionals as being counterlegals which do not, on the face of them, appear to be counterlegals at all. Through all the controversy concerning the analysis of conditionals, one principle which has been almost universally held has been that the greatest priority be given to the preservation of LAW in the analysis of conditionals. To give history a privileged position above law is *not* as Lewis implies the standard way of resolving the vagueness of conditionals. If we accept this tenet, then we must insist upon a non-miraculous account of temporal regularity. But then we must work out the details of a non-miraculous, deterministic account of conditionals in a way which I do not think has yet been done, or we must admit that a number of different pasts could have resulted in the same present. The latter seems to me to be the working hypothesis of most ordinary users of conditionals. Once we reject total determinism with respect to the past,

temporal regularity of the sort we observe becomes the most natural phenom-
enon imaginable.

NOTES

[1] The appeal is made here to a notion like the notion of similarity of worlds or to
Pollock's notion of minimal change. My account does not differ from Lewis's to the
extent that I do not utilize the notion of similarity of worlds. But the priorities in judging similarity are different. For me, law has the highest priority. While preserving the law,
it still seems likely that some changes in the history of the world will result in a greater
overall similarity to the way things actually are than will others. The point at which we
want the greatest similarity is at the time when the antecedent is to become true. To
achieve the greatest similarity at that one point might, however, result in extremely large
differences in some past period of the history of the two worlds. As a result, we are less
certain about the changes made in the past than we are about the changes made in the
future. In actual practice, we act in our hypothetical deliberations as if it is possible to
alter the past in such a way as to insure that nothing changes about the present except
that the antecedent we are considering becomes true. Pollock's Requirement of Temporal
Priority may in part be motivated by a desire to accomplish the kinds of changes which
will result in the observed temporal regularity. The RTP appears to prevent changes from
spreading too far into the past and thus altering the historical antecedents of too many
states of affairs which obtain in the present. But I am not sure how the RTP will help in
the sorts of situations we are considering since under complete determinism the kinds of
antecedents we are considering would apparently have historical antecedents extending
indefinitely far into the past.

[2] Have we begged the question here? One might maintain, after all, that a purpose of
Lewis's guidelines is to insure that in situations like this, the ZERO-ONE universe turns
out to be more similar to the ZERO universe than is the BUMP universe. After all, the
BUMP universe does require a larger and more wide-spread miracle than does the ZERO-
ONE universe. But this response doesn't seem to fit in with what Lewis says about convergence miracles and divergence miracles. The reason Lewis rejects convergence miracles
as a means of maximizing the region of spatio-temporal agreement is not that we then
have to countenance two miracles instead of only one. This would be a suspicious move
at any rate since *prima facie* two miracles are not more objectionable than one. Instead,
Lewis holds that convergence miracles are *bigger* than divergence miracles. Allowing convergence miracles doesn't just involve allowing additional miracles of the same scope as
the divergence miracles which they off-set; it involves 'upping the ante' on the kind of
miracle that we have to accept. But this line of reasoning does not apply in the case of
the BUMP universe. We can think of the BUMP universe as involving a *divergence* miracle
from time 0 to time 1 and a *convergence* miracle from time 1 to time 2. In this case, the
convergence miracle appears to be exactly as big and wide-spread as the divergence
miracle, no more and no less.

[3] One reason Lewis might object to the sorts of examples being used against him here is
that in the actual world, all or nearly all events have more post determinants than they
do predeterminates. This is not the case in our simplified universes. Suppose that in all of
the universes we consider, the counter ceases to exist at time 10. That means that for

each universe the function f becomes a partial function. This will be a particular problem in the case of the BUMP universe where our criticism depended upon the occurrence of a convergence miracle. The reason convergence miracles are bigger than divergence miracles is because events have more postdeterminants than they do predeterminants. But we can easily remedy this problem. Let the ZERO-0 universe be exactly like the ZERO universe except that the counter doesn't exist in the ZERO-0 universe at any time before 0. Now we alter Law 3 to apply only to times later than 0 and we add a new law which says that $f(0) = 0$. Then the ZERO-0 universe is completely deterministic, $f(0)$ has no predeterminants, and $f(0)$ has infinitely many postdeterminants. Yet the corresponding BUMP-0 universe is still more similar to the ZERO-0 universe according to Lewis's guidelines than is the corresponding ZERO-ONE-0 universe.

CHAPTER 6

SUBJUNCTIVE PROBABILITIES

6.1. A NEW SPECIES OF CONDITIONAL PROBABILITY

The probability that B is the case if A is, in symbols $p(B/A)$, is usually taken to be given by the formula $p(A \& B)/p(A)$. *Prima facie* there is another conditional probability different from $p(B/A)$. This is the probability that B *would* be the case if A *were* the case, which I will symbolize as $p(B//A)$. To see the difference, at least in the case of subjective probabilities, let A be 'Jones rolls a pair of fair dice at exactly 3 p.m. EST, January 1, 1980' and let B be 'Jones rolls a seven at exactly 3 p.m. EST, January 1, 1980'. Now I might have no opinion about the likelihood of either A or B and hence I can not compute $p(B/A)$. Since p represents a subjunctive probability based upon me, it seems to follow that $p(B/A)$ is not defined. But I have a very definite opinion about what Jones *would* roll if he were to roll, and $p(B//A) = 1/6$. So for subjective probabilities at least, $p(B//A)$ may be defined while $p(B/A)$ is undefined. In this chapter, we will explore the notion of the *subjunctive* probability represented by $p(B//A)$. For the purposes of the discussion, I will usually give probability statements a subjective interpretation although much of what will be said seems applicable given other interpretations of probabilities.

In his initial paper on subjective probabilities and conditionals, Robert Stalnaker (1970) made several assumptions including the following:

(1)   the logic of subjunctive conditionals is **C2** and

(2)   if $p(A) \neq 0$, then $p(A > B) = p(B/A)$.

As was mentioned in section 4.6, these two assumptions lead to unhappy results. David Lewis (1976a) demonstrated that (1) and (2) together with certain other reasonable assumptions can only be true in the case of certain trivial probability functions. Stalnaker himself (1976), however, provides the strongest 'triviality' result when he demonstrates that from (1), (2) and classical probability theory alone

(3)   there are at most two pair-wise incompatible propositions with non-zero probability.

Bas van Frassen (1976) develops a conditional logic **CE** which, when taken together with (2), does not lead to any triviality results like (3). While weaker than **C2**, **CE** preserves the controversial Stalnakerian thesis CEM. Lewis (1976a), taking a different approach, abandons (2) and develops a different account of the probabilities of Stalnaker's conditionals, i.e., conditionals for which **C2** is the proper logic. Lewis notes that for any proposition A such that $p(A) \neq 0$, the probability function $p(\ /A)$ is in some sense a minimal revision of p which raises the probability of A to 1. He suggests we consider other 'A-revisions' (my term) of p which are not the result of conditionalizing on p with respect to A but which are in some other sense minimal revisions of p. Beginning with **C2** and Stalnaker's semantics for conditionals, Lewis develops a method of revising probability functions which he calls *imaging*. First, to simplify the mathematics, Lewis supposes that p is a function which assigns probabilities to possible worlds, thus spreading the total probability out over the set W of worlds. To recover the notion of the probability that a proposition A is true, we let

(5) $p(A) = \Sigma_{w/A} p(w)$

We can revise p by shifting probability from one world to another. Let $\langle w, \langle s, R, \lambda \rangle \rangle$ be a WS-model. For any $A \in CL$ such that $p(A) \neq 0$ and $w \in W$, Lewis lets

(6) $p_A(w) = \Sigma_{w' \in w} p(w') . \begin{cases} 1 \text{ if } s(A, w') = w \\ 0 \text{ otherwise} \end{cases}$.

This method of shifting probability has the effect of pushing the probability of any world w onto s(A, w), i.e., the world at which A is true which is nearest to or most similar to w. Of course, this results in all probability finally residing in worlds at which A is true, and we have $p_A(A) = 1$. This is one way of producing a 'minimal' A-revision of p. Finally, Lewis shows that where $p(A) \neq 0$ and p_A comes from p by *imaging on A*, we have

(7) $p(A > B) = p_A(B)$.

With his technique of imaging, Lewis is introducing a new notion. There are really three distinct concepts involved in (2) and (7). In (2) we have $p(A > B)$ representing the probability that the subjunctive conditional 'If A were the case, B would be' is true and we have $p(B/A)$ representing the conditional probability that B is true if A is. It is well known that $p(A \rightarrow B)$ and $p(B/A)$ are not in general the same, so it should not come as a great shock that $p(A > B)$ and $p(B/A)$ are not in general the same either. In (7) a third notion is introduced; $p_A(B)$ represents one way of computing the subjunctive probability that B would be the case if A were the case. In the case of the very strong theory of WS-models, the subjunctive probability turns out to be the same as the probability of the subjunctive conditional when we interpret subjunctive probabilities as Lewis suggests. For this reason, it is not entirely clear in Lewis's article that a new concept has been introduced into the discussion. We shall see that in general, for a less restrictive model theory, the subjunctive probability and the probability of the subjunctive conditional are no more identical than are the conditional probability and the probability of the material implication.

The account of subjunctive probabilities to be offered here will be developed through applying Lewis's technique of imaging to the theory of CS-models. I will also employ a notion of relative reasonableness in my account, a notion which both resembles and is different from Lewis's notion of the relative similarity of worlds. Without the additional structure of the formal counterpart to the notion of relative reasonableness, it would not be possible to apply Lewis's technique to CS-models. After a model theory for subjunctive conditionals has been developed, it will be used in the investigation of Adams' notion of probabilistic entailment as it applies to subjunctive conditionals.

6.2. RELATIVE REASONABLENESS

Returning to our interpretation of the theory of CS-models, we must take a closer look at our notion of reasonableness conditions. Although all members of f(A, w) are *ex hypothesi* reasonable *enough* to be counterexamples to conditionals with antecedent A, some may still be more reasonable than others. This relativity of the notion of reasonableness shows up particularly well in the case of counterfactual antecedents, where an initial similarity between relative reasonableness and a difference in the degree to which suspension of belief is required can be seen. Where a proposition A is contrary-to-fact, or at least contrary-to-belief, consideration of any situations in which A is true should require suspension of belief. However, consideration of some situations may require that we suspend belief to a greater extent than do others. Suppose, for example, that Carter had not won the 1976 Presidential election. This might have been the case if he had not won in Ohio. It might also have been the case if he had lost in every state in the deep South. Perhaps either of these circumstances is reasonable *enough* to consider when we suppose that Carter had not won the election, but it seems *more* reasonable that he might not have won in Ohio than that he might have lost every state in the deep South. I'm not sure that I would want to say that one of these sets of circumstances is more *probable* than the other, but I'm quite sure that I would want to say that one is more *plausible* than the other. Since I *know* that Carter carried both Ohio (by a slim margin) and nearly all of the deep South, the subjective probability of his not carrying either of these is, for me, 0. If we in fact *knew* the truth values of all sentences, and hence *knew* which world was actual, it would in general be peculiar to talk of assigning *subjective* probabilities other than 0 to propositions other than those we knew to be true, or worlds other than the one we knew to be actual. To do so would be to admit that we do not know which situation is actual after all. In a case in which we have complete information about what is actually the case, at least, we cannot identify relative reasonableness with subjective probability. However, we can surely say that it is easier to believe that if the world were different in certain ways, it would be different in *this* way rather than in *that* way. Perhaps even consideration of subjunctive conditionals with true antecedents requires a certain suspension of belief in some cases. We may find the actual situation to be very implausible or unreasonable in certain ways, or at least no more plausible than any number of other situations. It is very implausible, for example, that if I were to roll a pair of dice seven consecutive times, I should roll a seven each time. Even if I were in fact to roll seven consecutive sevens, what I would have done would still be very 'unbelievable' and implausible. In considering what would happen if I were to roll the dice seven times, we may want to consider hypothetical situations other than the actual situation because the actual situation is so surprising that we do not feel justified in basing our decisions about subjunctive conditionals on an examination of the actual situation alone.

We cannot absolutely identify relative reasonableness with degree of suspension of belief, although these two notions are related. In the example in which I roll seven consecutive sevens at the dice table, I might have reason to consider what would happen had I *not* rolled seven consecutive sevens. Since I know that I *did* roll *six* consecutive sevens, it should require a lesser degree of suspension of belief to consider hypothetical situations in which I rolled six consecutive sevens, than it would be to consider cases in which I did not. Yet it seems to me, at least, that it is more plausible that I should *not* roll six consecutive sevens than that I *should*. The reason for this, I think, is that we consider any combination of rolls equally reasonable, and there are so few combinations involving the roll of six consecutive sevens. The *simple subjective* probability of my rolling six consecutive sevens on this occasion is 1 (since I in fact know that I *did* roll them) while the *subjunctive* probability of my having done this is only 1/46656. So relative reasonableness involves more than degree of suspension of belief. Another way of looking at this example is to treat the *reasonableness* of rolling six straight sevens *after* having rolled seven as being the same as the *probability* of rolling six straight sevens *before* the roll. This harkens back to Adams's suggestion that the probability of a counterfactual is the same as some prior conditional probability. Adams's suggestion may be correct in many situations, but we saw in Section 4.6 that it is at least not generally applicable. This example also relates to my earlier suggestion that while the actual situation must always be reasonable *enough* to consider in our subjunctive deliberations, it may be *less* reasonable in certain ways than are other merely hypothetical situations.

We can also use examples of this sort to demonstrate the difference between the notion of relative reasonableness on the one hand and the notions of the comparative similarity of worlds (Stalnaker and Lewis) and of minimal change (Pollock) on the other. Surely in the context of our example a situation in which I roll six sevens is more similar to what actually happened than is any situation in which I do not. Similarly, if we make a minimal change in what actually happens in order to produce a situation in which I do not roll seven consecutive sevens, we should expect the result to be a situation in which I roll six consecutive sevens. There is some similarity between these three notions, but each is distinct from the other two.

I clearly have not given a complete explication of the notion of relative reasonableness, but it seems clear that one situation may be more reasonable than another even when both are reasonable enough to be considered in our hypothetical deliberations on a particular occasion. A very important consideration in determining relative reasonableness appears to be 'objective' probabilities as in the dice examples. Besides that, further refinement of our determinations will depend upon degrees of suspension of belief, clearly a subjective notion, and perhaps other considerations which I have overlooked.

A new, complicated model theory is suggested.

DEFINITION 6.2.1. A *measured CS-model* is a model $\langle W, M \rangle$ such that:

(1)   M assigns to each $A \in CL$ and $w \in W$ a function $M_{A,w}$ from W into $[0, 1]$ such that either $M_{A,w}$ is the constant zero function on W or $\Sigma_{w' \in W} M_{A,w}(w') = 1$;

(2) $W/A > B = \{w \in W: \{w' \in W: M_{A,w}(w') \neq 0\} \subseteq W/B\}$.

We can easily show

THEOREM 6.2.2. Every measured CS-model is equivalent to some CS-model.

Where $\langle W, M \rangle$ is a measured CS-model, $A \in CL$, and $w \in W$, we let $f(A, w) =$ $\{w' \in W: M_{A,w}(w') \neq 0\}$. Then $\langle W, f \rangle$ is a CS-model. Since $\{w' \in W: M_{A,w}(w')$ $\neq 0\}$ must always be at most countable, we encounter insurmountable prob-lems in trying to construct a measured CS-model which is equivalent to an 'uncountable' CS-model. This leads us to suspect that the theories of CS-models and of measured CS-models may not be used to characterize the same logics. Fortunately, it is shown in Chapter 7 that all of the logics with which we are likely to be concerned have the finite model property. Since any finite CS-model can be transformed into a measured CS-model, we can put aside any worry we may have about being unable to determine our favorite con-ditional logics by means of classes of measured CS-models. Furthermore, we will eventually generalize our model theory for subjunctive probabilities in such a way to insure that every CS-model can be transformed into a model which can be used to interpret subjunctive probabilities.

The move to measured CS-models allows us to interpret comparative reasonableness claims in our model theory. The reasonableness relative to a model $\mathscr{M} = \langle W, M \rangle$ at $w \in W$ that B would be the case if A were is given by the following equality:

$$R_w(B/A) = \left\{ \begin{array}{l} \Sigma_{w' \in W/B} M_{A,w}(w') \text{ if } M_{A,w} \text{ is not} \\ \text{the constant zero function on W} \\ \\ 1 \text{ otherwise} \end{array} \right\}.$$

We can also think of relative reasonableness as itself being the subjunctive probability we are seeking in a certain special case. Suppose we know which situation is actual, i.e., we know exactly which propositions are true. Cer-tainly the probability that B would be the case if A were, depends upon which propositions are true. For example, the probability that famine would have resulted if we had had a bad wheat crop in 1977 depends upon the amount of surplus wheat we had available from previous seasons, etc. That the wheat stores are sufficient to avoid famine, may itself be only more or less probable, depending upon the birthrate, the availability of alternative grains, etc. But when we *know* what the surplus was, what the birthrate was, etc., our estimates of probabilities becomes easier. With complete knowledge, we should have $R_w(B/A) = p(B//A)$, where w is, of course, the possible world corresponding to the actual situation. As we become less certain about which propositions are in fact *true*, then we compound subjective probabilities and p(B//A) must be some function of the set of values $R_w(B/A)$ for all the w that *might* be the case.

Stalnaker (1970) defines an *absolute probability function* as any function p taking propositions into real numbers which meets the following six conditions for all propositions A, B, and C:

(1) $1 \geqslant p(A) \geqslant 0$

(2) $p(A) = p(A \& A)$

(3) $p(A \& B) = p(B \& A)$

(4) $p[A \& (B \& C)] = p[(A \& B) \& C]$

(5) $p(A) + p(\sim A) = 1$

(6) $p(A) = p(A \& B) + p(A \& \sim B)$

For any measured CS-model $\mathscr{M} = \langle W, M \rangle$, any $w \in W$, and any $A \in CL$, if $M_{A,w}$ is not the constant zero function, then $R_w(\ /A)$ is clearly an absolute probability function. This gives added reason for thinking of relative reasonableness as a peculiar species of conditional probability, one depending upon omniscience concering what is *actually* true or false.

Instead of a measure function, we might have used a relation to represent relative reasonableness in our models. This would have had the disadvantage that we would then lack a measure of the difference in reasonableness of two worlds with respect to a given antecedent. But the primary reason for representing relative reasonableness in this way is that we will need these measure functions in completing our general account of subjunctive probabilities. Lewis (1973a) suggests that we might augment his account of the comparative similarity of worlds by providing a quantitative measure of the relative similarity of two worlds, but he did not find this suggestion useful. Given a measured CS-model $\langle W, M \rangle$, we can certainly define a corresponding reasonableness relation or similarity-relation on W: We just say that w_1 is more-A-reasonable-from-w than is w_2 in case $M_{A,w}(w_1) > M_{A,w}(w_2)$. One important difference between relative-reasonableness-as-relation (or comparative similarity of worlds) and relative-reasonableness-as-measure is that we could have infinitely many infinite equivalence classes generated by a reasonableness-relation (or similarity-relation), but we can have at most one infinite equivalence class generated by a reasonableness-measure, a proposition A and a world w. There may be infinitely many worlds w′ such that $M_{A,w}(w') = 0$, but for any $n \in (0, 1]$ there can be at most n^{-1} worlds w′ such that $M_{A,w}(w') = n$; otherwise $\Sigma_{w' \in W} M_{A,w}(w') > 1$, contrary to definition.

Having a reasonableness measure available in our models allows us to apply Lewis's imaging technique to models which are not so restrictive as are those of Stalnaker's semantics. In this way we will be able to give an account of subjunctive probabilities to complement conditional logics weaker than Stalnaker's **C2**.

6.3. GENERAL SEMANTICS FOR SUBJUNCTIVE PROBABILITIES

We might say that an agent who knows exactly which propositions are true and has available to him an exact measure of plausibility with respect to every sentence is in a determinate epistemic situation. Of course, no one is ever in a determinate epistemic situation and one's information is always incomplete. When one does not *know* whether or not A is true, one still frequently has a greater tendency to believe, or degree of belief in, one of A or ~A than the other. Adapting from Lewis (1976a) I will represent an *epistemic situation* as a function which assigns to each possible world a value commensurate with the degree of rational belief an agent has that that is the actual world.

A feature of relative reasonableness which we have ignored until now is the possibility that two agents are in a determinate epistemic situation and yet each subscribes to a different relative reasonableness measure. Both, in other words, agree that w is the actual world, but they disagree about the probability that B would happen if A were to happen. Heretofore, we have been able to treat worlds simply as functions from CL to truth values. Now, however, we find an additional way in which we may want to distinguish worlds. This would require us to complicate our notion of a model. A model then becomes an ordered triple $\langle W, [\ ], X \rangle$ where W is a non-empty set of formally propertyless indices and $[\ ]$ is a function from CL to subsets of W. The intended interpretation is that for $A \in CL$, [A] is the set of worlds at which A is true. If we generalize the notion of a measured CS-model in this way, we can then allow that for some such model $\langle W, [\ ], M \rangle$, there are w, w' $\in$ W and A, B $\in$ CL such that $R_w(B/A) \neq R_{w'}(B/A)$ even through for all $C \in CL$, $w \in [C]$ iff $w' \in [C]$. This kind of distinction could not be made using the original definition of a measured CS-model. Having noted the possibility for such refinement, I will nevertheless confine myself to a discussion of the simpler notion of a model in which worlds are functions. All our results will still hold if we were to adopt this more complicated definition. This change in the definition of a model is one way in which the notion of subjunctive probability might be generalized beyond the suggestion of the previous section, that subjunctive probability be identified with relative reasonableness in a measured CS-model. But this alteration is still only applicable assuming a determinate epistemic situation, and this assumption is far too restrictive.

To capture the suggestion that *subjunctive* probabilities are a function (at least in part) of the probabilities that certain propositions are *true*, we need to develop a new kind of structure called a *probability model*.

DEFINITION 6.3.1. A probability model is a model $\langle W, \langle M, P \rangle \rangle$ such that:

(1) $\langle W, M \rangle$ is a measured CS-model; and

(2)   P is a function from W into $[0, 1]$ satisfying the condition that $\Sigma_W P(w) = 1$

Let $\mathcal{M} = \langle W, \langle M, P \rangle \rangle$ be a probability model. Then we can use P to determine a value for the probability of any wff A in a natural way:

$$p(A) = \Sigma_{w \in W/A} P(w)$$

This clearly makes of p an absolute probability function on the set of sentences of our conditional language. We can also use $\mathcal{M}$ to provide an interpretation of the subjunctive probability that B would be the case if A were:

$$p(B//A) = \Sigma_W P(w) \cdot R_w(B/A).$$

Suppose A is a proposition such that for each $w \in W$, either $P(w) = 0$ or $M_{A,w}$ is not the constant zero function. Then we can show that $p(//A)$ is also an absolute probability function. I will only sketch a proof of this claim. Assume our hypothesis and let $w \in W$. If $P(w) = 0$, then for any proposition B, $P(w) \cdot R_w(B/A) = 0$ and hence $P(w) \cdot R_w(/A)$ satisfies conditions (1)–(4) and (6) of Stalnaker's definition. However, $P(w) \cdot R_w(B/A) + P(w) \cdot R_w(\sim B/A) = 0 = P(w)$. If $P(w) \neq 0$, then by hypothesis $M_{A,w}$ is not the constant zero function and, as we noted earlier, $R_w(/A)$ is an absolute probability function. Then $P(w) \cdot R_w(/A)$ satisfies conditions (1)–(4) and (6) of Stalnaker's definition, and for any proposition B, $P(w) \cdot R_w(B/A) + P(w) \cdot R_w(\sim B/A) = P(w) \cdot [R_w(B/A) + R_w(\sim B/A)] = P(w) \cdot 1 = P(w)$. But then $P(//A)$ will surely satisfy conditions (1)–(4) and (6), and for any proposition B, $P(B//A) + P(\sim B//A) = \Sigma_W P(w) \cdot R_w(B/A) + \Sigma_W P(w) \cdot R_w(\sim B/A) = \Sigma_W [(P(w) \cdot R_w(B/A)) + (P(w) \cdot R_w(\sim B/A))] = \Sigma_W P(w) = 1$. So $P(//A)$ is an absolute probability function.

The condition that for all $w \in W$, $P(w) = 0$ or $M_{A,w}$ not be the constant zero function roughly corresponds here to the condition for the conditional probability $p(B/A)$ being defined that $p(A) \neq 0$. When our condition for p(//A) to be an absolute probability function is not met, however, the function p(//A) may nevertheless be defined but turn out to be rather peculiar. Suppose we have a model $\mathcal{M} = \langle W, \langle M, P \rangle \rangle$ such that $w \in W$, $P(w) \neq 0$, $M_{A,w}$ is the constant zero function, and for all $w' \in W$, either $w' = w$ or $P(w') = 0$ or $M_{A,w'}$ is not the constant zero function. We further assume that there exists at least one $w' \in W$ such that $w' \neq w$ and $P(w') \neq 0$. Then for any proposition B, $p(B//A) + p(\sim B//A) = 1 + P(w)$. Intuitively, we have here a situation in which a number of worlds are assigned some positive subjective probability and in exactly one of these worlds A is totally implausible. In this and similar cases, the subjunctive probability function has some rather peculiar features.

Recall that Lewis's imaging technique for Stalnaker's semantics was a method of producing minimal A-revisions of a probability function. p_A is produced by 'pushing' the probability p assigns to a world w onto the world most similar to w in which A is true. Here we have instead *spread* the probability that w is actual over the set of reasonable A-alternatives to w, i.e., onto those worlds w' for which $M_{A,w}(w') \neq 0$. The notion of a reasonableness measure is essential to this adaptation of Lewis's imaging technique since without the reasonableness measure we would have no way of deciding how much of the probability originally assigned to w to transfer to each of the reasonable A-alternatives to w.

A Stalnaker model for subjunctive conditionals is essentially a measured CS-model $\langle W, M \rangle$ satisfying the condition that for any proposition A and worlds w and w', either $M_{A,w}(w') = 0$ or $M_{A,w}(w') = 1$. Consequently, the present account of subjunctive probabilities and Lewis's account agree in the case of the conditional logic **C2** and the theory of WS-models. If $\langle W, M \rangle$ is a measured CS-model which is equivalent to a WS-model, we have $p(B//A) = p_A(B)$. Of course, the real advantage of the present account is that it is also compatible with logics weaker than **C2**. Weaker conditional logics can also be determined using Lewis's system-of-spheres semantics, but there does not appear to be any way to apply the imaging technique to SOS-models and thereby provide an account of subjunctive probabilities for these logics by this means.

The theory of probability models allows us to make a number of distinctions that we should wish to make. Consider once again an antecedent with subjective probability 0. Suppose I roll a die and it comes up an ace. Then the subjective probability (for me) that the die came up an even number is 0. Now consider 'If the die came up even, then it came up a deuce' and 'If the die had come up even, then it would have come up a deuce'. Figure 6.3.2.

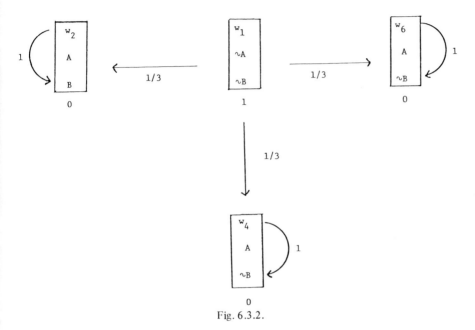

Fig. 6.3.2.

represents the relative features of the semantics of the situation. For each
$i = 1, 2, 4, 6$, let w_i be the world in which the die shows an i. We will assume
that I am in a determinate epistemic situation, so there is a particular world
w_1 in which the die comes up an ace and which I know to be the actual world.
Let A be 'the die comes up even' and let B be 'the die comes up a deuce'. We
assume that there is a unique alternative w_i to be considered for any number i
which the die shows. Then all of the initial probability is assigned to w_1. If
the die had come up even, then one of w_2, w_4, or w_6 would have been actual.
Assuming the toss of the die is fair and the die itself is fair, each of w_2, w_4,
and w_6 is equally reasonable given A. So we have arrows with $1/3$ attached
to them going from w_1 to each of w_2, w_4, and w_6. (We have additional arrows
indicating that $M_{A,w_i}(w_i) = 1$ for $i = 2, 4, 6$, but these values don't actually
affect our results in this example.) Then in this case we have $p(A \rightarrow B) = 1$,
$p(A > B) = 0$, $p(B/A)$ is undefined (since $p(A) = 0$), and $p(B//A) = 1/3$. No
two of these quantities are the same, and the values of these subjective probabilities are just what we would intuitively expect them to be.

Our model theory can accommodate such differences even when the probability of the antecedent is not 0. Where A is our antecedent and B our consequent, consider Figure 6.3.3.

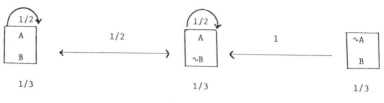

Fig. 6.3.3.

Here we have $p(A \to B) = 2/3$, $p(A > B) = 0$, $p(B/A) = 1/2$, and $p(B//A) = 1/3$. Of course, the possibility of such models may be of no particular value if they cannot correspond to any situations which we would take to be intuitively plausible. However, an example of an intuitively plausible situation in which these four subjective probabilities would take exactly the values indicated is available. Let A be 'the die comes up even' and let B be 'the die comes up showing a six'. Suppose we know only that the die showed some number larger than 3. Then, we assign probability 1/3 to each of w_4, w_5, and w_6. Further, $M_{A,w_i}(w_j) = 1/3$ for each $i = 1, 2, 3, 4, 5, 6$, and $j = 4, 5, 6$. This gives us the same values as in Figure 6.3.3. Furthermore, it is *intuitively* clear that the probability that the die *actually* came up six if it came up even is 1/2 (since we know the die didn't come up a deuce) while the probability that it *would have* come up a six if it *had* come up even is 1/3. John Pollock has suggested in conversation that examples of this sort lend evidence to the claim that $p(B//A)$ must represent some *real* probability rather than a *subjective* probability. However, it seems that even in this case $p(B//A)$ is subjective since it depends upon beliefs about the fairness of the die, the fairness of the roll, etc.

So far we have developed a model theory which is only suitable if we have only countably many worlds with positive probability. Where $\langle W, \langle M, P \rangle \rangle$ is a probability model, P can assign positive value to at most countably many worlds. Furthermore, for each $w \in W$ and $A \in CL$, $M_{A,w}$ can assign positive value to at most countably many worlds. To generalize our model theory we will need to replace P and M with functions giving us *probability densities*.

DEFINITION 6.3.4. A *full (probability) model* is a model $\langle W, \langle f, \mu, \nu \rangle \rangle$ such that

(1) $\langle W, f \rangle$ is a CS-model;

(2) μ is a partial function from $\mathscr{P}(W)$ into $[0, 1]$;

(3) $\{W/A: A \in CL\} \subseteq$ domain of $\mu = \mathscr{A}$;

(4) $\langle W, \mathscr{A}, \mu\}$ is a probability space; and

(5)   for each $A \in CL$ and $w \in W$ such that $f(A, w) \neq \emptyset$, ν assigns to A
        and w a function $\nu_{A,w}$ from $\mathscr{B} = \{S \cap f(A, w): S \in \mathscr{A}\}$ into
        [0, 1] such that $\langle W, \mathscr{B}, \nu_{A,w} \rangle$ is a probability space.

Where $\mathscr{M} = \langle W, \langle f, \mu, \nu \rangle\rangle$ is a full model, $A, B \in CL$ and $w \in W$, we let

$$M_{A,B}(w) = \left\{ \begin{array}{l} \nu_{A,w}(W/B \cap f(A, w)) \text{ if } f(A, w) \neq \emptyset \\ 1 \text{ otherwise} \end{array} \right\}.$$

Now we can use $\mathscr{M}$ to interpret the subjunctive probability $p(B//A)$ for any
$A, B \in CL$ such that $M_{A,B}$ is $\mathscr{A}$ measurable. We simply let

$$p(B//A) = \int M_{A,B}(w)d\mu.$$

This analysis reduces to the analysis presented in terms of probability models
in those cases where we never need consider sets which are uncountable.

6.4. SUBJUNCTIVE PROBABILITIES
AND PROBABILISTIC ENTAILMENT

In Section 4.6. we noted that Ernest Adams (1975) insists that in ordinary
discourse we are concerned to limit ourselves to inferences which preserve
high subjective probability rather than just to inferences which preserve the
truth. To review briefly, Adams says indicative conditionals do not have truth
value at all. Instead, we assert an indicative conditional when the corresponding subjective conditional probability is high and this conditional probability
then plays a certain role in our arguments. Since indicative conditionals lack
truth value, they cannot properly occur as arguments for truth functions. So
Adams develops a logic of what we can call first-degree conditional statements, statements in which the indicative conditional connective never itself
occurs within the scope of any other connective. Adams than stipulates that
the first-degree premises $A_1, \ldots, A_n$ *probabilistically entail* or *p-entail* the
first-degree conclusion B just in case for any $\delta > 0$ there is an $\epsilon > 0$ such that
for any probability function p, if $p(A_i) > 1 - \epsilon$ for all $i \leqslant n$, then $p(B) >$
$1 - \delta$. Adams identifies the probability of the conditional $p(A \gg B)$ (where
$A \gg B$ is an indicative conditional) with the conditional probability $p(B/A)$.
On this account, the logic of the indicative conditional turns out to be considerably weaker than the logic of material implication.

Since the interpretation of subjunctive probabilities offered here applies to compounds of conditionals, we can get some interesting results of our own concerning p-entailments among subjunctive conditionals, even without confining ourselves to first-degree statements.

First, if we restrict ourselves to full models $\langle W, \langle f, \mu, \nu \rangle\rangle$ such that for all $A \in CL$ and $w \in W$, $f(A, w) \subseteq W/A$, we have a probabilistic counterpart to ID:

IDp. Anything p-entails $A > A$.

Proof. IDp will follow immediately once we show that for any probability function p, $p(A//A) = 1$. Let $\mathscr{M} = \langle W, \langle f, \mu, \nu \rangle$ be a full model and let $w \in W$. Since $\langle W, \{S \cap f(A, w): S \in$ domain $\mu\}, \nu_{A,w}\rangle$ is a probability space and since $W \in$ domain μ, $\nu_{A,w}(W \cap f(A, w)) = 1$. But since $f(A, w) \subseteq W/A$, $M_{A,A}(w) = \nu_{A,w}(W/A \cap f(A, w)) = \nu_{A,w}(W \cap f(A, w)) = 1$. Thus, for the probability function p interpreted in $\mathscr{M}$, $p(A//A) = \int 1 \, d\mu = 1$.

We also have a counterpart to the rule RCK. Suppose we confine our attention to some class Γ of CS-models. Then let **L** be the logic determined by Γ and let Γ^* be the class of all full models $\langle W, \langle f, \mu, \nu \rangle\rangle$ such that $\langle W, f \rangle$ is in Γ. In the next rule, we will confine our attention to probability functions which can be interpreted in some full model in Γ^* and to the corresponding notion of p-entailment.

RCKp. If $(A_1 \& \ldots \& A_n) \to B \in$ **L**, then $C > A_1, \ldots, C > A_n$ p-entail $C > B$.

Proof. Assume the hypothesis, let $\epsilon > 0$, and let $\mathscr{M} = \langle W, \langle f, \mu, \nu \rangle\rangle \in \Gamma^*$ such that $p(A_i//C) > 1 - \epsilon/n$ for the probability function p determined by $\mathscr{M}$ and each $i = 1, \ldots, n$. Then $\int M_{C,A_i}(w)d\mu > 1 - \epsilon/n$ for each $i = 1, \ldots, n$. However, $M_{C,A_i}(w) \geq \nu_{C,w}(W/A_i \cap f(C, w))$ for each $w \in W$ and $i = 1, \ldots, n$. Then for each $w \in W$, $M_{C,B}(w) \geq \nu_{C,w}(W/B \cap f(C, w)) \geq \nu_{C,w}(W/A_1 \& \ldots \& A_n \cap f(C, w))$, since $(A_1 \& \ldots \& A_n) \to B \in$ **L**. So $M_{C,B}(w) \geq \nu_{C,w}((W/A_1 \cap f(C, w)) \cap \ldots \cap (W/A_n \cap f(C, w))) \geq 1 - [(1 - \nu_{C,w}(W/A_1 \cap f(C, w))) + \ldots + (1 - \nu_{C,w}(W/A_n \cap f(C, w))] = 1 - [(1 - M_{C,A_1}(w)) + \ldots + (1 - M_{C,A_n}(w))]$ for each $w \in W$. So $p(B//C) = \int M_{C,B}(w)d\mu \geq \int 1 - [(1 - M_{C,A_1}(w)) + \ldots + (1 - M_{C,A_n}(w))]d\mu = 1 - [(1 - \int M_{C,A_1}(w)d\mu) + \ldots + (1 - \int M_{C,A_n}(w)d\mu)] = 1 - \epsilon$.

Without special restrictions on the class of full models to be used in interpreting probability functions, we can establish neither a probabilistic counterpart for MP nor a probabilistic rule of detachment for subjunctive conditionals, i.e., we have neither of the following:

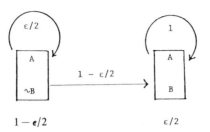

Fig. 6.4.1.

MPp. A > B p-entails A → B.

Cp-Detachment. A and A > B p-entail B.

We can show the failure of MPp and Cp-Detachment using Figure 6.4.1. This figure gives us a partial measured CS-model, which is a kind of full model. The arrows indicate values for the function M with A as argument.

Here we have $p(A) = 1$ and $p(B//A) = (1 - \epsilon/2)^2 + \epsilon/2 > 1 - \epsilon$, but we have $p(A \to B) = \epsilon/2$ and $p(B) = \epsilon/2$. Thus, we are able to set the values of $p(A)$ and $p(B//A)$ as high as we wish while keeping the values of $p(B)$ and $p(A \to B)$ arbitrarily low. While it does not help us so far as MPp is concerned, we can at least secure Cp-Detachment if we are prepared to accept the thesis CS and the corresponding semantic restriction that for any full model ⟨W, ⟨f, μ, ν⟩⟩, any $w \in W$, and any $A \in CL$, if $w(A) = 1$, then $f(A, w) = \{w\}$.

Proof of Cp-Detachment assuming CS: Let $\epsilon > 0$ and let $\mathcal{M} = ⟨W, ⟨f, \mu, \nu⟩⟩$ be a full model such that for the corresponding probability function $p, p(A) = \mu(W/A) > 1 - \epsilon/2$ and $p(B//A) = \int M_{A,B} d\mu > 1 - \epsilon/2$. For $w \in W/A \& B$, $M_{A,B}(w) = 1$; for $w \in W/A \& {\sim}B$, $M_{A,B}(w) = 0$. So $\int_{W/A} M_{A,B}(w)d\mu = \int_{W/A \& B} 1 d\mu = \mu(W/A \& B) = p(A \& B)$. But $\int_{W/{\sim}A} M_{A,B}(w)d\mu \leqslant \int_{W/{\sim}A} 1 d\mu = \mu(W/{\sim}A) < \epsilon/2$. Then $p(B) \geqslant p(A \& B) = \int_{W/A} M_{A,B}(w)d\mu = \int M_{A,B}(w)d\mu - \int_{W/{\sim}A} M_{A,B}(w)d\mu > (1 - \epsilon/2) - \epsilon/2 = 1 - \epsilon$, and our probabilistic rule of detachment for subjunctive conditionals is established.

I have offered various arguments against the thesis CS throughout this work. Yet the rule Cp-Detachment is very plausible, and it can only be insured if we accept CS. This lends considerable support to CS despite all arguments to the contrary. Note, however, that even CS will not give us MPp. We can have $p(B//A)$ as high as we wish (short of 1 if we preserve MP) and yet have $p(B/A)$ as low as we wish (even 0). This is possible where we make $p(A)$

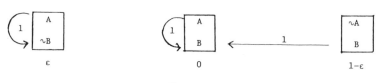

Fig. 6.4.2.

extremely low, as is illustrated in Figure 6.4.2. For a full model satisfying the conditions of the diagram, we have $p(B/A) = 0$ and $p(B/\!/A) > 1 - \epsilon$ for arbitrarily small $\epsilon > 0$. I can find no interesting condition on full models which insures MPp.

6.5. CONDITIONALS, PROBABILITY, AND DECISION THEORY

Very few people know what a probability density is, and not many more know much about the theory of integration. These facts suggest that the foregoing account of subjunctive probability lacks relevance to everyday concerns, such as the need to make decisions in various circumstances. Even the simplified account of subjunctive probabilities in terms of finite probability models does not clearly avoid descriptive inadequacy. What exactly is the relationship between our formal analysis and the ordinary use of conditional language which originally motivated this volume?

Ernest Adams, in Chapter 3 of (1975), proposes that conditional probabilities play an important role in a theory of decision under risk which he calls *expected utility theory*. We consider, says Adams, the subjective probabilities of certain outcomes given different actions performed and the occurrence of different contingencies. When we combine these with the subjective probabilities of the various contingencies considered and with the relative utilities of the different outcomes, we determine the utilities which we expect will result from the different courses of action contemplated. We then act to maximize the expected utility. The probabilities of the outcomes given the contingencies and the possible courses of action are supposed by Adams to be standard conditional probabilities.

I suspect that this is not a very good description of the way in which we actually make decisions under risk. The problem is that we very likely do not determine the conditional probabilities upon which we base our decisions in the manner which the equation $p(B/A) = p(A \& B)/p(A)$ requires. For example, we might reason that if we do such and such and A is true, then B will probably come to be true. But A is probable and B is much to be desired, so we should do such and such. Presumably in this case we are trying to decide whether or not to do such and such. One important consideration is whether B will result from doing such and such. Is the important probability, then, p(B/we do such and such)? If so, we must despair, for we surely cannot determine the probability of the antecedent as an intermediate step in making our decision in such a case since what we are trying to decide is whether or not to *bring it about* that the antecedent is true. And the same holds true for p(B/A & we do such and such). What we are concerned to know, I think, is what *would* happen if A *were* true and we *were* to do such and such. Whatever this conditional probability is, it must not be the standard conditional probability of which Adams treats since otherwise it can in no wise enter into our deliberations.

Let us consider another, particular example of the use of subjunctive conditionals in decision making which is of some interest. In this example, unlike the general sort of case just considered, it is possible for us to arrive at a satisfactory determination of both the subjunctive probability and the standard conditional probability. We will see, however, that it is the subjunctive probability which influences our decision. Suppose I need to talk to my friend Victor within the next half hour. Victor has told me that he will be either at Margaret's party or at the bowling alley. I first go to Margaret's party and find hundreds of people present. If I spend time looking for Victor among the crowd at Margaret's and he is at the bowling alley, I will not be able to speak with him within the half hour. On the other hand, if Victor is at the party and I leave the party to look for him at the bowling alley, I again will not reach him in time. What to do? Fortunately, I see Stanley at the party and he tells me that he has been there for hours. I say that this is fortunate because I know that Stanley owes Victor money and has been avoiding him, and I also know that Victor walks into a party very late. I now reason that if Victor were at the party, Stanley probably would not be at the party. But Stanley is at the party. So I rush to the bowling alley, thinking that Victor is probably there. Formally, I have decided that $p(\sim B//A)$ is very high where A is 'Victor is at the party' and B is 'Stanley is at the party'. But $p(\sim B) = 0$ since I know that Stanley is at the party. So $p(A)$ is very low although it may not be zero. (With our model theory, this rule of probabilistic *modus tollens* follows from acceptance of CS in much the same manner as does Cp-Detachment.) But why do we have to attend to $p(\sim B//A)$ to arrive at the decision to look for Victor at the bowling alley? Why won't the standard conditional probability serve our need as well? The answer is that $p(\sim B/A) = p(A \& \sim B)/p(A) = 0/p(A) = 0$, since $0 = p(\sim B) \geqslant p(A \& \sim B)$. The standard conditional probability that Stanley wouldn't be at the party if Victor were is zero while the subjunctive probability is very high. But perhaps the relevant probability is $p(\sim A/B) = p(\sim A \,\&\, B)/p(B)$, which is surely high enough. In this case, though, I think we implicitly *use* the fact that $p(\sim B//A)$ is high in *determining* that $p(\sim A \,\&\, B)$ is high. This is not the case with $p(A \,\&\, \sim B)$ since we know that B is true.

If we accept the conclusion towards which these considerations point, that standard conditional probabilities cannot play the role in decision making in which Adams casts them, while subjunctive probabilities clearly do influence decision in at least some cases, it still is not clear that the model theory developed here for subjunctive probabilities provides an adequate analysis of these probabilities. Of course, we should keep in mind that our possible worlds semantics is intended at best to be a formalization of an idealized version of what goes on in our actual deliberations.

What I think we in fact do in estimating $p(B//A)$ is to consder all *reasonable* situations in which A is true and see 'how many' of these are situations in which B is true. Furthermore, we weigh the A-situations in terms of relative reasonableness. This sounds very much like an informal parallel of our theory of full probability models with one important exception. The details of our model theory more or less require us to go through this sort of procedure for each situation which seems to us at all likely, but in fact I think we consider a single set of situations with weights provided through considerations of relative reasonableness. This suggests that instead of individual worlds, the function M in a probability model $\langle W, M, P \rangle$ or the function f in a full model $\langle W, \langle f, \mu, \nu \rangle \rangle$ takes the entire set of worlds which are of 'non-zero probability' as argument. But this isn't quite right either, for the particular probabilities of the individual worlds of this set (or the probability densities involved) affect the outcome. It is not simply the set of worlds of 'non-zero probability', but the set of these worlds, together with a probability density function defined upon the set which determines the relative reasonableness weightings we give to the worlds we consider. In some vague and imprecise way, the functions of the two functions M and P in the probability model, or the functions μ and ν in the full model, are combined in actual deliberations concerning subjunctive probabilities. What we get is a sort of super-weighting of the single set of reasonable worlds in which the antecedent is true. The idealization which takes place in our theory of full probability models is that the subjective probabilities of various propositions being true and the relative reasonableness estimations which would be adopted in case of complete knowledge about what is actually true, which are amalgamated into a fuzzy but simple thought process in actual deliberation, get separated so that each is given a precise role in the model theory. I suspect that the way in which we ordinarily estimate subjunctive probabilities is so imprecise that no model theory can both accurately represent it and also serve some heuristic function. At the same time, the model theory developed here seems to be compatible, intuitively, with those processes and to parody them in an instructive way. I must appeal to the normative function of formalization as well as the descriptive function in justifying my analysis. Subjunctive probabilities seem to play an important role in our decision-making processes, and the present theory provides some suggestions for more accurately estimating these probabilities, even if it does not give us an entirely adequate picture of the manner in which these estimations are commonly made. Of course, the notion of probabilities as degrees of *rational* belief already involves some sort of idealization. The present account of subjunctive probabilities suggests one direction in which this kind of interpretation of probabilities, complete with its optimistic, prescriptive character, can be extended fruitfully.

CHAPTER 7

ALGEBRAIC SEMANTICS

7.1. INTRODUCTION

In Chapter 3 we investigated the formal properties of a number of possible worlds semantics for conditional logics. I would have been willing to follow the example of Lewis (1973) in segregating this more technical material at the end of the volume, but locating it where it is, made subsequent discussion of the philosophical merits of these model theories in Chapter 4 much easier. As is well known, the possible worlds semantics was developed earlier for modal logics. Another, algebraic semantics has also been developed for modal logics, e.g. in Lemmon (1966) and (1966a). So far, algebraic semantics have received little attention from investigators of conditional logics. The only papers I know of which discuss such semantics are my (1975) and (1979), and van Fraassen's (1976). In this chapter, algebraic semantics for conditional logics will be presented following the line of development of my two earlier papers and in many ways parallelling Lemmon's work in modal logics.

We will look at a number of conditional logics in this chapter, including those defined in Chapter 3. All of these logics can be defined in terms of the following rules and axiom schemata:

RCEA: from $A \leftrightarrow B$, to infer $(A > C) \leftrightarrow (B > C)$

RCEC: from $A \leftrightarrow B$, to infer $(C > A) \leftrightarrow (C > B)$

RCK: from $(A_1 \& \ldots \& A_n) \to B$, to infer $[(C > A_1) \& \ldots \& (C > A_n)] \to (C > B), n \geqslant 0$

RCE: from $A \to B$, to infer $A > B$.

CM: $[A > (B \& C)] \to [(A > B) \& (A > C)]$

CC: $[(A > B) \& (A > C)] \to [A > (B \& C)]$

ID: $A > A$

MP: $(A > B) \to (A \to B)$

MOD: $(\sim A > A) \to (B > A)$

CSO: $[(A > B) \mathbin{\&} (B > A)] \rightarrow [(A > C) \leftrightarrow (B > C)]$

RT: $[(A \mathbin{\&} B) > C] \rightarrow [(A > B) \rightarrow (A > C)]$

CV: $[(A > B) \mathbin{\&} \sim (A > \sim C)] \rightarrow [(A \mathbin{\&} C) > B]$

CA: $[(A > B) \mathbin{\&} (C > B)] \rightarrow [(A \mathbin{\&} C) > B]$

CS: $(A \mathbin{\&} B) \rightarrow (A > B)$

CEM: $(A > B) \vee (A > \sim B)$

We define our logics in each case as the smallest conditional logic closed under certain rules and containing certain axiom schemata. The logics with which we shall be concerned are:

$$\mathbf{Ce} = \langle \mathrm{RCEC} \rangle$$
$$\mathbf{CE} = \langle \mathrm{RCEC}, \mathrm{RCEA} \rangle$$
$$\mathbf{Cm} = \langle \mathrm{RCEC}; \mathrm{CM} \rangle$$
$$\mathbf{CM} = \langle \mathrm{RCEC}, \mathrm{RCEA}; \mathrm{CM} \rangle$$
$$\mathbf{Cr} = \langle \mathrm{RCEC}; \mathrm{CM}, \mathrm{CC} \rangle$$
$$\mathbf{CR} = \langle \mathrm{RCEC}, \mathrm{RCEA}; \mathrm{CM}, \mathrm{CC} \rangle$$
$$\mathbf{Ck} = \langle \mathrm{RCEC}, \mathrm{RCK} \rangle$$
$$\mathbf{G} = \langle \mathrm{RCEC}, \mathrm{RCEA}, \mathrm{RCE} \rangle$$
$$\mathbf{CK} = \langle \mathrm{RCEC}, \mathrm{RCEA}, \mathrm{RCK} \rangle$$
$$\mathbf{Ck} + \mathrm{ID} = \langle \mathrm{RCEC}, \mathrm{RCK}; \mathrm{ID} \rangle$$
$$\mathbf{CK} + \mathrm{ID} = \langle \mathrm{RCEC}, \mathrm{RCEA}, \mathrm{RCK}; \mathrm{ID} \rangle$$
$$\mathbf{Ck} + \mathrm{MP} = \langle \mathrm{RCEC}, \mathrm{RCK}; \mathrm{MP} \rangle$$
$$\mathbf{CK} + \mathrm{MP} = \langle \mathrm{RCEC}, \mathrm{RCEA}, \mathrm{RCK}; \mathrm{MP} \rangle$$
$$\mathbf{CO} = \langle \mathrm{RCEC}, \mathrm{RCK}; \mathrm{ID}, \mathrm{MP}, \mathrm{MOD}, \mathrm{CSO} \rangle$$
$$\mathbf{CA} = \langle \mathrm{RCEC}, \mathrm{RCK}; \mathrm{ID}, \mathrm{MP}, \mathrm{MOD}, \mathrm{CSO}, \mathrm{CA} \rangle$$
$$\mathbf{WC} = \langle \mathrm{RCEC}, \mathrm{RCK}; \mathrm{ID}, \mathrm{MP}, \mathrm{MOD}, \mathrm{CSO}, \mathrm{CA}, \mathrm{RT} \rangle$$
$$\mathbf{V} = \langle \mathrm{RCEC}, \mathrm{RCK}; \mathrm{ID}, \mathrm{MOD}, \mathrm{CSO}, \mathrm{CV} \rangle$$
$$\mathbf{VW} = \langle \mathrm{RCEC}, \mathrm{RCK}; \mathrm{ID}, \mathrm{MOD}, \mathrm{CSO}, \mathrm{CV}, \mathrm{MP} \rangle$$

$$\mathbf{VC} = \langle \text{RCEC, RCK; ID, MOD, CSO, CV, MP, CS} \rangle$$
$$\mathbf{SS} = \langle \text{RCEC, RCK; ID, MP, MOD, CSO, CA, CS} \rangle$$
$$\mathbf{C2} = \langle \text{RCEC, RCK; ID, MOD, CSO, CV, MP, CEM} \rangle$$

Any logic closed under RCEC is called *half-classical*, any half-classical logic closed under RCEA is called *classical*, and any classical logic closed under RCE is called *entailment preserving*, and any classical logic closed under RCK is called *normal*. Any half-classical extension of **Cm** is called *half-monotonic*, any half-classical extension of **Cr** is called *half*-regular, and any half-classical extension of **Ck** is called *half-normal*. Any classical extension of **CM** is called *monotonic* and any classical extension of **CR** is called *regular*. All normal extensions of **CK** + ID are called *dependable* and all normal extensions of **CK** + MP are called *weakly material*. A logic is said to be *ordered* iff, in addition to being dependable, it contains MOD and CSO. Normal extensions of **V** are called *variably strict*. A logic is said to be *material* iff it is dependable and it contains both MP and CS. Every normal extension of **CA** is called *additive*. Since the logic **WC** has been suggested in this volume as the classical logic most adequately representing the conditional of ordinary discourse, I shall call normal extensions of **WC** *preferred*. The definitions of **Ce, CE, Cm, CM, Cr, CR, Ck, CK, Ck** + ID, **CK** + ID, **Ck** + MP and **CK** + MP, as well as the terms 'half-classical,' 'classical,' 'monotonic,' 'regular' and 'normal' are all taken from Chellas (1975). An alternative axiomatization of CO is included in Lewis (1971), and axiomatizations of **V**, **VW** and **VC** are found in Lewis (1973). **SS** was first discussed in Pollock (1975) and **C2** made its debut in Stalnaker (1968).

We can easily show that all of these logics are consistent. For any A ∈ CL, let A + be the result of replacing all occurrences of '>' in A by '→'. We will call A *trivially valid* iff A + is a tautology. Examination shows that all our axiom schemata are trivially valid and that each of our rules preserves trivial validity. But ∼ (A → A) + is not trivially valid and hence is not a member of any of the logics we have defined.

We arrange **Ce–C2** according to containment to produce Figure 7.1.1. One logic contains another if the former is above or to the right of the latter in the diagram. All of the containment relations indicated are proper. In Section 7.4, we will provide proofs that some of these containments are proper using the techniques developed in the next two sections. Sections 7.2 and 7.3 are concerned with algebraic semantics for classical logics, while 7.5 deals with the special problems involved in developing algebraic semantics for half-classical logics.

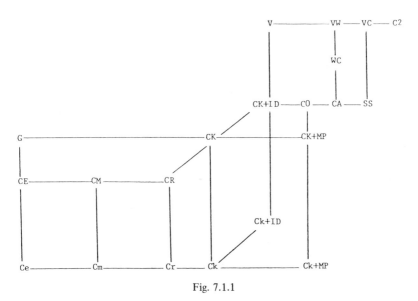

Fig. 7.1.1

7.2. ALGEBRAS

Lemmon interpreted modal systems in terms of matrices, i.e. algebras with certain elements designated. His most interesting results, however, concerned algebras which had Boolean algebras as substructures. In such algebras, the only designated element was the unit of the Boolean algebra. Since all of our results will involve such algebras, we will interpret our conditional logics directly in terms of algebras rather than matrices.

DEFINITION 7.2.1. A structure $\mathscr{A} = \langle M, \cup, \cap, -, * \rangle$ is a *basic algebra* iff M is a set of elements closed under unary operation $-$ and binary operations $\cup$, $\cap$ and $*$ such that $\langle M, \cup, \cap, - \rangle$ is a Boolean algebra. Where $\mathscr{A} = \langle M, \cup, \cap, -, * \rangle$ is a basic algebra and x, y $\in$ M, we let $x \gg y = - x \cup y$ and $x \equiv y = (x \gg y) \cap (y \gg x)$.

DEFINITION 7.2.2. An *interpretation* in a basic algebra $\mathscr{A} = \langle M, \cup, \cap, -, * \rangle$ is a function f which assigns to each A $\in$ CL a member f(A) of M such that

(i) $f(\sim A) = - f(A)$;

(ii) $f(A \& B) = f(A) \cap f(B)$;

(iii) $f(A \lor B) = f(A) \cup f(B)$;

(iv) $f(A \to B) = f(A) \gg f(B)$;

(v) $f(A \leftrightarrow B) = f(A) \equiv f(B)$;

(vi) $f(A > B) = f(A) * f(B)$.

A basic algebra $\mathscr{A}$ *satisfies* a wff A (or A is *true* in $\mathscr{A}$) iff for every interpretation f in $\mathscr{A}$, $f(A) = 1$. $\mathscr{A}$ satisfies a set $S \subseteq CL$ iff $\mathscr{A}$ satisfies every member of S. $\mathscr{A}$ *characterizes* a logic L iff $\mathscr{A}$ satisfies all and only members of L.

DEFINITION 7.2.3. An algebra is *entailment preserving* iff, in addition to being basic, it satisfies the condition that $x * y = 1$ for all $x \leqslant y$ (where $x \leqslant y$ iff $x \cup y = y$ iff $x \cap y = x$).

DEFINITION 7.2.4. An algebra is *monotonic* iff, in addition to being basic, it satisfies the following postulate:

(i) $x * (y \cap z) \leqslant (x * y) \cap (x * z)$.

DEFINITION 7.2.5. An algebra is *regular* iff, in addition to being basic, it satisfies the following postulate:

(i) $x * (y \cap z) = (x * y) \cap (x * z)$.

DEFINITION 7.2.6. An algebra is *normal* iff, in addition to being regular, it satisfies the following postulate:

(i) $x * 1 = 1$.

DEFINITION 7.2.7. An algebra is *dependable* iff, in addition to being normal, it satisfies the following postulate:

(i) $x * x = 1$.

DEFINITION 7.2.8. An algebra is *weakly material* iff, in addition to being normal, it satisfies the following postulate:

(i) $x * y \leqslant x \gg y$.

DEFINITION 7.2.9. An algebra is *ordered* iff, in addition to being dependable, it satisfies the following postulates:

(i) $-x * x \leqslant y * x;$

(ii) $x * (y \cap z) \leqslant (x \cap y) * z.$

DEFINITION 7.2.10. An algebra is *additive* iff, in addition to being weakly material and ordered, it satisfies the following postulate:

(i) $(x * y) \cap (z * y) \leqslant (x \cup z) * y.$

DEFINITION 7.2.11. An algebra is *preferred* iff, in addition to being additive, it satisfies the following postulate:

(i) $[(x \cap y) * z] \cap (x * y) \leqslant (x * z).$

DEFINITION 7.2.12. An algebra is *variably strict* iff, in addition to being ordered, it satisfies the following postulate:

(i) $(x * y) \cap - (x * - z) \leqslant (x \cap z) * y.$

DEFINITION 7.2.13. An algebra is *material* iff, in addition to being dependable and weakly material, it satisfies the following postulate:

(i) $x \cap y \leqslant x * y.$

DEFINITION 7.2.14. An algebra is *singular* iff, in addition to being material and additive, it satisfies the following postulate:

(i) $- (x * y) \leqslant x * - y.$

The names applied to the different algebras defined here, of course, are not accidental; they indicate a connection between a kind of algebra and a kind of logic for which we use the same term. We get the expected soundness results.

LEMMA 7.2.15. Every monotonic algebra satisfies the following condition:

(i)   if $x \leqslant y$, then $z * x \leqslant z * y.$

Proof. Let $\mathscr{A} = \langle M, \textbf{U}, \textbf{\cap}, -, * \rangle$ be a monotonic algebra and let x, y, $z \in M$ such that $x \leqslant y$. Then $x = x \cap y$, and $z * x = z * (x \cap y) \leqslant (z * x) \cap (z * y) \leqslant z * y.$

THEOREM 7.2.16. Every basic (entailment preserving, monotonic, regular,

normal, dependable, weakly material, ordered weakly material, additive, preferred, variably strict, variably strict weakly material, material, variably strict
material, singular) algebra satisfies **CE (G, CM, CR, CK, CK + ID, CK + MP,
CO, CA, WC, V, VW, SS, VC, C2)**.

Proof. The proofs are all similar and we will take the case of **CK** as
example. Let $\mathscr{A} = \langle M, \cup, \cap, -, * \rangle$ be a normal algebra and let f be an interpretation in $\mathscr{A}$. Since $\langle M, \cup, \cap, - \rangle$ is a Boolean algebra, $f(A) = 1$ if A is a
tautology, and $f(B) = 1$ if $f(A) = 1$ and $f(A \rightarrow B) = 1$. Suppose A, B, C $\in$ CL
such that $f(A \leftrightarrow B) = f(A) \equiv f(B) = 1$. $f(A) = f(B)$ by Boolean algebra, so
$f(A) * f(C) = f(B) * f(C)$ and $f(A > C) \equiv f(B > C) = 1$. But this means that
$f((A > C) \leftrightarrow (B > C)) = 1$. Similarly, if $f(A \leftrightarrow B) = 1$, then $f((C > A) \leftrightarrow (C > B)) = 1$. If $f(B) = 1$, then $f(A > B) = f(A) * f(B) = f(A) * 1 = 1$. So for RCK,
let $n > 0$ and $A_1, \ldots, A_n$, B, C $\in$ F such that $f((A_1 \& \ldots \& A_n) \rightarrow B) = 1$.
Then $f(A_1 \& \ldots \& A_n) \leqslant f(B)$ by Boolean algebra, and $f((C > A_1) \& \ldots \&$
$(C > A_n)) = (f(C) * f(A_1)) \cap \ldots \cap (f(C) * f(A_n)) = f(C) * (f(A_1) \cap \ldots \cap$
$f(A_n))$ (since $\mathscr{A}$ is regular) $\leqslant f(C) * f(B)$ (by Lemma 7.2.15) $= f(C > B)$. But
then by Boolean algebra and Definition 7.2.2, $f([(C > A_1) \& \ldots \& (C >$
$A_n)] \rightarrow (C > B)) = 1$. Hence, $\mathscr{A}$ satisfies **CK**.

Let **L** be any classical logic. For any A, B $\in$ CL, let $A \simeq B$ iff $A \leftrightarrow B \in$ **L**.
Then $\simeq$ is a congruence relation on CL. For each $A \in$ CL, let $E(A) = \{B \in CL :$
$A \simeq B\}$. Let $M_L = \{E(A) : A \in CL\}$. For $E(A), E(B) \in M_L$, let

$$E(A) \cup_L E(B) = E(A \vee B),$$

$$E(A) \cap_L E(B) = E(A \& B),$$

$$\neg_L E(A) = E(\sim A), \text{ and}$$

$$E(A) *_L E(B) = E(A > B).$$

Let $\mathscr{A}_L = \langle M_L, \cup_L, \cap_L, \neg_L, *_L \rangle$.

THEOREM 7.2.17. If **L** is a consistent classical logic closed under substitution on sentential variables, then $\mathscr{A}_L$ is a basic algebra which characterizes
L.

Proof. Let **L** be a consistent classical logic closed under substitution on
sentential variables. Since every tautology is in **L** and **L** is closed under
modus ponens, $\langle M_L, \cup_L, \cap_L, \neg_L \rangle$ is clearly a Boolean algebra with unit **L**,
and hence $\mathscr{A}_L$ is a basic algebra. Let $A \in$ **L** and let f be an interpretation in
$\mathscr{A}_L$. Then there must be a $B \in f(A)$ such that B is a substitution instance of
A. But **L** is closed under substitution on sentential variables, so $B \in$ **L** and

$f(A) = L$. Thus, $\mathscr{A}_L$ satisfies **L**. Suppose $\mathscr{A}_L$ satisfies $A \in CL$. Since the function E is itself an interpretation in $\mathscr{A}_L$, $E(A) = L$ and $A \in L$. So $\mathscr{A}_L$ characterizes **L**.

THEOREM 7.2.18. $\mathscr{A}_G$, ($\mathscr{A}_{CM}$, $\mathscr{A}_{CR}$, $\mathscr{A}_{CK+ID}$, $\mathscr{A}_{CK+MP}$, $\mathscr{A}_{CO}$, $\mathscr{A}_{CA}$, $\mathscr{A}_{WC}$, $\mathscr{A}_V$, $\mathscr{A}_{VW}$, $\mathscr{A}_{SS}$, $\mathscr{A}_{VC}$, $\mathscr{A}_{C2}$) is entailment preserving (monotonic, regular, normal, dependable, weakly material, ordered weakly material, additive, preferred, variably strict, variably strict weakly material, material, variably strict material, singular).

Proof. Again, we use **CK** as our example. It is left to the reader to show that **CK** is closed under substitution on sentential variables. By Theorem 7.2.17, we know that $\mathscr{A}_{CK}$ is a basic algebra. Let $E(A), E(B), E(C) \in M_{CK}$. Then $E(A) *_{CK} (E(B) \cap_{CK} E(C)) = E(A > (B \& C)) = E((A > B) \& (A > C))$ (since **CK** contains both **CM** and **CC**) $= (E(A) *_{CK} E(B)) \cap_{CK} E(A) *_{CK} E(C))$, and $\mathscr{A}_{CK}$ is regular. If $A \in CK$ then $B > A \in CK$ by RCK. So $E(A) *_{CK} CK = E(A > (A \rightarrow A)) = CK$ and $\mathscr{A}_{CK}$ is normal.

Combining the results we have achieved so far, we immediately get a completeness result for each of our conditional logics.

THEOREM 7.2.19. $A \in CE$ (**G**, etc.) iff A is satisfied by every basic (monotonic, etc.) algebra.

Lemmon was able to use a certain elegant technique to establish the finite model property and decidability for each of the modal logics discussed in (1966). Lemmon's technique can be adapted for use in the cases of **CM, CR, CK, CK + MP**, but not in the case of our other conditional logics. This technique could also be used in the cases of other logics which have not been defined here and which have not attracted attention in the literature.

THEOREM 7.2.20. If $\mathscr{A} = \langle M, \cup, \cap, -, * \rangle$ is a monotonic (regular, normal, dependable, weakly material) algebra and $a_1, \ldots, a_n$ is a finite sequence of elements of M, then there is a monotonic (regular, normal, dependable, weakly material) algebra $\mathscr{A}_1 = \langle M_1, \cup_1, \cap_1, *_1 \rangle$ with at most 2^{2^n} elements such that:

(i) $a_1, \ldots, a_n \in M_1$;

(ii)   for $x, y \in M_1, x \cup_1 y = x \cup y$;

(iii)   for $x, y \in M_1, x \cap_1 y = x \cap y$;

(iv)   for $x \in M_1, -_1 x = -x$;

(v)   for $x, y \in M_1$, if $x * y \in M_1$, then $x *_1 y = x * y$.

Proof. Assume $\mathscr{A} = \langle M, \cup, \cap, -, * \rangle$ is a monotonic algebra and let $a_1, \ldots, a_n$ be a finite sequence of elements of M. Let M_1 be the set of elements of M obtained from $a_1, \ldots, a_n$ by any finite number of applications of $\cup, \cap$, and $-$. Let $\cup_1, \cap_1$, and $-_1$ be the operations $\cup, \cap$, and $-$ restricted to M_1. $\langle M_1, \cup_1, \cap_1, -_1 \rangle$ is a Boolean algebra with at most 2^{2^n} elements which satisfies (i)–(iv). For $x, y \in M_1$ and $z \in M$, we say y *x-covers* z iff $z \leqslant y$, $z \in M_1$, and $x * z \in M_1$. For $x, y \in M_1$, we put $x *_1 y = (x * y_1) \cup \ldots \cup (x *_1 y_k) \cup 0$, where $y_1, \ldots, y_k$ are all the elements x-covered by y. Since $0 \in M_1, x *_1 y \in M_1$ for each $x, y \in M_1$. Thus, $\mathscr{A}_1 = \langle M_1, \cup_1, \cap_1, -_1, *_1 \rangle$ is a basic algebra.

Let $x, y \in M_1$, and let $y_1, \ldots, y_k$ be all those elements which y x-covers. For each $0 \leqslant i \leqslant k$, $y_i \leqslant y$, $y_i \in M_1$, and $x * y_i \in M_1$. But then by Lemma 7.2.15, for each $y_i, x * y_i \leqslant x * y$, and $(x * y_1) \cup \ldots \cup (x * y_k) \cup 0 \leqslant x * y$. On the other hand, if $x * y \in M_1$, then y x-covers itself and $x * y \leqslant (x * y) \cup (x * y_1) \cup \ldots \cup (x * y_k) \cup 0 = x *_1 y$. So $\mathscr{A}_1$ satisfies (v).

Let $x, y, z \in M_1$. If $y \cap_1 z$ x-covers w, then $w \leqslant y \cap_1 z = y \cap z$, $w \in M_1$, and $x * w \in M_1$. But then $w \leqslant y$, $w \leqslant z$, and both y and z x-covers w. Therefore, $x *_1 (y \cap_1 z) = (x * w_1) \cup \ldots \cup (x * w_k) \cup 0 \leqslant (x *_1 y) \cap (x *_1 z) = (x *_1 y) \cap_1 (x *_1 z)$, where $w_1, \ldots, w_k$ are all the elements which $y \cap_1 z$ x-covers. So $\mathscr{A}_1$ is monotonic.

Suppose $\mathscr{A}$ is regular and let $x, y, z \in M_1$. As we just saw, if $y \cap_1 z$ x-covers w, then both y and z x-cover w. So since $w = w \cap w$, w equals the union of a pair of elements such that y x-covers the first and z x-covers the second. On the other hand, if y x-covers y_1 and z x-covers z_1, then $y_1 \leqslant y$, $y_1 \in M_1$, $x * y_1 \in M_1$, $z_1 \leqslant z$, $z_1 \in M_1$, and $x * z_1 \in M_1$. But then $y_1 \cap_1 z_1 \leqslant y \cap_1 z$, $x * (y_1 \cap_1 z_1) = (x * y_1) \cap (x * z_1) \in M_1$, and $y \cap_1 z$ x-covers $y_1 \cap_1 z_1$. So the elements which $y \cap_1 z$ x-covers consist of all pairs of elements such that y x-covers the first and z x-covers the second. Let $y_1, \ldots, y_k$ be all the elements which y x-covers, let $z_1, \ldots, z_m$ be all the elements which z x-covers, and let $w_1, \ldots, w_s$ be all the elements which $y \cap_1 z$ x-covers. Then $(x *_1 y) \cap_1 (x *_1 z) = [(x * y_1) \cup \ldots \cup (x * y_k) \cup 0] \cap [(x * z_1) \cup \ldots \cup (x * z_m) \cup 0] = [(x * y_1) \cap (x * z_1)] \cup [(x * y_1) \cap (x * z_2)] \cup \ldots \cup [(x * y_k) \cap (x * z_m)] \cup [(x * y_1) \cap 0] \cup \ldots \cup [0 \cap (x * z_m)] \cup [0 \cap 0] = (x * w_1) \cup \ldots \cup (x * w_s) \cup 0 = x *_1 (y \cap_1 z)$, and $\mathscr{A}_1$ is regular.

Suppose $\mathscr{A}$ is normal and $x \in M_1$. Then $x * 1 = 1 \in M_1$, so by (v) $x *_1 1 = x * 1 = 1$. Hence, $\mathscr{A}_1$ is normal.

Suppose $\mathscr{A}$ is dependable and let $x \in M_1$. Then $x * x = 1 \in M_1$, so by (v), $x *_1 x = x * x = 1$. Hence $\mathscr{A}_1$ is dependable.

Suppose $\mathscr{A}$ is weakly material and $x, y \in M_1$. Then $x *_1 y \leqslant x * y \leqslant x \rightarrow y = x \rightarrow_1 y$, and $\mathscr{A}_1$ is weakly material.

We use Theorem 7.2.20 to show that **CM**, **CR**, **CK**, **CK** + ID, and **CK** + MP are all decidable.

THEOREM 7.2.21. Let $A \in CL$ and let n be the number of subformulas of A. Then $A \in$ **CM** (**CR**, **CK**, **CK** + ID, **CK** + MP) iff A is satisfied by every monotonic (regular, normal, dependable, weakly material) algebra with at most 2^{2^n} elements.

Proof. Assume the hypothesis. If $A \in$ **CM** (for example), then A is satisfied by all monotonic algebras (by Theorem 7.2.16). If $A \notin$ **CM**, let $\mathscr{A}$ be a monotonic algebra and f an interpretation in $\mathscr{A}$ such that $f(A) \neq 1$ (by Theorem 7.2.19). Let $S = \{f(B): B$ is a subformula of $A\}$. By Theorem 7.2.20 let $\mathscr{A}_1 = \langle M, \cup, \cap, -, * \rangle$ be a monotonic algebra such that $S \subseteq M$, $\mathscr{A}_1$ satisfies conditions (i)–(v) of Theorem 7.2.20, and M has at most 2^{2^n} elements. We define a function g which assigns to each $B \in CL$ an element $g(B) \in M$ as follows:

$$g(B) = \begin{cases} \text{the largest } x \in M \text{ such that } x \leqslant f(B) \text{ if B is a sentence letter} \\ \text{the smallest } x \in M \text{ such that } - g(C) \leqslant x \text{ if } B = \sim C \\ g(C) \cap g(D) \text{ if } B = C \,\&\, D \\ g(C) \cup g(D) \text{ if } B = C \vee D \\ \text{the largest } x \in M \text{ such that } x \leqslant f(B) \text{ if } B = C > D \end{cases}$$

g is an interpretation in $\mathscr{A}_1$ and $g(B) = f(B)$ for all subformulas B of A. So $g(A) = f(A) \neq 1$, and $\mathscr{A}_1$ does not satisfy A.

We will provide additional decidability results after we have explored the relationships between basic algebras and the possible worlds models in the next section.

7.3. ALGEBRAS AND MODELS

In Chapter 3, we examined a number of interesting model theories for conditional logics. Now we will look at the relationship between two of those theories, the theory of E-models and the theory of PCS-models, and the algebraic semantics of the last section. Three important results reported in Chapter 3 are that every PCS-model is equivalent to some E-model, that **CE** is determined by the class of all E-models, and that **CK** is determined by the class of all PCS-models.

The connection between E-models and basic algebras is fairly obvious. In effect, an E-model is little more than a basic algebra on the power set of some set. For any E-model $\mathscr{M} = \langle W, f \rangle$, let $\mathscr{M}+ = \langle \{W/A : A \in CL\}, \cup, \cap, -, f \rangle$, where $\cup, \cap$, and $-$ are the usual set-theoretic operations. Then we have the following result:

THEOREM 7.3.1. If $\mathscr{M}$ is an E-model, then $\mathscr{M}+$ is a basic algebra.

Proof. By the definition of a possible world, $\langle \{W/A : A \in CL\}, \cup, \cap, - \rangle$ is a Boolean algebra with unit element W.

Corresponding to our notions of entailment preserving (monotonic, etc.) algebras, we need notions of entailment preserving (monotonic, etc.) models.

DEFINITION 7.3.2. An entailment preserving model is any E-model $\langle W, f \rangle$ satisfying the following condition for all $S, T \subseteq W$:

(i)   if $S \subseteq T$, then $f(T, S) = W$.

DEFINITION 7.3.3. A *monotonic* model is any E-model $\langle W, f \rangle$ satisfying the following condition for all $S, T, U \subseteq W$:

(i) $f(S, T \cap U) \subseteq f(S, T) \cap f(S, U)$.

DEFINITION 7.3.4. A *regular* model is any E-model $\langle W, f \rangle$ satisfying the following condition for all $S, T, U \subseteq W$:

(i) $f(S, T \cap U) = f(S, T) \cap f(S, U)$.

DEFINITION 7.3.5. A *normal* model is any regular model $\langle W, f \rangle$ satisfying the following condition for all $S \subseteq W$:

(i) $f(S, W) = W$.

More interesting because they have greater heuristic value for the analysis of ordinary language conditional are PCS-models. Since **CK** is determined by the class of all PCS-models, we might say that PCS-models are also normal models.

DEFINITION 7.3.6. A PCS-model $\langle W, f \rangle$ is *dependable* iff it satisfies the following condition for all $w \in W$ and $S \subseteq W$:

(i) $f(S, w) \subseteq S$.

DEFINITION 7.3.7. A PCS-model $\langle W, f \rangle$ is *weakly material* iff it satisfies the following condition for all $w \in W$ and $S \subseteq W$:

(i)   if $w \in S$, then $w \in f(S, w)$.

DEFINITION 7.3.8. A PCS-model $\langle W, f \rangle$ is *ordered* iff, in addition to being dependable, it satisfies the following conditions for all $w \in W, S \subseteq W$, and $A, B \in CL$:

(i)   if $f(W/A, w) = \emptyset$, then $f(S, w) \cap W/A = \emptyset$;

(ii)   if $f(W/A, w) \subseteq W/B$ and $f(W/B, w) \subseteq W/A$, then $f(W/A, w) = f(W/B, w)$.

DEFINITION 7.3.9. A PCS-model $\langle W, f \rangle$ is *additive* iff, in addition to being weakly material and ordered, it satisfies the following condition for all $w \in W$ and $A, B \in CL$:

(i) $f(W/A \vee B, w) \subseteq f(W/A, w) \cup f(W/B, w)$.

DEFINITION 7.3.10. A PCS-model $\langle W, f \rangle$ is *preferred* iff, in addition to being additive, it satisfies the following condition for all $w \in W$ and $A, B, C \in CL$:

(i)   if $f(W/A, w) \subseteq W/B$, then $f(W/A, w) \subseteq f(W/A \& B, w)$.

DEFINITION 7.3.11. A PCS-model $\langle W, f \rangle$ is *variably strict* iff, in addition to being ordered, it satisfied the following condition for all $w \in W$ and $A, B, C \in F$:

(i)   if $f(W/A, w) \subseteq W/B$, then $f(W/A, w) \subseteq W/\sim C$ or $f(W/A \& C, w) \subseteq W/B$.

DEFINITION 7.3.12. A PCS-model $\langle W, f \rangle$ is *material* iff, in addition to being both weakly material and dependable, it satisfies the following condition for all $w \in W$ and $S \subseteq W$:

(i)   if $w \in S$, then $f(S, w) = \{w\}$.

DEFINITION 7.3.13. A PCS-model $\langle W, f \rangle$ is *singular* iff, in addition to being both material and additive, it satisfies the following condition for all $w \in W$ and $S \subseteq W$:

(i) $f(S, w)$ has at most one member.

Note that Definitions 7.3.8, 7.3.9, 7.3.10 and 7.3.11 involve a weaker sort of condition than do the other definitions. We find this necessary if we are to provide completeness results for certain of our logics.

We construct corresponding algebras for PCS-models in much that same way we did for E-models. Let $\mathscr{M} = \langle W, f \rangle$ be a PCS-model. Let $M + = \{W/A : A \in CL\}$ and let $\cup, \cap$, and $-$ be the set-theoretic operations on $M +$ and for all $W/A, W/B \in M +$ we put $W/A * W/B = W/A > B$. Let $\mathscr{M} + = \langle M +, \cup, \cap, -, * \rangle$.

THEOREM 7.3.14. If $\mathscr{M}$ is an entailment preserving (monotonic, etc.) model, then $\mathscr{M} +$ is an entailment preserving (monotonic, etc.) algebra.

THEOREM 7.3.15. If $\mathscr{M}$ is a PCS-model (dependable PCS-model, etc.), then $\mathscr{M} +$ is a regular (dependable, etc.) algebra.
    Proof. As an example, we will prove that if $\mathscr{M} = \langle W, f \rangle$ is an ordered weakly material PCS-model, then $\mathscr{M} +$ is an ordered weakly material algebra. Assume the hypothesis. By the definition of a possible world, $\langle M +, \cup, \cap, - \rangle$ is a Boolean algebra with unit element W. Let $W/A, W/B, W/C \in M$. $W/A *$ $(W/B \cap W/C) = W/A * (W/B \& C) = W/A > (B \& C) = \{w \in W: f(W/A, w) \subseteq W/B \& C\} = \{w \in W: \quad f(W/A, w) \subseteq W/B \cap W/C\} = \{w \in W: \quad f(W/A, w) \subseteq W/B\} \cap \{w \in W: f(W/A, w) \subseteq W/C\} = W/A > B \cap W/A > C = (W/A * W/B) \cap (W/A * W/C)$, and $\mathscr{M} +$ is regular. Moreover, $W/A * W = W/A * W/A \to A = W/A > (A \to A) = \{w \in W: \quad f(W/A, w) \subseteq W/A \to A\} = \{w \in W: f(W/A, w) \subseteq W\} = W$, and $\mathscr{M} +$ is normal. $W/A * W/A = W/A > A = \{w \in W: f(W/A, W) \subseteq W/A\} = W$, since $\mathscr{M}$ is a dependable PCS-model; so $\mathscr{M} +$ is dependable. If $w \in W/A * W/B$, i.e., $w \in W/A > B$, then $f(W/A, w) \subseteq W/B$. If $w \in W/A$, then since $\mathscr{M}$ is weakly material, $w \in f(W/A, w)$, $w \in W/B$, and $w \in W/A \to B$. On the other hand, if $w \in -W/A = W/\sim A$, then $w \in W/A \to B$. So in either case,

$w \in W/A \to B$, $W/A * W/B \subseteq W/A \to B = W/A \geqslant W/B$, and $\mathscr{M} +$ is weakly material. Assume $w \in -W/A * W/A$, i.e., $w \in W/\sim A > A$. Then $f(W/\sim A, w)$ $\subseteq w/A$. But since $\mathscr{M}$ is dependable, $f(W/\sim A, w) \subseteq W/\sim A$. Hence, $f(W/\sim A, w)$ $\subseteq W/A \cap W/\sim A = W/A \cap -W/A = \emptyset$. By 7.3.8 (i), $f(W/B, w) \cap W/\sim A =$ $\emptyset$, $f(W/B, w) \subseteq -W/\sim A$, and $w \in W/B > A$. $-W/A * W/A \subseteq W/B * W/A$, and $\mathscr{M} +$ satisfies Condition 7.3.8(i). Assume further that $w \in W/A * (W/B \cap W/C)$, i.e., $w \in W/A > (B \& C)$. Then $f(W/A, w) \subseteq W/B \& C = W/B \cap W/C$, $f(W/A, w) \subseteq W/B$, and $f(W/A, w) \subseteq W/C$. But since $\mathscr{M}$ is dependable, $f(W/A * B, w) \subseteq W/A \& B = W/A \cap W/B \subseteq W/A$. Then by 7.3.8(ii), $f(W/A, w) =$ $f(W/A \& B, w)$, and $f(W/A \& B, w) \subseteq W/C$. So $w \in W/(A \& B) > C = (W/A \cap W/B) * W/C$, $W/A * (W/B \cap W/C) \subseteq (W/A \cap W/B) * W/C$, $\mathscr{M} +$ satisfies Condition 7.3.8(ii), and $\mathscr{M} +$ is ordered.

We have representation theorems for both E-models and PCS-models.

THEOREM 7.3.16. *Every finite basic (entailment preserving, monotonic, regular, normal) algebra $\mathscr{A}$ is isomorphic to $\mathscr{M} +$ for some finite E-model (entailment preserving, monotonic model, regular model, normal model) $\mathscr{M}$.*

Proof. Let $\mathscr{A} = \langle M, \cup, \cap, -, * \rangle$ be a finite basic algebra. Let K be the set of atoms of the Boolean algebra $\langle M, \cup, \cap, - \rangle$, and let h be an interpretation in $\mathscr{A}$ such that h is *onto* M. For each $a \in K$ and $A \in CL$, let $w_a(A) = \begin{cases} 1 \text{ if } a \leqslant h(A) \\ 0 \text{ otherwise} \end{cases}$. Since h is an interpretation, and since for each $a \in K$ and $A \in CL$, $a \leqslant h(A)$ or $a \leqslant -h(A) = h(\sim A)$, w_a is a possible world for each $a \in K$. Let $W = \{w_a: a \in K\}$. For each $x \in M - \{0\}$, there are $a_1, \ldots, a_n \in K$ such that $x = a_1 \cup \ldots \cup a_n$, by Boolean algebra. Define a function g from M onto $\mathscr{P}(W)$ as follows: let $f(0) = \emptyset$ and for each $x \in M - \{0\}$, let $g(x) = \{w_{a_1}, \ldots, w_{a_n}\}$ where $a_1, \ldots, a_n \in K$ and $x = a_1 \cup \ldots \cup a_n$. g is an isomorphism from $\langle M, \cup, \cap, - \rangle$ onto the algebra $\langle \mathscr{P}(W), \cup_1, \cap_1, -_1 \rangle$ of all subsets of W.

For $S, T \subseteq W$, let $f(S, T) = g(g^{-1}(S) * g^{-1}(T))$. $\mathscr{M} = \langle W, f \rangle$ is an E-model. Since h is onto, $\mathscr{P}(W) = \{W/A: A \in CL\}$ and g is an isomorphism from $\langle M, \cup, \cap, - \rangle$ onto $\langle \{W/A: A \in CL\}, \cup_1, \cap_1, -_1, f \rangle$. Entailment preservation etc., follow from the fact that g is an isomorphism.

THEOREM 7.3.17. *Every finite normal (dependable, etc.) algebra is isomorphic to $\mathscr{M} +$ for some finite PCS-model (dependable PCS-model, etc.) $\mathscr{M}$.*

Proof. Let $\mathscr{A} = \langle M, \cup, \cap, -, * \rangle$ be a finite normal algebra and let h, g and W be defined for $\mathscr{A}$ as in the proof for Theorem 7.3.16. So W is a set of possible worlds, g is an isomorphism from $\langle M, \mathsf{U}, \mathsf{\cap}, - \rangle$ onto $\langle \{W/A: A \in CL\}, \mathsf{U}_1, \mathsf{\cap}_1, -_1 \rangle$, and h is an interpretation in $\mathscr{A}$ which is onto M. For each $w \in W$ and $A \in CL$, let $f(W/A, w) = \{w' \in W:$ for all $B \in CL$, if $w(A > B) = 1$, then $w'(B) = 1\}$. Since $\mathscr{P}(W) = \{W/A : A \in CL\}$, $\mathscr{M} = \langle W, f \rangle$ is a PCS-model.

I omit the simple inductive proof that for each $x \in M$ and $A \in CL$, if $h(A) = x$, then $g(x) = W/A$. Let $x, y \in M$. Since h is onto, let $A, B \in CL$ such that $h(A) = x$, $h(B) = y$, and $h(A > B) = x * y$. Suppose $w_a \in g(x * y)$. Then $a \leqslant x * y = h(A > B)$ and $w_a(A > B) = 1$. So $w_a \in W/A > B = W/A *_1 W/B = g(x) *_1 g(y)$ and $g(x * y) \leqslant g(x) *_1 g(y)$. Suppose $w_a \in g(x) *_1 g(y) = W/A *_1 W/B = W/A > B$. So $w_a(A > B) = 1$ and $a \leqslant h(A > B) = x * y$. But then $w_a \in g(x * y)$ and $g(x) *_1 g(y) \leqslant g(x * y)$. Thus, $g(x * y) = g(x) *_1 g(y)$ and g is also an isomorphism from $\mathscr{A}$ onto $\mathscr{M}+$.

Dependability, etc., follow from the fact that g is an isomorphism. We provide a proof for the case where $\mathscr{A}$ is dependable as an example. Let $\mathscr{M}$ be as constructed above, let $w_a \in W$, and let $A \in CL$. Since $\mathscr{A}$ is dependable, $h(A > A) = 1$. But this means that $a \leqslant 1 = h(A > A)$ and $w_a(A > A) = 1$. By the definition of f, $f(W/A, w_a) \subseteq W/A$. Therefore, $\mathscr{M}$ is dependable.

THEOREM 7.3.18. If $A \in \mathbf{CE}$ (**G**, etc.), then A is true in every E-model (entailment preserving model, etc.).

Proof. Let $A \in \mathbf{CE}$ and let $\mathscr{M} = \langle W, f \rangle$ be an E-model. By Theorem 7.3.1, $\mathscr{M}+ = \langle \{W/A: A \in CL\}, \mathsf{U}, \mathsf{\cap}, -, f \rangle$ is a basic algebra. By Theorem 7.3.16, $\mathscr{M}+$ satisfies A. For each $B \in CL$, let $g(B) = W/B$. g is an interpretation in $\mathscr{M}+$, so $W/A = g(A) = W$ and A is true in $\mathscr{M}$. Proofs for **G**, etc., are similar but utilize Theorems 7.3.14 and 7.2.16.

THEOREM 7.3.19. If $A \in \mathbf{CK}$ (**CK** + ID, etc.), then A is true in every PCS-model (dependable PCS-model, etc.).

Proof. Proofs are similar to those for Theorem 7.3.18 but utilize Theorems 7.3.15 and 7.2.16.

In the cases of **CM**, **CR**, **CK**, **CK** + ID, and **CK** + MP we can get an even stronger result using our decidability result for these logics.

THEOREM 7.3.20. Let $A \in CL$ and let n be the number of subformulas of A. Then $A \in \mathbf{CM}$ (**CF**, **CK**, **CK** + ID, **CK** + MP) iff A is true in every monotonic regular, normal, dependable, weakly material) model with at most 2^{2^n} members.

Proof. Assume the hypothesis. By Theorem 7.3.18, if $A \in CM$, then A is true in every E-model. Suppose $A \notin CM$. By Theorem 7.2.19, let $\mathscr{A}$ be a normal algebra and g an interpretation in $\mathscr{A}$ such that $g(A) \neq 1$. By the construction for Theorem 7.2.21, let $\mathscr{A}_1$ be the monotonic algebra generated by $\{g(B): B$ is a subformula of $A\}$. Let h be an interpretation in $\mathscr{A}_1$ such that for all subformulas B of A, $h(B) = g(B)$. Then $h(A) \neq 1$. Finally, let $\mathscr{M} = \langle W, f \rangle$ be the monotonic model constructed from $\mathscr{A}_1$ and h according to the instructions in the proof for Theorem 7.3.16. W has, at most, 2^{2^n} members and $W/A \neq W$. The arguments for CR, CK, $CK + ID$, and $CK + MP$ are exactly parallel.

We can get completeness results by a more direct route for these and all the rest of our conditional logics.

THEOREM 7.3.21. G, (CM, CR, CK) is determined by the class of all entailment preserving (monotonic, regular, normal) models.
Proof. We take CK as our example. Let W be the set of all *maximally CK-consistent* subsets of CL, $(S \subseteq F$ is *maximally CK-consistent* iff $S \neq CL$, $CK \subseteq S$, S is closed under *modus ponens*, RCEA, RCEC, and RCK, and for every $A \in CL$, $A \in S$ or $\sim A \in S)$. Since CK contains all tautologies and is closed under *modus ponens*, we have a Lindenbaum lemma, compactness theorem, deduction theorem, and other familiar results for CK. Since CK is consistent, $W \neq \emptyset$. For each $w \in W$ and $A \in CL$, let $w(A) = 1$ if $A \in w$ and let $w(A) = 0$ if $A \notin w$. W so construed is a non-empty set of possible worlds. For each $w \in W$ and $S, T \subseteq W$, let

$$f(S, T) = \begin{cases} \bigcup \{W/A > B: W/B \subseteq T\} \text{ if } S = W/A \\ W \text{ if } T = W \text{ and there is no } A \in CL \text{ such that } S = W/A \\ \emptyset \text{ otherwise} \end{cases}.$$

We need to show that $\mathscr{M}_{CK} = \langle W, f \rangle$ is a normal model. Suppose $x \in f(W/A, W/B) = \bigcup \{W/A > C: W/C \subseteq W/B\}$. Then $x \in W/A > C$ for some $W/C \subseteq W/B$. But then $W/C = W/C \cap W/B = W/C \& B$, and by the definition of W, $C \leftrightarrow (C \& B) \in CK$. By RCEC, $(A > C) \leftrightarrow [A > (B \& C)] \in CK$, $W/A > C = W/A > (B \& C)$, and $x \in W/A > (B \& C)$. Then by CM, *modus ponens* and the definition of W, $x \in W/A > B$. So $f(W/A, W/B) \subseteq W/A > B$. Since the converse is obvious, $\mathscr{M}_{CK}$ is an E-model. Let $S, T, U \subseteq W$ and suppose $x \in f(S, T \cap U)$.
Case 1. $S = W/A$. Then $f(S, T \cap U) = \bigcup \{W/A > B: W/B \subseteq T \cap U\}$. Then

W/B $\subseteq$ T and W/B $\subseteq$ U, so x $\in \bigcup$ {W/A > C: W/C $\subseteq$ T} $\cap \bigcup$ {W/A > C: C $\subseteq$ U} = f(S, T) $\cap$ f(S, U).

Case 2. There is no A $\in$ CL such that S = W/A. If T $\cap$ U $\neq$ W, then f(S, T $\cap$ U) = $\emptyset \subseteq$ f(S, T) $\cap$ f(S, U). If T $\cap$ U = W, then T = W, U = W, and f(S, T $\cap$ U) = W = f(S, T) $\cap$ f(S, U). In either case, f(S, T $\cap$ U) $\subseteq$ f(S, T) $\cap$ f(S, U) and $\mathscr{M}_{CK}$ is monotonic. Suppose x $\in$ f(S, T) $\cap$ f(S, U).

Case 1. S = W/A. Then there exist B, C $\in$ CL such that W/B $\subseteq$ T, W/C $\subseteq$ U, x $\in$ W/A > B and x $\in$ W/A > C. By CC and *modus ponens*, x $\in$ W/A > (B & C). But W/B & C = W/B $\cap$ W/C $\subseteq$ T $\cap$ U, so x $\in \bigcup$ {W/A > D: W/D $\subseteq$ T $\cap$ U} = f(S, T $\cap$ U).

Case 2. There is no A $\in$ CL such that S = W/A. If T = U = W, then T $\cap$ U = W and f(S, T) $\cap$ f(S, U) = W = f(S, T $\cap$ U). If T $\neq$ W or U $\neq$ W, then T $\cap$ U $\neq$ W and f(S, T) $\cap$ f(S, U) = $\emptyset$ = f(S, T $\cap$ U). In either case, $\mathscr{M}_{CK}$ is regular.

Finally, consider f(S, W). If S = W/A, then f(S, W) = f(W/A, W/A $\vee \sim$ A) = W/A > (A $\vee \sim$ A) = W by RCK. So $\mathscr{M}_{CK}$ is normal. Since Theorem 7.3.18 gives us soundness, we only need completeness. If A $\in$ CL is true in every normal model, then A is true in $\mathscr{M}_{CK}$, A is a member of every maximally CK-consistent subset of CL, and A $\in$ **CK**.

THEOREM 7.3.22. **CK** + ID (**CK** + MP, etc.) is determined by the class of all dependable (weakly material, etc.) PCS-models.

Proof. We take **C2** as our example. Let W be the set of all maximally **C2**-consistent subsets of CL, construed as possible worlds. Since **C2** is consistent, W $\neq \emptyset$. For each w $\in$ W and S $\subseteq$ W, let

$$f(S, w) = \left\{ \begin{array}{l} \{w' \in W: \text{for all } B \in CL, \text{ if } A > B \in w, \text{ then } B \in w'\} \\ \text{if } S = W/A. \\ (S \cap \{w\}) \cup \bigcup \{f(W/A, w): f(W/A, w) \subseteq S \subseteq W/A\} \\ \text{if there is no } A \in CL \text{ such that } S = W/A. \end{array} \right\}.$$

$\mathscr{M}_{C2}$ = $\langle$ W, f $\rangle$ is clearly a PCS-model. Let S, T $\subseteq$ W and let w $\in$ W. If there is no A $\in$ CL such that S = W/A, then obviously f(S, w) $\subseteq$ S. So suppose S = W/A. By ID, A > A $\in$ W and f(S, w) $\subseteq$ W/A. Thus, $\mathscr{M}_{C2}$ is dependable. Suppose w $\in$ S. If there is no A $\in$ CL such that S = W/A, then obviously w $\in$ f(S, w). So suppose S = W/A. Then A $\in$ w. Suppose A > B $\in$ w. Since (A > B) $\rightarrow$ (A $\rightarrow$ B) $\in$ w by MP, A $\rightarrow$ B $\in$ w and B $\in$ w by *modus ponens*. Thus, B $\in$ w for all B $\in$ CL such that A > B $\in$ w, w $\in$ f(W/A, w), and $\mathscr{M}_{C2}$ is weakly material. Next assume A $\in$ CL such that f(W/A, w) = $\emptyset$. If w' $\in$ f(S, w) $\cap$ W/A, then w' $\in$ W/A or there is a B $\in$ CL such that f(W/B, w) $\cap$

$W/A \neq \emptyset$. If $w' \in W/A$, then $w' \in f(W/A, w)$ (since $\mathscr{M}_{C2}$ is weakly material), contrary to hypothesis. So suppose $f(W/B, w) \cap W/A \neq \emptyset$. Now $A > \sim A \in w'$ since $f(W/A, w) \subseteq W/\sim A$, and $\sim\sim A > \sim A \in w'$ by RCEA. But $(\sim\sim A > \sim A)$ $\to (B > \sim A) \in w'$ by MOD, so $B > \sim A \in w'$ and $f(W/B, w) \subseteq W/\sim A$, but this is impossible if $f(W/B, w) \cap W/A \neq \emptyset$; so $f(S, w) \cap W/A = \emptyset$, and $\mathscr{M}_{C2}$ satisfies 7.3.8 (i). Let $A, B \in CL$ and suppose $f(W/A, w) \subseteq W/B$ and $f(W/B, w)$ $\subseteq W/A$. Then $A > B, B > A \in w$. Since for each $C \in CL$, $[(A > B) \& (B > A)]$ $\to [(A > C) \equiv (B > C)] \in w$ by CSO, then for each $C \in CL$, $(A > C) \leftrightarrow (B > C)$ $\in w$, and $f(W/A, w) = f(W/B, w)$. Thus, $\mathscr{M}_{C2}$ is ordered. In similar fashion we use CA and CV to show that $\mathscr{M}_{C2}$ is additive and variably strict. Next suppose $w \in S$ and $x \in f(S, w)$. $w \in f(S, w)$ since $\mathscr{M}_{C2}$ is weakly material. Either $x = w$ or there is an $A \in CL$ such that $f(W/A, w) \subseteq S \subseteq W/A$. But in the latter case, $w \in W/A$ and $A \in w$. If $B \in w$, then $B \in x$ since $(A \& B) \to (A > B) \in w$ by CS. Thus, $x \subseteq w$. Since x and w are maximally C2-consistent subsets of CL, it follows that $x = w$. So in any case $x = w$, $f(S, w) = \{w\}$, and $\mathscr{M}_{C2}$ is material. Finally, suppose $x, y \in f(S, w)$. If $x \neq y$, then $x \neq w$ or $y \neq w$. Suppose $x \neq w$. Then there is an $A \in CL$ such that $x \in f(W/A, w) \subseteq S \subseteq W/A$. If $w \in W/A$, then $f(W/A, w) = \{w\}$ and $x = w$, so assume $w \notin W/A$ and hence $w \notin S$. Then $y \neq w$ and there is a $B \in CL$ such that $y \in f(W/B, w) \subseteq S \subseteq W/B$. But then $f(W/A, w) \subseteq W/B$ and $f(W/B, w) \subseteq W/A$, so $f(W/A, w) = f(W/B, w)$ since $\mathscr{M}_{C2}$ is ordered. Hence, $x, y \in f(W/A, w)$. Since $x \neq y$, let $C \in CL$ such that $C \in x$ and $\sim C \in y$. By CEM, $(A > C) \vee (A > \sim C) \in w$. By the maximal C2-consistency of w, $A > C \in w$ or $A > \sim C \in w$. If $A > C \in w$, then $C \in y$; if $A > \sim C \in w$, then $\sim C \in x$. Since neither of these is possible, $x = y$, $f(S, w)$ has at most one member, and $\mathscr{M}_{C2}$ is singular. Completeness follows as in Theorem 7.3.21.

As the last result of this section, we will prove decidability for all our logics, including those which were not included in Theorems 7.2.21 and 7.3.20.

THEOREM 7.3.23. Let $A \in CL$ and let n be the number of subformulas of A. Then $A \in CE$ (G, etc.) iff A is satisfied by every basic (entailment preserving, etc.) algebra with at most 2^{2^n} elements.

Proof. As our example, we will take $CK + MP$ and weakly material algebras. Let $A \in CL$ and n be the number of subformulas of A. By Theorem 7.2.19, if $A \in CK + MP$, then every weakly material algebra satisfies A. Suppose $A \notin CK + MP$. By Theorem 7.3.18, let $\mathscr{M} = \langle W, f \rangle$ be a weakly material model such that $W/A \neq W$. Let $K = \{W/B: B$ is a subformula of $A\}$, and let $M = \{S \subseteq W: S$ is the result of some finite number of applications of the set-theoretic operations $\cup, \cap$, and $-$ to the members of K}. $\langle M, \cup, \cap, - \rangle$ is a Boolean algebra with unit element W, M has at most 2^{2^n} members, and for every $x \in M$ there is a $B \in CL$ such that $x = W/B$. For W/B, W/C $\in M$, let $W/B * W/C = \cup \{W/D \in M: W/D \subseteq W/B > C\}$. Then $\mathcal{M}_A = \langle M, \cup, \cap, -, * \rangle$ is a basic algebra.

Let W/B, W/C, W/D $\in M$. Since $\mathcal{M}$ is regular, W/B > (C & D) = f(W/B, W/C & W/D) = f(W/B, W/C) $\cap$ f(W/B, W/D) = W/B > C $\cap$ W/B > D.   W/B * (W/C $\cap$ W/D) = $\cup \{W/E \in M: W/E \subseteq W/B > (C \& D)\} = \cup \{W/E \in M: W/E \subseteq W/B > C \cap W/B > D = \cup \{W/E \in M: W/E \subseteq W/B > C\} \cap \cap \{W/E \in M: W/E \subseteq W/B > D\} = (W/B * W/C) \cap (W/B * W/D)$, and $\mathcal{M}_A$ is regular. Since $\mathcal{M}$ is normal, W/B > (B v ~ B) = f(W/B, W/B v ~ B) = f(W/B, W) = W. So W/B * W = W/B * (W/B $\cup$ $-$ W/B) = W/B * W/B v ~ B = $\cup \{W/C \in M: W/C \subseteq W/B > (B v ~ B)\} = \cup \{W/C \in M: W/C \subseteq W\} = W$, and $\mathcal{M}_A$ is normal. Since $\mathcal{M}$ is weakly material, W/B > C = f(W/B, W/C) $\subseteq$ W/B $\gg$ W/C = W/B $\rightarrow$ C. So W/B * W/C = $\cup \{W/D \in M: W/D \subseteq W/B > C\} \subseteq \cap \{W/D \in M: W/D \subseteq W/B \rightarrow C\}$ = W/B $\rightarrow$ C = W/B $\gg$ W/C, and $\mathcal{M}_A$ is weakly material. For each $B \in CL$, let

$$g(B) = \begin{cases} \cup \{W/C \in M: W/C \subseteq W/B\} \text{ if B is a sentence letter} \\ -g(C) \text{ if } B = \sim C \\ g(C) \cup g(D) \text{ if } B = C \vee D \\ g(C) \cap g(D) \text{ if } B = C \& D \\ g(C) * g(D) \text{ if } B = C > D \end{cases}.$$

g is an interpretation in $\mathcal{M}_A$ such that for each subformula B of A, g(B) = W/B. But since A is not true in $\mathcal{M}$, g(A) = W/A $\neq$ W and $\mathcal{M}_A$ does not satisfy A.

7.4. SOME INDEPENDENCE RESULTS

Possible worlds model theories can be used to establish independence results for conditional logics. Although different authors have developed different model theories, the strategy for proving independence is always the same: to show that a wff A is not a member of logic L, we construct a possible worlds model of some sort for L in which A is not true. Typically, this involves devising a 'partial' model which rejects A and then expanding this partial model into a 'complete' model for L. Expanding the partial model into a complete model involves providing simultaneous recursive definitions for the items in the model. Such constructions can be very complicated and 'untidy'. An alternative method, which frequently provides simpler and more elegant results, is to use the partial model as a basis for constructing a finite basic algebra which satisfies **L** but does not satisfy **A**. It is this latter technique which will be applied here, using the connections we have established between possible worlds model theories and basic algebras. The algebras we will develop will be similar to the many-valued matrices developed by early researchers working on modal logics, but we enjoy a considerable advantage over those authors. While those early 'modal' matrices had to be developed in a hit-or-miss, *ad hoc* fashion, we will be able to pursue our goal in a much more orderly fashion since both a sophisticated possible worlds model theory and a workable algebraic semantics are available to us.

Our results concern the systems **CE, G, CO, CA, VW, SS**, and **VC**. We shall show that all the containment relations involving these logics, which were indicated in our earlier figure, are proper. A number of the independence results proved here were assumed in the arguments of Section 3.8.

THEOREM 7.4.1. **CE** is not closed under RCE.

Proof. In this case, the required model is very simple. Let $W = \{w\}$ and let $f(\{w\}, w) = \{w\}$. The basic technique in our construction of algebras will be to treat sets of worlds as *truth values* with the set of all worlds as the only designated value. Our algebras then become many-valued truth matrices for the operations $-, \cap, \cup$ and $*$. We treat $-, \cap$ and $\cup$ in each case as complementation, intersection and union, respectively, of the sets of worlds. In the present instance, our truth matrices are two-valued with $0 = \emptyset$ and $1 = \{w\}$. We have the standard truth tables for $-, \cap$ and $\cup$ and for $*$ we have:

TABLE 7.4.2

$*$	0	1
0	0	1
1	0	1

$\langle \mathscr{P}\{w\}, \cup, \cap, -, * \rangle$ is a basic algebra and hence satisfies **CE**. But $0 \geqslant 0 = 1$ while $0 * 0 = 0$, so RCE does not hold in $\langle \mathscr{P}\{w\}, \cup, \cap, -, * \rangle$ and **CE** is not closed under RCE.

THEOREM 7.4.3. **G** is not closed under RCK.

Proof. As it turns out, RCK holds in every PCS-model in which RCE holds.

We cannot, then, prove our theorem by constructing an appropriate partial PCS-model and then using this to develop our matrices. However, we could use the theory of DPR-models for this purpose. Rather than do this, though, I will attack the problem of constructing the required matrices directly.

Suppose we begin with one world w. This gives us a two-element Boolean algebra $\langle \mathscr{P}\{w\}, \cup, \cap, - \rangle$. We want RCE to hold in our basic algebra, so we will need to have $\emptyset * \emptyset = \{w\}$, $\emptyset * \{w\} = \{w\}$, and $\{w\} * \{w\} = \{w\}$. Thus, we can only have $\{w\} * \emptyset$ taking the nondesignated value $\emptyset$. Letting $\emptyset = 0$ and $\{w\} = 1$, this gives us the following matrix for $*$:

TABLE 7.4.4

$*$	0	1
0	1	1
1	0	1

But this is just the usual table for $\geqslant$. Hence, $*$ collapses into $\geqslant$ in any two-element basic algebra in which RCE holds, and RCK must also hold in such an algebra.

Let us, then, try two worlds a and b and a basic algebra with four elements: $1 = \{a, b\}$, $2 = \{b\}$, $3 = \{a\}$ and $4 = \emptyset$. For RCE to hold, we must have $x * y = 1$ whenever $x \leqslant y$, i.e., whenever $x \subseteq y$. Thus, our matrix for $*$ must look like this:

TABLE 7.4.5

$*$	1	2	3	4
1	1	–	–	–
2	1	1	–	–
3	1	–	1	–
4	1	1	1	1

We should be able to fill in the missing values in such a way as to invalidate RCK. Let's begin by considering an x and y such that $x \geqslant y = 1$. For example, $4 \geqslant 3 = 1$. I choose this example because 4 represents the value 'true in no world', a value which seems perverse enough to work. Now we could use a value x such that $x * 4 = 1$ and $x * 3 = 4$. Since this would give us $(x * 4) \geqslant (x * 3) = 1 \geqslant 4 = 4$. Notice that we have assigned no values to $2 * 4$ and $2 * 3$. We assign the values 1 and 4 respectively to $2 * 4$ and $2 * 3$ and we are done. In fact, we might as well fill all the spaces in Table 7.4.5 with 1 except for the space for $2 * 3$ which we fill with 4. This gives us:

TABLE 7.4.6

*	1	2	3	4
1	1	1	1	1
2	1	1	4	1
3	1	1	1	1
4	1	1	1	1

Then $\langle \mathscr{P}\{a, b\}, \cup, \cap, -, * \rangle$, where $*$ is defined by Table 7.4.6, is an entailment preserving algebra in which RCK does not hold. Hence, **G** is not closed under RCK.

THEOREM 7.4.7. CA is not contained in **CO**.

Proof. We could establish this result if we had a PCS-model $\langle \{a, b, c\}, f \rangle$ for **CO** which satisfied the following conditions:

$$a(A) = 1, b(A) = 1, c(A) = 1,$$
$$a(B) = 0, b(B) = 0, c(B) = 0,$$
$$a(C) = 0, b(C) = 0, c(C) = 1,$$
$$f(\{a\}, a) = \{a\}, f(\{c\}, a) = \{c\}, f(\{a, b, c\}, a) = \{a, b\}$$

To show that there exists such a PCS-model is rather complicated. The completed model will satisfy the following condition for $S \subseteq \{a, b, c\}$:

$$f(S, a) = \begin{cases} \{a\} \text{ if } a \in S \text{ and } S \neq \{a, b, c\} \\ \{c\} \text{ if } S = \{b, c\} \\ \{a, b\} \text{ if } S = \{a, b, c\} \\ S \text{ otherwise} \end{cases}.$$

To simplify matters, we make b and c trivial worlds, i.e., worlds such that for each $S \subseteq \{a, b, c\}$:

$$f(S, b) = \begin{cases} \{b\} \text{ if } b \in S \\ \emptyset \text{ otherwise} \end{cases} \text{ and } f(S, c) = \begin{cases} \{c\} \text{ if } c \in S \\ \emptyset \text{ otherwise} \end{cases}.$$

Rather than complete this construction, however, we will use the same basis to construct a finite basic algebra which does the same job.

The elements of our algebra will be the eight subsets of $\{a, b, c\}$ and $\cup, \cap$, and $-$ will be the set-theoretic operations. We let $1 = \{a, b, c\}$, $2 = \{b, c\}$, $3 = \{a, c\}$, $4 = \{a, b\}$, $5 = \{c\}$, $6 = \{b\}$, $7 = \{a\}$, and $8 = \emptyset$. Then we use our 'partial PCS-model' to devise the following table for $*$:

TABLE 7.4.8

*	1	2	3	4	5	6	7	8
1	1	2	5	4	5	6	8	8
2	1	1	2	6	5	6	8	8
3	1	2	1	4	2	6	4	6
4	1	2	2	1	5	2	3	5
5	1	1	1	6	1	6	6	6
6	1	1	5	1	5	1	5	5
7	1	2	1	1	2	2	1	2
8	1	1	1	1	1	1	1	1

It turns out that $\langle \mathscr{P}\{a, b, c\}, \cup, \cap, -, * \rangle$ is an ordered algebra and hence satisfies **CO**. However $[(4 * 7) \cap (2 * 7)] \geqslant [(4 \cup 2) * 7] = 5$, so **CA** is not satisfied by this algebra.

From THEOREM 7.4.7 we conclude that **CA** $\nsubseteq$ **CO** and **CA** $\nsubseteq$ **G**.

THEOREM 7.4.9. The axiom schema CS is not contained in **CA** or **VW**.

Proof. We could show this if we could construct a PCS-model $\langle \{a, b\}, f \rangle$ for which $a(A) = b(A) = a(B) = 1$, $b(B) = 0$, and $f(\{a, b\}, a) = \{a, b\}$. Again, we use this basis to construct a finite basic algebra, this time with only four elements: $1 = \{a, b\}$, $2 = \{b\}$, $3 = \{a\}$, and $4 = \emptyset$. Our table defining $*$ is:

TABLE 7.4.10

*	1	2	3	4
1	1	2	4	4
2	1	1	4	4
3	1	2	1	2
4	1	1	1	1

Then $\langle \mathscr{P}\{a, b\}, \cup, \cap, -, f \rangle$ is variably strict weakly material, but $(1 \cap 3) \geqslant (1 * 3) = 2$, so CS is contained in neither **CA** nor **VW**.

From Theorem 7.4.9 we conclude that none of **G**, **CO**, **CA**, and **VW** contain either of **SS** and **VC**.

One thing we should note about the algebras we have defined so far: certain properties of these algebras can be discovered immediately by a quick glance at the table defining ∗. For example, an algebra satisfies the characteristic condition for normality iff nothing but 1 appears in the column under 1, and it satisfies the characteristic condition for dependability iff nothing but 1 appears in the diagonal from upper left to lower right. A bit more complicated, an algebra satisfies condition 7.2.9(i) iff each entry in the diagonal from lower left to upper right is the smallest (in terms of containment) entry in its column.

Pollock reports the following result in (1975) but offers no proof.

THEOREM 7.4.11. CV is not contained in **SS**.

Proof. The partial model upon which this proof is based involves four possible worlds, so the elements of our algebra will be sixteen in number: $1 = \{a, b, c, d\}$, $2 = \{b, c, d\}$, $3 = \{a, c, d\}$, $4 = \{a, b, d\}$, $5 = \{a, b, c\}$, $6 = \{c, d\}$, $7 = \{b, d\}$, $8 = \{b, c\}$, $9 = \{a, d\}$, $10 = \{a, c\}$, $11 = \{a, b\}$, $12 = \{d\}$, $13 = \{c\}$, $14 = \{b\}$, $15 = \{a\}$, $16 = \emptyset$. We let b, c and d be trivial worlds, and for each $S \subseteq \{a, b, c, d\}$ we let

$$f(S, a) = \begin{cases} \{a\} \text{ if } a \in S \\ \{b, c\} \text{ if } S = \{b, c, d\} \\ S \text{ otherwise} \end{cases}.$$

Using this partial model, we construct the following table for ∗:

TABLE 7.4.12

∗	1	2	3	4	5	6	7	8	9	10	11	12	13	14	15	16
1	1	2	3	4	5	6	7	8	9	10	11	12	13	14	15	16
2	1	1	6	7	5	6	7	5	12	13	14	12	13	14	16	16
3	1	2	1	4	5	2	7	8	4	5	11	7	8	14	11	14
4	1	2	3	1	5	6	2	8	3	10	5	6	13	8	10	13
5	1	2	3	4	1	6	7	2	9	3	4	12	6	7	9	12
6	1	1	1	7	8	1	7	8	7	8	14	7	8	14	14	14
7	1	1	6	1	8	6	1	8	6	13	8	6	13	8	13	13
8	1	1	6	7	1	6	7	1	12	6	7	12	6	7	12	12
9	1	2	1	1	5	2	2	8	1	5	5	2	8	8	5	2
10	1	2	1	4	1	2	7	2	4	1	4	7	2	7	4	7
11	1	2	3	1	1	6	2	2	3	3	1	6	6	2	3	6
12	1	1	1	1	8	1	1	8	1	8	8	1	8	8	8	8
13	1	1	1	7	1	1	7	1	7	1	7	7	1	7	7	7
14	1	1	6	1	1	6	1	1	6	6	1	6	6	1	6	6
15	1	2	1	1	1	2	2	2	1	1	1	2	2	2	1	2
16	1	1	1	1	1	1	1	1	1	1	1	1	1	1	1	1

Then $\langle \mathscr{P}\{a, b, c, d\}, \cup, \cap, -, * \rangle$ is an additive material logic, but $[(2 * 8) \cap -(2 * -7)] \geqslant [(2 \cap 7) * 8] = 2$, so **SS** does not contain **CV**.

From Theorem 7.4.11, we conclude that none of **G**, **CO**, **CA** and **SS** contain either of **VW** and **VC**.

I end this section by correcting an error in my (1975). There I suggested that **CO** = **VW**, a claim which we now see to be false.

7.5. NON-CLASSICAL LOGICS

Since basic algebras always validate RCEA, the foregoing development of algebraic semantics for conditional logics cannot be applied in the case of half-classical logics. In this section, we will consider alternative ways of providing semantics for half-classical logics.

One way of providing an algebra-like semantics for half-classical logics is suggested by a remark made by David Lewis in (1971). Lewis proposes that many weak logics, including half-classical logics, should not be called conditional logics at all. Instead, he suggests that they be called *logics of sententially indexed modalities*. If we follow this suggestion, we will not treat $A > B$ as involving a binary sentence connective; instead, we will treat '$A >$' as a unary modal operator. Formally, we will eschew basic algebras in favor of Boolean algebras supplemented by countably many unary operations.

DEFINITION 7.5.1. A structure $\mathscr{A} = \langle M, \cup, \cap, -, 0_1, 0_2, 0_3, \ldots \rangle$ is an *α-structure* iff $\langle M, \cup, \cap, - \rangle$ is a Boolean algebra and M is closed under each of the countably many unary operations $0_1, 0_2, 0_3, \ldots$

I am inclined to call these *α-structures* rather than *α-algebras* simply because algebras usually involve only finitely many operations on a set of elements.

DEFINITION 7.5.2. An *interpretation* in an α-structure $\mathscr{A} = \langle M, \cup, \cap, -, 0_1, 0_2, 0_3, \ldots \rangle$ is an ordered pair $\langle g, f \rangle$ such that:

(1)   g is a function which assigns to each $A \in CL$ a positive integer $g(A)$;

(2)   f is a function which assigns to each $A \in CL$ a member $f(A)$ of M such that:

   (i) $f(\sim A) = -f(A)$;

    (ii) $f(A \mathrel{\&} B) = f(A) \cap f(B)$;

    (iii) $f(A \vee B) = f(A) \cup f(B)$;

    (iv) $f(A \to B) = f(A) \geqslant f(B)$;

    (v) $f(A \leftrightarrow B) = f(A) \equiv f(B)$;

    (vi) $f(A > B) = 0_{g(A)}f(B)$.

An α-structure $\mathscr{A}$ satisfies a wff A iff for every interpretation $\langle g, f \rangle$ in $\mathscr{A}$, $f(A) = 1$. $\mathscr{A}$ satisfies a set Γ of wffs iff $\mathscr{A}$ satisfies every member of Γ. $\mathscr{A}$ *characterizes* a logic **L** iff $\mathscr{A}$ satisfies all and only members of **L**.

THEOREM 7.5.3. Every α-structure satisfies **Ce**.

Let **L** be any half-classical logic. For any A, $B \in CL$, let $A \simeq B$ iff $A \leftrightarrow B \in \mathbf{L}$. Then $\simeq$ is a congruence relation on CL. For each $A \in CL$, let $E(A) = \{B \in CL : A \simeq B\}$. Let $M_L = \{E(A) : A \in CL\}$. Let the sequence $s = \langle A_1, A_2, A_3, \ldots \rangle$ be an enumeration of CL. For each $E(A), E(B) \in M_L$, let $E(A) \cup_L E(B) = E(A \vee B)$, $E(A) \cap_L E(B) = E(A \mathrel{\&} B)$, $-_L E(A) = E(\sim A)$, and $0_n^s E(A) = E(A_n > A)$. Let $\mathscr{A}_L^s = \langle M_L, \mathbf{U}_L, \mathbf{\cap}_L, -_L, 0_1^s, 0_2^s, 0_3^s, \ldots \rangle$.

THEOREM 7.5.4. If **L** is a consistent half-classical logic closed under substitution on sentential variables and s is an enumeration of CL, then $\mathscr{A}_L^s$ is an α-structure which characterizes **L**.

From Theorems 7.5.3 and 7.5.4 we derive our completeness result.

THEOREM 7.5.5. $A \in \mathbf{Ce}$ iff every α-structure satisfies A.

Another way of providing semantics for half-classical logics, which I find more attractive, is suggested if we admit that members of CL have more than one kind of semantic content (cf. Chapter 2). We might call the two kinds of content of a wff A the *indicative* content and the *subjunctive* content. When A is a subformula of another wff B, both the indicative and the subjunctive contents of B are functions of one or the other of the indicative or subjunctive contents of A. Which of these contents is involved depends upon the form of B. In most cases, it is the indicative content of A which is involved. Both contents of B are functions of the subjunctive content of A iff A occurs as the antecedent of the connective '>' in B. This approach allows us to

continue to use basic algebras in our semantics. What we require is an interpretation of the members of CL in an algebra which takes into account the
two kinds of content each wff can have.

DEFINITION 7.5.6. A *dual-interpretation* on a basic algebra $\mathscr{A} = \langle M, \cup, \cap,$
$-, * \rangle$ is an ordered pair $\langle g, f \rangle$ such that:

(1)   g is a function which assigns to each $A \in CL$ a member $g(A)$ of M;

(2)   f is a function which assigns to each $A \in CL$ a member $f(A)$ of M
         such that:
   (i)–(v) same as for Definition 7.5.1;
   (vi) $f(A > B) = g(A) * f(B)$.

The logic **Ce** has no substitution principles for conditional antecedents. Even
without RCEA, we may well want some substitution principles. These are to
be provided by restricting the first member of the dual-interpretation in
various ways. When the first and second members of a dual-interpretation on
a basic algebra $\mathscr{A}$ are identical, the dual-interpretation has essentially col-
lapsed into an *interpretation* and we have recovered the algebraic semantics
of the previous sections. This amounts to identifying the indicative and subjunctive contents of wffs. Thus, our earlier semantics is a special case of the
semantics we are now considering.

A basic algebra $\mathscr{A}$ *sub-satisfies* a wff A iff for every dual-interpretation
$\langle g, f \rangle$ in $\mathscr{A}$, $f(A) = 1$. $\mathscr{A}$ sub-satisfies a set Γ of wffs iff $\mathscr{A}$ subsatisfies every
member of Γ. $\mathscr{A}$ *sub-characterizes* a logic **L** iff $\mathscr{A}$ subsatisfies all and only
members of **L**.

THEOREM 7.5.7. Every basic algebra sub-satisfies **Ce**.

For any half-classical logic **L** and any A, $B \in CL$, let $A \simeq B$ if $A \leftrightarrow B \in L$ and
let $A \approx B$ if for every $C \in CL$, $(A > C) \leftrightarrow (B > C) \in L$. Both $\simeq$ and $\approx$ are congruence relations on CL. For each $A \in CL$, let $E(A) = \{B \in CL: A \simeq B\}$ and
let $H(A) = \{B \in CL; A \approx B\}$. Let $M_L = \{E(A): A \in CL\} \cup \{H(A): A \in CL\} \cup$
$\{CL - H(A): A \in CL\}$. For $x, y \in M_L$, let:

$$
x \cup_L y = \left\{ \begin{array}{l} E(A \vee B) \text{ if there exist } A, B \in CL \text{ such that} \\ x = E(A) \text{ and } y = E(B) \\ CL \text{ otherwise} \end{array} \right\};
$$

$$x \cap_L y = \left\{ \begin{array}{l} E(A \And B) \text{ if there exist } A, B \in CL \text{ such that} \\ x = E(A) \text{ and } y = E(B) \\ E(A \And \sim A) \text{ for any } A \in CL \text{ otherwise} \end{array} \right\};$$

$$-_L x = CL - x \text{ (which is } E(\sim A) \text{ when } x = E(A); \text{ and}$$

$$x *_L y = \left\{ \begin{array}{l} E(A > B) \text{ if there exist } A, B \in CL \text{ such that} \\ x = E(A) \text{ and } y = E(B) \\ E(A \And \sim A) \text{ for any } A \in CL \text{ otherwise} \end{array} \right\}.$$

Let $\mathscr{A}_L = \langle M_L, \cup_L, \cap_L, -_L, *_L \rangle$.

THEOREM 7.5.8. $\mathscr{A}_{Ce} (\mathscr{A}_{Cm}, \mathscr{A}_{Cr}, \mathscr{A}_{Ck})$ is a basic algebra which sub-characterizes Ce (Cm, Cr, Ck).

THEOREM 7.5.9. $A \in Ce$ (Cm, Cr, Ck) iff every basic (monotonic, regular, normal) algebra sub-satisfies A.

THEOREM 7.5.10. Let $A \in CL$ and let n be the number of subformulas of A. Then $A \in Cm$ (Cr, Ck) iff A is sub-satisfied by every monotonic (regular, normal) algebra with at most 2^{2^n} elements.

Proof. Assume the hypothesis. If $A \in Cm$ (for example), then A is sub-satisfied by all monotonic algebras. If $A \notin Cm$, let $\mathscr{A}$ be a monotonic algebra and $\langle g, f \rangle$ a dual-interpretation in $\mathscr{A}$ such that $f(A) \neq 1$. Let $S = \{g(B): B \text{ is a subformula of } A\} \cup \{f(B): B \text{ is a subformula of } A\}$. S has at most 2n elements, and by Theorem 7.2.20 we can let $\mathscr{A} = \langle M, \cup, \cap, -, * \rangle$ be a monotonic algebra such that $S \subseteq M$, $\mathscr{A}$ satisfies conditions (i)–(v) of Theorem 7.2.20 and M has at most 2^{2^n} elements. For each $B \in CL$, let $h(B) =$ the largest $x \in M$ such that $x \leqslant g(B)$, and let

$$k(B) = \left\{ \begin{array}{l} \text{the largest } x \in M \text{ such that } x \leqslant f(B) \text{ if B is a} \\ \text{sentence letter} \\ \text{the smallest } x \in M \text{ such that } -k(c) \leqslant x \text{ if } B = \sim C \\ k(C) \cap k(D) \text{ if } B = C \And D \\ k(c) \cup k(D) \text{ if } B = C \vee D \\ h(c) * k(D) \text{ if } B = C > D \end{array} \right\}.$$

$\langle h, k \rangle$ is a dual-interpretation in $\mathscr{A}$, and for all subformulas B of A $h(B) = g(B)$ and $k(B) = f(B)$. So $k(A) = f(A) \neq 1$, and $\mathscr{A}$ does not sub-satisfy A.

We might expect that we would not have to add any special restrictions upon the first members of our dual-interpretations in order to obtain completeness results until we started adding substitution principles for antecedents to our logic. Unfortunately, this is not the case. Notice that both $Ck + ID$ and $Ck + MP$ are deleted from Theorems 7.5.7, 7.5.8 and 7.5.9. Both ID and MP involve the particular content of the antecedent of the conditional in ways in which the characteristic rules and axioms of the simpler logics do not. We must, then, provide special theorems for the logics $Ck + ID$ and $Ck + MP$. I will close by providing soundness results for each.

THEOREM 7.5.11. If $\mathscr{A}$ is a dependable algebra and $\langle g, f \rangle$ is a dual-interpretation in $\mathscr{A}$ such that for all $A \in CL$, $g(A) \leqslant f(A)$, then for all $B \in Ck + ID$, $f(B) = 1$.

Proof. Assume the hypothesis. Since we have Theorem 7.5.8 we need only show that $f(A > A) = 1$. We have that $f(A > A) = g(A) * f(A)$. In a normal algebra, if $x \leqslant y$, then $z * x \leqslant z * y$. Since $g(A) \leqq f(A)$, $g(A) * g(A) \leqq g(A) * f(A)$. But since $\mathscr{A}$ is dependable, $g(A) * g(A) = 1$. Thus $1 \leqslant g(A) * f(A)$ and $f(A > A) = 1$.

THEOREM 7.5.12. If $\mathscr{A}$ is a weakly material algebra and $\langle g, f \rangle$ is a dual-interpretation in $\mathscr{A}$ such that for all $A, B \in CL$, $f(A > B) \leqslant f(A) * f(B)$, then for all $C \in Ck + MP$, $f(C) = 1$.

Proof. Assume the hypothesis. Since $\mathscr{A}$ is weakly material, $f(A > B) \leqslant f(A) * f(B) \leqslant f(A) \geqslant f(B) = f(A \to B)$ for all $A, B, \in CL$. This establishes the theorem.

BIBLIOGRAPHY

Adams, Ernest: 1975, *The Logic of Conditionals*, Reidel, Dordrecht, Holland.

Åqvist, Lennart: 1971, *Modal Logic with Subjunctive Conditionals*, Uppsala.

Bennett, Jonathan: 1974, 'Counterfactuals and Possible Worlds', *Canadian Journal of Philosophy* 4, 381–402.

Bigelow, John C.: 1976, 'If-Then Meets the Possible Worlds', *Philosophia* 6, 215–236.

Chellas, Brian F.: 1975, 'Basic Conditional Logic', *Journal of Philosophical Logic* 4, 133–153.

Creary, Lewis G. and Christopher S. Hill: 1975, 'Review (of *Counterfactuals*, David Lewis)', *Philosophy of Science* 43, 341–344.

Daniels, Charles B. and James B. Freeman: 1977, 'An Analysis of the Subjunctive Conditional', Pacific Division, American Philosophical Association, Portland, March 27, 1977.

Fine, Kit: 1974, 'An Incomplete Logic Containing S4', *Theoria* 40, 23–39.

Fine, Kit: 1975, 'Review (of *Counterfactuals*, David Lewis)', *Mind* 84, 451–458.

Gabbay, Dov M.: 1972, 'A General Theory of the Conditional in Terms of a Ternary Operator', *Theoria* 38, 97–104.

Gerson, Martin: 1975, 'The Inadequacy of the Neighborhood Semantics for Modal Logic', *The Journal of Symbolic Logic* 40, 141–148.

Hansson, Bengt and Peter Gärdenfors: 1973, 'A Guide to Intensional Semantics', *Modality, Morality, and Other Problems of Sense and Non-sense*, CWK Gleerup.

Kim, Jaegwon: 1973, 'Causes and Counterfactuals', *The Journal of Philosophy* 70, 570–572.

Kripke, Saul A.: 1963, 'Semantical Analysis of Modal Logics, I', *Zeitschrift für mathematische Logik und Grundlagen der Mathematik* 9, 67–96.

Kripke, Saul A.: 1972, 'Naming and Necessity', *Semantics of Natural Language*, (eds. Davidson and Harmon), Reidel, Dordrecht, Holland.

Lemmon, E. J.. 1966, 'Algebraic Semantics for Modal Logics, I', *The Journal of Symbolic Logic* 31, 46–65.

Lemmon, E. J.: 1966a, 'Algebraic Semantics for Modal Logics, II', *The Journal of Symbolic Logic* 31, 191–218.

Lewis, David: 1971, 'Completeness and Decidability of Three Logics of Counterfactual Conditionals', *Theoria* 37, 74–85.

Lewis, David: 1973, *Counterfactuals*, Harvard.

Lewis, David: 1973a, 'Counterfactuals and Comparative Possibility', *Journal of Philosophical Logic* 2, 418–446.

Lewis, David: 1973b, 'Causation', *The Journal of Philosophy* 70, 556–567.

Lewis, David. 1976, 'Counterfactual Dependence and Time's Arrow', *Noûs* 13, 455–476.

Lewis, David: 1976a, 'Proabilities of Conditionals and Conditional Probabilities', *The Philosophical Review* 85, 297–315.

Loewer, Barry: 1976, 'Counterfactuals with Disjunctive Antecedents', *The Journal of Philosophy* **73**, 531–536.

McKay, Thomas and Peter van Inwagen: 1977, 'Counterfactuals with Disjunctive Antecedents', *Philosophical Studies* **31**, 353–356.

Montague, R.: 1970, 'Pragmatism', *Contemporary Philosophy I: Logic and Foundations of Mathematics* (ed. Klibansky), La Nuova Italia.

Nute, Donald: 1975, 'Counterfactuals', *Notre Dame Journal of Formal Logic* **16**, 476–482.

Nute, Donald: 1975a, 'Counterfactuals and the Similarity of Worlds', *The Journal of Philosophy* **72**, 773–778.

Nute, Donald: 1978, 'An Incompleteness Theorem for Conditional Logic', *Notre Dame Journal of Formal Logic* **19**, 634–636.

Nute, Donald: 1978a, 'Do Proper Names Always Designate Rigidly?', *Canadian Journal of Philosophy* **8**, 475–484.

Nute, Donald: 1978b, 'Simplification and Substitution of Counterfactual Antecedents', *Philosophia* **7**, 317–326.

Nute, Donald: 1979, 'Algebraic Semantics for Conditional Logics', *Reports on Mathematical Logic* **10**, 79–101.

Nute, Donald: 1980, 'Critical Study (of *Subjunctive Reasoning*, John Pollock)', to appear in *Noûs*. *15 (1981), pp. 432 –*

Nute, Donald and William Mitcheltree: 1980, 'Critical Study (of *The Logic of Conditionals*, Ernest Adams)', to appear in *Noûs*.

Pollock, John: 1974, *Knowledge and Justification*, Princeton.

Pollock, John: 1976, *Subjunctive Reasoning*, Reidel, Dordrecht, Holland.

Pollock, John: 1978, *Language and Thought*, unpublished manuscript.

Post, John: 1979, 'Review (of *Subjunctive Reasoning*, John Pollock)', to appear in *Philosophia*. *1981 vol. 9 pp. 405–20*

Scott, Dana: 1970, 'Advice on Modal Logic', *Philosophical Problems in Logic*, (ed. Lambert), Reidel, Dordrecht, Holland.

Stalnaker, Robert: 1968, 'A Theory of Conditionals', *American Philosophical Quarterly*, monograph series 2 (ed. Rescher), 98–112.

Stalnaker, Robert: 1970, 'Probabilities and Conditionals', *Philosophy of Science* **28**, 64–80.

Stalnaker, Robert: 1976, 'Stalnaker to van Fraassen', *Foundations of Probability Theory, Statistical Inference, and Statistical Theories of Science* (eds. Harper and Hooker), Reidel, Dordrecht, Holland.

Stalnaker, Robert and Richmond Thomason: 1970, 'A Semantic Analysis of Conditional Logic', *Theoria* **36**, 23–42.

Swain, Marshall: 1978, 'A Counterfactual Analysis of Event Causation', *Philosophical Studies* **34**, 1–19.

Thomason, S. K.: 1972, 'Semantic Analysis of Tense Logics', *The Journal of Symbolic Logic* **37**, 150–158.

Van Fraassen, Bas: 1976, 'Probabilities of Conditionals', *Foundations of Probability Theory, Statistical Inference, and Statistical Theories of Science* (eds. Harper and Hooker), Reidel, Dordrecht, Holland.

LIST OF FREQUENTLY MENTIONED
RULES AND THESES

RULES

GCP: if Γ is a set of sentences, and for each $B \in \Gamma$, $A > B$ is true, and $\Gamma \vdash C$, then $A > C$ is true.

NEC: from A, to infer $\square A$.

RCE: from $A \to B$, to infer $A > B$.

RCEA: from $A \leftrightarrow B$, to infer $(C > A) \leftrightarrow (C > B)$.

RCEC: from $A \leftrightarrow B$, to infer $(A > C) \leftrightarrow (B > C)$.

RCK: from $(A_1 \& \ldots \& A_n) \to B$, to infer $[(C > A_1) \& \ldots \& (C > A_n)] \to (C > B)$, $n \geqslant 0$.

RCKp: if $(A_1 \& \ldots \& A_n) \to B \in L$, then $C > A_1, \ldots, C > A_n$ p-entail $C > B$.

SE: from $A \leftrightarrow B$, to infer $C \leftrightarrow D$, provided that D is the result of replacing one of more occurrences of A by B in C.

ST1: $A \vee B :: B \vee A$

ST2: $A \vee (B \vee C) :: (A \vee B) \vee C$

ST3: $A \vee A :: A$

ST4: $A \& B :: B \& A$

ST5: $A \& (B \& C) :: (A \& B) \& C$

ST6: $\sim (A \& B) :: \sim A \vee \sim B$

ST7: $\sim (A \vee B) :: \sim A \& \sim B$

ST8: $A \& B :: \sim (\sim A \vee \sim B)$

ST9: $A \& (B \vee C) :: (A \& B) \vee (A \& C)$

ST11: $A \& A :: A$

ST12: $A \vee (B \& C) :: (A \vee B) \& (A \vee C)$

THESES

(A1) $\square(A \to B) \to (\square A \to \square B)$

(A2) $\square(A \to B) \to (A > B)$

(A3) $(A > (B \to C)) \to ((A > B) \to (A > C))$

(A4) $(A > B) \to (A \to C)$

(A5) $\square \sim A \leftrightarrow \sim \lozenge A$

159

(A6) $((A \& B) > C) \to ((A > B) \to (A > C))$
(A7) $((A > B) \& (C > B)) \to ((A \lor C) > B)$
CA: Same as (A7)
CC: $[(A > B) \& (A > C)] \to [A > (B \& C)]$
CEM: $(A > B) \lor (A > \sim B)$
CG: $[(A > B) \& (A > \sim B)] \leftrightarrow [A > (B \& \sim B)]$
CM: $[A > (B \& C)] \to [(A > B) \& (A > C)]$
CS: $(A \& B) \to (A > B)$
CSO: $[(A > B) \& (B > A)] \to [(A > C) \leftrightarrow (B > C)]$
CV: $[(A > B) \& \sim (A > \sim C)] \to [(A \& C) > B]$
CV*: $(\sim [(A \lor B) > A] \& \sim \{[(A \& C) \lor B] > B\}] \to \sim [(A \lor B) > \sim C]$
ID: $A > A$
IDp: Anything p-entails $A > A$.
MOD: $(\sim A > A) \to (B > A)$ (or, $\Box A \to (B > A)$)
MP: Same as (A4)
MPp: $A > B$ p-entails $A \to B$.
RT: Same as (A6)
S*: $[\sim (A \& B) > C] \to [(\sim A > C) \& (\sim B > C)]$
SDA: $[(A \lor B) > C] \to [(A > C) \& (B > C)]$
ST10: $(A > B) \leftrightarrow (\sim\sim A > B)$

Cp-detachment: A and $A > B$ p-entail B.
Transitivity: $(A > B) \to [(B > C) \to (A > C)]$
Transposition: $(A > B) \to (\sim B > \sim A)$
Triviality: $(A > B) \to \Box(A \to B)$
Weakening Antecedents: $(A > B) \to [(A \& C) > B]$

INDEX OF NAMES

161

INDEX OF SUBJECTS

PHILOSOPHICAL STUDIES SERIES
IN PHILOSOPHY